# Debating the Past

# DEBATING THE PAST

*Music, Memory, and Identity in the Andes*

Raúl R. Romero

OXFORD

UNIVERSITY PRESS

2001

# OXFORD

UNIVERSITY PRESS

Oxford   New York
Athens   Auckland   Bangkok   Bogotá   Buenos Aires   Cape Town
Chennai   Dar es Salaam   Delhi   Florence   Hong Kong   Istanbul   Karachi
Kolkata   Kuala Lumpur   Madrid   Melbourne   Mexico City   Mumbai   Nairobi
Paris   São Paulo   Shanghai   Singapore   Taipei   Tokyo   Toronto   Warsaw

and associated companies in
Berlin   Ibadan

Copyright © 2001 by Oxford University Press

Published by Oxford University Press, Inc.
198 Madison Avenue, New York, New York 10016

Oxford is a registered trademark of Oxford University Press, Inc.

Library of Congress Cataloging-in-Publication Data
Romero, Raúl R.
Debating the past : music, memory, and identity in the Andes /
Raúl R. Romero.
p.   cm.
Includes bibliographical references and index.
ISBN 0-19-513881-3
1. Music—Peru—History and criticism. 2. Folk music—
Andes Region—History and criticism.
3. Music—Social aspects—Peru. I. Title.
ML236 R66   2001
780'.985—dc21      00-047825

1 3 5 7 9 8 6 4 2
Printed in the United States of America
on acid-free paper

# *Acknowledgments*

This book could not have been written without the guidance of many people throughout the years. I wish to thank Gerard Béhague for publishing my initial analysis of the music of the Mantaro Valley in the pages of *Latin American Music Review*. I am also indebted to Dieter Christensen who first encouraged me to publish my research early on in my graduate studies. I also wish to thank Kay Shelemay, my adviser at Harvard University, for her valuable comments. Most of this book was written while I was living on the University of Chicago campus, where my wife was concluding a doctoral degree in the Department of Anthropology. Many of the arguments developed in this book were the result of our daily conversations, which also allowed me to benefit indirectly from the sapience of her professors. During that time many people offered valuable support and friendship, especially Pablo and Mónica Silva, Petra and Fritz Lehmann, Mirta Schattner and Ricardo Gomez, Francisco and Viviana, Laura and Luis, and Philip Bohlman, all of whom made me feel welcome in Hyde Park; so, too, the many friends and fellow parents we met at the Blackstone Building. I also want to thank my friends in Boston, including Patty Tang and Eric Sommers, Alejandra and Marcelo Amati, "Mencha" Ramirez de la Jara and Gonzalo de la Jara, Matt McGuire, Paola Uccelli, Bob Kendrick, and Bart and Michelle Dean.

Many other friends and colleagues have supported and nurtured my studies in the Andes. For a long time Chuck Walker and Zoila Mendoza have been loyal comrades and supporters. The same for Tony Seeger, who throughout the years has been not only a generous friend but also a source of steady support. During the final stages of this book I received support from a number of people. From Marisol de la Cadena, Marta Savigliano, Gage Averill, and Veit Erlmann I received warm encouragement. I thank Prof. Robert Stevenson for his interest in my work and for sharing his enthusiasm for the study of Latin American music and culture. Enrique Iturriaga, my professor at the National Conservatory of Music, always supported my musical undertakings, including this one. The same for maestros

Edgar Valcárcel, Celso Garrido Lecca, and the late Enrique Pinilla. Thanks go as well to Gonzalo Portocarrero, Carlos Iván Degregori, and Norma Fuller for their positive remarks to portions of the last chapter of this book, which assured me that it was pointed in the right direction. I also benefited from the lucid discussions with the graduate students enrolled in the seminar I taught in the Department of Ethnomusicology of the University of California, Los Angeles, in the fall of 1999, including Jonathan Ritter, Heidi Feldman, Brad Shank, Cristian Amigo, and Rebecca Rehman. I also want to thank Paul Gelles, who commented on different sections of this book and made useful suggestions.

In the Mantaro Valley, Hugo Orellana, from the town of Ataura, in the province of Jauja, always provided a warm place to rest and a wealth of information about regional popular culture. At the other end of the valley, Luis Cárdenas, owner of a of local handicrafts store in Huancayo, provided me with much needed data on festivals and dance-dramas on a regular basis. In Lima, I rediscovered two old acquaintances from the Mantaro Valley: performer and musicologist Rubén Valenzuela from the town of Sicaya and violinist Mencio Sovero from Huaripampa. Both kindly listened to my numerous questions and shared their knowledge with me. A friend and colleague, Manuel Ráez, joined me on many of my field trips, and his passion for fieldwork was, fortunately, contagious. Another Peruvian anthropologist and dear friend, the late Mary Fukomoto, joined me in Paccha and helped me collect valuable research data. Two research assistants whom I contacted in the valley, Oscar Zamudio Cabezas from Huancayo and Luis David Valenzuela from Acolla, elaborated useful reports about festivals. Conversations with Josafat Roel Pineda and Mildred Merino de Zela, two of the foremost scholars of folklore studies in Peru, were always enlightening. To all these individuals and to the participants in the seminar organized in 1999 by the Faculty of Sociology of the Universidad Nacional del Centro (National University of Central Peru) in the city of Huancayo, I wish to offer my sincere appreciation.

Funding for most of my research and fieldwork was provided through the Project of Preservation of Andean Music at the Catholic University of Peru, a program sponsored by the Ford Foundation (Grant 870–0657). Antonio Muñoz Nájar and the members of the advisory committee to the foundation's program of cultural preservation deserve special thanks for their help in assuring the continuity of this project in its initial years. Additional research was possible thanks to a Tinker summer travel grant in 1994 and a Paine travel fellowship in 1996, both through Harvard University. The Center for Andean Ethnomusicology of the Riva-Agüero Institute of the Catholic University of Peru allowed me the time and resources to travel and facilitated the writing process. The presence of my colleagues at the center through the years (Manuel Ráez, Gisela Cánepa-Koch, Alex Huerta-Mercado, Maria Eugenia Ulfe, Juan M. Ossio, "Leito" Casas, Mariela

Cosio, Marimeña Jiménez, Ana María Béjar, Giuliana Borea, and Omar Ráez) and the numerous students of the Catholic University of Peru who participated in our field trips and audiovisual productions have been more than motivating. Thanks to all.

Finally, I want to thank my parents, Catalina and Emilio, for their love and constant aid throughout the years, my brother and sisters and their families for reminding me that I am not alone, and particularly my sister Ruth for her sustained support during the years that I have been working on this book. My in-laws César and Gerhild and their family have been a constant source of support as well. Last but certainly not least, thanks to my dear wife, Gisela Cánepa, and my lovely children, Amanda and Sebastian, to whom I promise to leave more time on the computer for their games now that this book is finished.

# Contents

Debating the Past

# INTRODUCTION

Dispute over the past is only possible when conflicting memories coexist. In the summer of 1996 I was witness to important new developments in the city of Huancayo, the bustling commercial center of the Mantaro Valley in the Peruvian Andes. Every single block along Giraldez Avenue, one of the most important boulevards of the city, had been embellished with the statue of a regional dancer. Each of these colorful and well-maintained statues was fully costumed in the elaborate dress of native dance traditions. Since Huancayo had always given me the impression that it favored the "modern" and industrial aspects of urban development over its indigenous heritage, I was intrigued by the vision that these statues conveyed.[1]

But this was not the only monumental transformation that I noticed in Huancayo. The Parque de la Identidad Wanka (Park of Wanka Identity) was being built in one of the more affluent neighborhoods of Huancayo, as part of a new cultural policy of the municipality that is dedicated to celebrating the most distinguished figures of Wanka identity in the twentieth century.[2] Seven statues were being built, among which were the figures of three popular musicians: the acclaimed singers the Picaflor de los Andes and the Flor Pucarina and the legendary composer and violinist Zenobio Dagha.[3] Only the latter statue was finished, and it portrayed Dagha standing up on two *wakrapukus* (*cachos*), the spiral-shaped horn trumpets used in the ritual branding of cattle. The statue was noteworthy in two respects. First, Dagha was still alive. Second, he had played in urban public festivals using "modern" instruments such as saxophones and clarinets. The wakrapukus, in contrast, were old ritual instruments that pertained exclusively to a rural domain. What was the purpose of this fusion?

From my point of view, this representation reinforced the balance between the modern and the traditional, the new and the old, the recent

The statue of a regional dancer (*chonguinada*) on
Giraldez Avenue in Huancayo. Photo: Raúl R.
Romero.

past and the distant past of the Mantaro Valley. Thus, conflicting pasts are
represented in one single image in order to reinforce cultural continuity,
transcending the conflicting representations of history. This image was in
tune with the everyday observations of the people of the valley in debating the past as a way of interpreting the present. I never sensed confrontation but rather a negotiation of different cultural projects directed at a
common objective: the protection of cultural difference. This objective, in
spite of the sometimes heated debate, was clearly manifest in the public
park.

This book examines the dispute over the past, the search for cultural authenticity, and the role of modernity, through the study of the regional
music culture of the Mantaro Valley in central Peru. Through an exploration of the role of rituals with significant musical content, dance-dramas,

Statue of violinist Zenobio Dahga standing near two *wakrapukus* in the Park of Wanka Identity. Photo: Raúl R. Romero.

musical ensembles, and popular Andean music, I illustrate how the search for authenticity emerges within a complex public debate characterized by antagonistic discourses and cultural practices. At the same time, these seemingly conflictive modes converge in a project of collective identity defined in opposition to that of the established national elite.

If "memory can be stored in traces, obliterated, or overwritten" (Karrer 1994:128), then a social memory is almost necessarily a contested one, since it pertains to hundreds or thousands of individuals. This is certainly the case in the Mantaro Valley, where the inhabitants can be said to have both short-term and long-term memory. The former is usually choreographed and dramatized in popular culture, and the later is ritualized following inherited patterns, the origins of which no one remembers. The former is celebratory, while the latter speaks of nostalgia and remorse. The inhabitants of the Mantaro Valley have resolved their concern over

Map of Peru

the loss of ancient customs (mostly agricultural practices and beliefs) by restructuring colonial and pre-Hispanic traditions within dance-dramas and the festival system. For example, as I explore in chapter 2, the revival of the nocturnal harvest ritual in the form of a dance-drama is mobilized as an image of the valley's rural past, and this has given rise to a heated debate about cultural authenticity. A similar controversy has occurred over the use of saxophones in the most representative instrumental ensemble of the valley (see chapter 3). In these and other cases that I cover in this book, there is no unanimity concerning the past as a unique cultural legacy, that is, there is no agreement on where tradition or modernity ought to reside. There is a constant dispute in everyday life over which kind of past represents the local culture and which one should determine its future direction.[4]

The Mantaro Valley is a region within a "modern" nation-state that has maintained a unique cultural temperament and identity in spite of the fact that it produces goods for national and international markets. The proximity of the valley to the nation's capital and the fluidity of communications due to the existence of an efficient railroad and highway system have accelerated regional integration into the wider national economy. How is it possible for a regional culture, subordinated by a dominant national economic and ideological system, to maintain autonomy in terms of popular culture and aesthetics? How are the people of the Mantaro Valley struggling to maintain their singularity in the face of the intensification of mass migration and the alluring homogenizing voices of the mass media? What kinds of cultural debates are developing inside the valley concerning the shape and profundity of their identity? What is the role of music in these processes, and is this role an influential one?

In attempting to answer these questions, I suggest that this regional cultural sovereignty was attained by generating a vigorous popular culture within which the fiesta system, ritual, and dance, and the vitality and overall presence of music figure importantly.[5] All of these manifestations constitute transcendent opportunities for social and cultural revelation in an otherwise compliant practical existence characterized by the everyday endorsement of capitalist enterprise and market-wise decision making. Popular culture in the valley, however, is not free of social conflicts and ideological controversies. Conflicting trends are constantly being negotiated, and those who resist its cultural baggage regularly challenge the power of modern capitalism. Hence, the postures assumed by "traditionalists" and "innovators" are perpetually in creative conflict, as are the discussion about authenticity and modernity and the definition of what is new and what is old.

Music is the common central element in festivals, rituals, and dance-dramas. And it is the single element that transcends these settings and emerges in supraregional contexts. For example, the music from the Mantaro Valley is central to the reproduction of identity in the nation's capital, where it not only constitutes a central element in the fiestas of urban-based migrants but also is a powerful presence in the recording industry, from which it reroutes itself back to the Mantaro Valley and other regions. Musical practice emerges, therefore, as a key element to understanding this region's social and cultural singularity.

I believe that by itself, however, music (understood as sound structure) does not have the power to significantly alter other domains.[6] In the Mantaro Valley music does not exist in a vacuum but is intermingled with other manifestations of popular culture (festivals, rituals, dance-dramas, and collective memories). It is only in its association with these other realms of culture and social organization that music as a cultural practice has the power to affect local consciousness.[7] Hence, I focus on the festivals, rituals, and dances as musically organized manifestations around which people of the valley consolidate, adjust, and generate their cultural projects. My goal, then, is to analyze how processes of cultural resistance, assimilation, and creativity take effect in the realm of musical practice and contexts and to understand how these processes operate to preserve or reinvent regional traditions that maintain cultural difference vis-à-vis national hegemonic ideologies.

I am also interested in the extent to which the idea of modernization has impacted the identity of the valley's residents. There are many ethnographies about the economic development and social change of the region that have not answered basic questions as to how and why the cultural identity of the valley exhibits such a healthy and powerful presence in the national context. The domain of musical practice offers a unique perspective for answering these questions. It was José María Arguedas, a Peruvian anthropologist and writer, who, focusing on the cultural configuration of the Mantaro Valley and paying due attention to expressive culture (music as a primary target), suggested prospects hereafter for a regional development within the contexts of current national constraints. Arguedas suggested that the cultural *mestizaje* in the valley constituted a model of successful ethnic revival, which gave him new hopes for the continuity of a renovated yet vigorous Andean culture in the context of the modern nation-state (1975). This book finds inspiration and is also motivated by such a view.

## Being an "Insider/Outsider"

As a middle-class Spanish-speaking Limeño from the coast, working at more than 3,000 meters above sea level in Quechua-speaking villages I experienced much the same problems of adaptation that any foreign scholar would have. Yet, as a Peruvian, I was in my own "country of origin," already familiarized with the crucial dilemmas of Peruvian multiethnic and multiclass society and irrevocably involved with its future as a nation. In this sense, I could be considered an "insider," an "indigenous scholar" making sense of his own society, studying his own people. But this view does not correspond with the way people of the Mantaro Valley saw me, as a Limeño, an outsider, a newcomer who had to ask a lot of questions in order to understand the culture of the valley.

The ambivalent condition of "indigenous scholars" has been debated by several authors (see Asad 1973; Fahim 1982; Bennoune 1985; Jones 1970; Said 1990; Kay Trask 1991; and Narayan 1993). The basic assumption has been that, on the one hand, "insiders," "indigenous," or native scholars are intimate with the cultures they are studying, that is, that they are members of the social group under study. On the other hand, the "foreign" scholar is thought of as someone arriving from afar who knows nothing about that culture (see Nettl 1983:259–269). Today such a dichotomy has been called into question in relation to the current condition of globalization and massive international migrations (see Gupta and Ferguson 1997).

However, I find myself frequently dealing with these issues in some academic circles. So it bears repeating that such a view ignores the multicultural character, pluriethnic presence, and class differences that pervade modern nation-states. Is the native scholar defined in relation to a village, a region, a nation-state? Such a question is flawed from various perspectives. First, the distinction implies the false assumption that the countries of the native scholars are ethnically and culturally homogeneous. Second, the separation between insiders and outsiders is essentialized in relation to national origins. "Insiders" are placed in an eternal and inescapable position for life, destined to act as insiders just because they were born within the limits of the nation-states within which the community under study was located. The Western and non-Western dichotomy further reinforces this essentialization by ascribing and imposing the obligation on the non-Western to be "different," to develop novel methods, new approaches, and original perspectives.[8]

Kirin Narayan notices that the distinction appeared from the colonial settings in which anthropology originated: "the days in which natives were genuine natives (whether they liked it or not) and the observer's objectivity in the scientific study of Other societies posed no problem" (1993:672). Today, however, it is a widely accepted fact that this dichotomy is ineffective in defining the different styles and aims of regional scholarships in the world. In times when the borders between the traditional and the modern break apart and processes of globalization mark the passage into the twenty-first century, speaking of insiders and outsiders, native and foreign, seems part of another time and another place. With the increasing number of Third World scholars working in American universities, as well as professors in Third World institutions with doctoral degrees obtained in Europe and the United States, the distinction between natives and foreigners becomes blurred and irrelevant. In this line of thought, Lila Abu-Lughod has proposed the term *halfie* to refer to "people whose national or cultural identity is mixed by virtue of migration, overseas education, or parentage" (1991:137).

In this context I wish to clarify several important issues that may inform the reader about the author of this book. First, in a multicultural and multiethnic nation like Peru, I am not a native of or indigenous to the various regional cultures that constitute the nation. As a "native" of Lima, the nation's capital, a city of 8 million inhabitants, I have been raised in an urban middle-class environment. Although my father was born in the Andes, my cultural background stems from modern Lima, with all that implies. I attended a bilingual American school and a private university more similar to than different from similar institutions of higher learning in the world.

Second, I argue, following Néstor García Canclini (1995) and Roberto Da Matta (1995), that Peru and the rest of Latin America have been part of the Western Hemisphere since the late sixteenth century, when the European multitudes arrived and built towns, cities, governments, schools, and universities upon the ruins of the previous indigenous institutions. The historical dilemma of Latin American nation-states in postcolonial times (the nineteenth century onward) has indeed been deciding which developmental project to follow, a European liberal model or a nationalist venture based on the rescue of indigenous legacies. But since the second alternative has frequently been based on cultural issues rather than economic ones, all of Latin American developmental enterprises imply modernity within the Western area of influence.[9]

Third, I want to stress the question of audience. My audience (except when I publish in English) is different from that of the scholars who reside in Europe and North America.[10] My primary readership is Peruvian and Latin American. Despite the multicultural and multiethnic presence in Peru, the integrative mechanisms of the nation-state (i.e., commercial distribution) make access to national publications in Spanish attainable by everyone. Unlike the "foreign" scholar, I can feel assured that my subjects of study—or some of them—will eventually read what I write about them. Several other nuances derive from the question of audience. In my writing any suggestion of exoticism will be avoided whenever possible, such as narratives of distance and de-familiarization, common in Euro-American writings. As Dale Eickelman attests in explaining the differences between Moroccan scholarship and "Western" social sciences, the writing style directed to local audiences will tend to avoid those passages, definitions, and descriptions considered too obvious. Those same texts would be written differently when directed to a foreign audience (1989:391–392). For example, it is conceivable that detailed descriptions about the location of the region under study and careful depictions about recent political events would probably be reduced to a minimum in a Spanish edition of this book because they would appear as trivial and commonsensical to my local audience.

Fourth, another difference between my work as an ethnomusicologist who resides in Peru and many foreign ones is my lifelong commitment to my "subjects of study." This commitment may be emotional, but it is also political—not in the partisan sense but in the sense of being committed to a collective project. This of course is not a prerogative of "indigenous scholars" alone. There are plenty of "foreign" academics involved in what is technically called long-term field research, which inevitably leads to this kind of emotional and political involvement with the group under study and with the nation at large. George M. Foster, for example, has presented several testimonies of foreign researchers with a lifelong involvement in particular regions and nations (Foster et al. 1979). However, the Malinowskian model of fieldwork, which commended the short-term permanence at a foreign site based exclusively on "pure" academic and intellectual reasons, after which the researcher "comes back home" and reports to his own academic community, has functioned as an archetype in the past and is still a dominant trend in the ethnographic disciplines (Gupta and Ferguson 1997:11).[11]

## Fieldwork and Organization

As with the first researchers of folklore studies in Central Europe, my fieldwork was not constrained by one or two years of intense residence, because "the field" was always near home (Gupta and Ferguson 1997:28). One can get from Lima to the Mantaro Valley in six hours by car or twelve by train. My first visit to the valley was in 1984, and after a couple of field trips I became convinced that it was an ideal place to carry out my fieldwork. I became interested in the regional scope of such a study, instead of a community approach. The valley is comprised of sixty-four rural districts, all of them within a two-hour drive. The valley is roughly thirty miles long, and despite the diversity of each district, the cultural homogeneity of the valley became a revelation.

While I was a Limeño arriving in towns with my yellow Volkswagen Bug, the people of the valley were always very friendly, and I was warmly received in each village. The residents of the valley, whether poor or affluent peasants, influential townsmen, merchants, or white-collar professionals, greeted my interest in their lives with respect and collaboration. My questions about the music of the Mantaro Valley were well taken because its inhabitants are extremely proud of their popular culture and their music. The people of the valley are well traveled, their contacts with Lima constant, and many of them have relatives and friends abroad. The majority of the inhabitants of the valley are peasants in the sense that they live from, own, or obtain supplementary income from agricultural enterprises. But they do not correspond to Eric Wolf's portrait of the constituent of a "closed corporate peasant community" (1966). Nor do they conform to the "peasants becoming farmers" notion (Mallon 1983). The residents of the Mantaro Valley are an ethnically homogenous mestizo group, differentiated only along economic lines. Thus, the strong feelings regarding regional identity are equally dispersed throughout the districts of the valley as well as in the dynamic urban center of Huancayo and the less prosperous town of Jauja.

The peasants of the valley have frequently been described as "prosperous" in the literature, in relation to other peasants in Peru. When years later I visited the northern province of Cajamarca, some five hundred miles away, I confirmed this to be the case when, instead of being served a three-course meal, I would be greeted with only a bowl of soup (Cajamarca peasants are among the poorest in Peru). The pride and self-assurance of the residents of the Mantaro Valley have a strong material basis. Most people own their own land, even when its size is often insufficient to maintain a family. But this land is a solid support for basic subsistence and a stable foundation upon which additional income can be obtained through commerce and other nonagricultural activities. These factors make valley residents highly successful when they arrive in Lima, where they integrate into a solid social and economic network (Altamirano 1984b).

My first entrance into serious fieldwork was devoid of any of the harsh or dramatic stories that so frequently inhabit ethnographic narratives. Throughout 1985 (January–December), which I devoted to continuous research in the valley, I was lucky enough to run into the same friendliness and cooperation. During that year I made several field trips from Lima, staying several weeks on each trip. I visited and revisited several districts, observing public festivals, private rituals, staged contests, and civic presentations. I recorded live music intensively in every one of these contexts, collecting nearly eighty hours of music on a Sony cassette recorder TC-D5M. The following year I embarked on other research ventures and interrupted my visits to the valley. I kept interviews, tapes, and documentation until I had time to reflect and "do something" with the material I had gathered. Eventually, I decided to go back to the valley during three consecutive summers (1994, 1995, and 1996). On those summer trips I found some new developments, but I mostly confirmed the trends I had observed in 1985.[12] The reflections presented in this book, therefore, are the results of over a ten-year span of visiting the Mantaro Valley.

This book can be read in conjunction with the compact disc I edited in 1995 for Smithsonian Folkways Recordings called *The Mantaro Valley* (SF CD 40467), volume 2 of the series *Traditional Music of Peru*. Most of the ritual and festival music and musical ensembles analyzed in this book are included in this compilation.

In the first chapter of this book I present a historical and cultural overview of the Mantaro Valley, with special emphasis on its ethnic demographics, the role of migration to the urban centers, and the dynamics of regional culture within the context of the nation at large. I also explore the relevance of concepts such as tradition and modernity, power and resistance, in interpreting sociocultural processes of the Mantaro Valley.

Three rituals with extensive musical content that are linked with economic activities are examined in chapter 2. In comparing the branding of animals (*herranza*) with other rituals of ceremonial agricultural labor, I address the issue of the endurance and prominence of some rituals in comparison with the vanishing of other rituals in the valley. I also focus on the festival system of the Mantaro Valley and the overall features of the numerous dance-dramas that are enacted within it. Here I explain how one dance-drama linked to Carnival and peasantry (the *huaylas*) has been reinvented in the form of two main variants (the "new" and the "old"), around which heated debates about "authenticity" are taking place.

A historical sketch of the formation of the *orquesta típica*, the most popular musical ensemble in the Mantaro Valley, is presented in chapter 3.[13] I will explain how this "modern" ensemble is in many ways a result of the impact of the mining industry, its influence manifest in its repertoire, musical style, and performance. I also explain how in Huaripampa, a town in the valley, the debate over cultural authenticity focuses on the orquesta típica and the disputed use of the saxophone.

In chapter 4 I address the search for cultural authenticity as it moved to Lima in the context of increasing migration. Until the 1950s the quest for a regional identity was blurred by the ideal of a homogenizing Andean symbol: the precolonial Inca. However, since the 1950s the musicians from the Mantaro Valley have taken on leading roles in the recording industry, introducing their unique regional style. Case studies of two Andean popular singing "stars" from the valley and their respective repertoires elucidate these processes.

Finally, in chapter 5 I discuss how the inhabitant of the Mantaro Valley—especially its younger generations—perceive themselves moving into the future in relation to the nation-state and its official ideologies. In so doing, I survey how the state has rationalized "Andean culture" and the role of local governments. Here I explain the manner in which the younger generations of the valley assume experimental identities in their search for cultural authenticity and the contradictions between what is here termed *traditionalist, modernist*, and *radical* perspectives. Within all of these spheres, music remains the main arena in which identity, authenticity, and social memory are defined and debated.

# I

# REGION, CULTURE, AND IDENTITIES

*The Mantaro Valley: History and Regional Development*

Some colonial sources suggest that when the first Spanish troops arrived in the Mantaro Valley (see map) in 1533 they expected war. Instead, they were surprised to be hailed by thousands of natives who celebrated their coming with songs and feasts (Arguedas 1975:81). It was later that the invaders would realize that the native inhabitants of the valley—the Wankas—had been subdued by the imperial Incas long ago and since then had been their fierce adversaries.[1] Thus, they saw in the arrival of the conquerors an opportunity for revenge and liberation from Inca rule. An alliance, which was considered mutually beneficial, soon followed. The Wanka leaders saw in their collaboration a way of recovering the regional autonomy they had lost when the Incas arrived in the valley around 1460 (Espinoza Soriano 1973:68). The Inca state, while allowing the regional chieftains to maintain many of their privileges, had undermined their political power to a great extent. They were closely supervised and severely punished if they did not comply with the policies of the empire. However, the Spaniards needed the local support to compensate for the greater forces of the Inca army. They were coming from Cajamarca in the north and were on their way to Cuzco, the capital of the Inca empire. For the journey they were in need of provisions and servicemen, which the *caciques*, the native

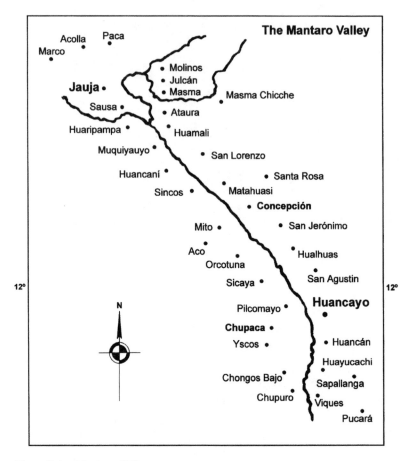

Map of the Mantaro Valley

leaders, promptly provided. Many natives fought and died with members of the Spanish army. In the military campaign against Quisquis 300 Indians of the Mantaro Valley died in battle. In the expedition from Cajamarca to Jauja 196 Indians and 109 Indian women were lost on the way (Arguedas 1975:83). The alliance seemed to satisfy both Wankas and Spaniards, and eventually the Spaniards chose the town of Jauja as the capital of the new conquered territory.

The town of Jauja is indeed considered the first capital of Peru. It is located at the south edge of the valley, on a site from which the entire valley can be watched. The impression of the first Spaniards on entering the town was illustrative:

It is large and it is located in a beautiful valley, and is a mild land; a powerful river crosses by one part of the town; it is organized like a Spanish town, very tight and with well-sorted streets. We have seen the people of other towns and there were so many more people congregated as in no other town in the Indias because many Spaniards saw that in the main plaza more than one hundred thousand souls gathered, and there were markets, other plazas and streets of the same town full of people, that such a large multitude seemed marvelous.[2]

A few decades later, when the Spanish armies continued conquering southern territories, they abandoned Jauja as their center of operations. Very few Spaniards remained in the valley in spite of the agricultural richness of the region. It has been suggested by Arguedas that the lack of gold mines—one of the primary goals of the conquerors—and the founding of Lima on the coast were the main reasons the valley was forsaken by the Spaniards (1975:91). This fact was later to prove beneficial for the regional development of the valley, because due to the departure of most of the Spaniards from the valley most of the land remained in local hands. This was unusual in the Peruvian Andes, since in the rest of the former Inca empire agricultural and pasturelands were taken from the Indians and given to Spaniards in the form of *encomiendas*—a colonial system of land tenure by which a landlord was given the rights over portions of land and its residents. Under this colonial system the Indian, with no land or income to survive on his own, surrendered to serfdom and total submission and exploitation by a Spanish authority. In the Mantaro Valley this colonial system was not put into practice, primarily because of the privileged treatment given to the allies, the Wanka leaders who had supported the Spanish armies in their quest for conquest.

The town of Jauja, then, went from being the first capital of Peru to a strictly local borough. Arguedas has observed that, as a result, Jauja does not have the Spanish flavor that other colonial capitals, in which the Spaniards settled in larger numbers, have in the southern Andes (1975:100). Notwithstanding the fact that in 1616 the colonial chronicler Guaman Poma described Huancayo as being so poor that he was unable to find lodging, Jauja ultimately yielded to Huancayo—located at the opposite end of the valley—the role of economic and political center of the valley.

Today, "the valley" refers to not only to the actual valley itself—the plains that surround the river—but also to its highland areas. Several districts, located between 3,500 and 4,000 meters above sea level, are located in those areas that emerge on the margins of the Mantaro River's tributaries. Above them there is an even higher ecological zone rising over 4,000 meters that surrounds the valley (*puna*) and mainly consists of pastures, with little or no agricultural activity (Mayer 1981). The region encompasses four provinces: Jauja, Concepción, Chupaca, and Huancayo. Its population is over half a million inhabitants, of whom nearly 100,000 reside in the city of Huancayo, the main urban and commercial center of

The town of Masmachicche, one of the villages along one of the Mantaro River's tributaries. Photo: Raúl R. Romero.

the valley (Long and Roberts 1978:8). The rest of the population is dispersed throughout the nearly sixty-four towns of the rural areas of the Mantaro Valley. It is in these towns that most of the mestizo peasantry of the valley reside, working in the fields, raising livestock, or turning to small-scale commercial activities for supplementary income.[3]

One of the turning points in the recent history of the Mantaro Valley was the beginning of Cerro de Pasco Corporation activities in the central Andes of Peru in 1901, when it acquired several preexisting small local mining companies. Since then the mining centers have constituted one of the main migration focal points for the peasants of the valley. This was a temporal migration, because the peasants went to the mines only for periods of two to three months and never lost control of their lands (Bonilla 1974:32). This condition has been noted by many authors (Bonilla 1974; Manrique 1987; Mallon 1983) as "resistance to proletarization," meaning the opposition of the peasants to abandoning their land (means of production) and transforming themselves into a proletariat (miners) who can only depend on their labor for survival. This "resistance" to becoming miners was primarily determined by the fact that, first, the "miner" was at the same time a peasant who owned land and, second, the peasant-miner worked only for supplementary earnings, since his main income derived from agricultural activities. Heraclia Bonilla has reproduced a technical report from 1905 on the state of a mining center in the region that says:

A view of the main street of Huancayo. Photo: Raúl R. Romero.

Morococha did not and does not have a distinct population. The workers in the mines are from Jauja, and they do not come at random but they are hired, usually for two or three months, rarely for five or six months. . . . Most of those who sign a contract have some kind of property which they cultivate and from which they earn their living, thus the wage that they earn in the mines is for additional expenses, the fiestas of the villages encouraged by the priests that are so expensive, and sometimes too to acquire more land.[4]

Bonilla, Florencia E. Mallon, and Nelson Manrique dramatize the mining experience of the peasantry of the valley as tragic, tarnished by exploitation and harsh labor conditions. Bonilla, who describes the mines as "centers for exploitation," illustrates with *huayno* song texts the blunt testimonies of what he depicts as the peasant's painful mining experience ("miner, sad miner, cheer your heart, soothe your pain, singing your misery," in Bonilla 1974:28). Manrique affirms that the nature of mining labor in the central Andes was that of "a brutal capitalist accumulation" and as an example cites the report from 1908 of a public relations manager from the mining company in which it is stated that work in the mines was performed day and night and that most of them worked for thirty-six consecutive hours (1987:253). What I want to highlight here is, rather than the extent to which the mining corporation wanted to capitalize upon the peasants or the relations of exploitation in the mines, how the peasants

The town of Orcotuna, situated on the plains that surround the Mantaro River. Photo: Raúl R. Romero.

utilized the mines for their own convenience, to obtain supplementary wages to further enhance their agricultural operations, and how they managed to migrate and be miners only for a short period of time, after which they would go back to the valley.

While it is undeniable that working in the mines was an unkind assignment, the temporary quality of the mining labor suggests that the mining experience was rude, perhaps brutal, but tolerable because of its short-term span. Systems like the *enganche* (a method of paying for labor in advance) were indeed designed to exercise total control upon a worker over a specific period of time, but by 1918 enganche was already being replaced by other employment strategies. Mallon herself explains that the system never worked in the valley because of the high rate of runaways (peasants who received payment but never showed up), the practice of signing up with different *enganchadores*, and the high commissions of the local merchants in charge of enganche (1983:220). Finally, the system was abandoned in favor of direct hiring by the mining company. It is possible that for the Mantaro Valley's residents who did not have access to land or other source of income mining labor was indeed seen as a tragic and more permanent destiny, but this seems to have been a rare occurrence. In my interviews in the valley with elder residents, seasonal migration to work in the mines was always referred to as a routine stage in the life cycle of particular individuals, and never in my interviews did I encounter tragic stories or tales of destruction of lives or families during or after work in the mines.[5]

Tragic indeed were the effects of mining on the ecology of the region. In 1922 the main offices of the Cerro de Pasco Corporation moved to the town of La Oroya and established there one of the largest refineries on the continent for all the minerals (copper, lead, zinc) that came from their mines in neighboring areas (Espinoza 1973:348). Once it started operating, "between 100 and 125 tons of arsenic, sulphur dioxide, lead, bismuth, and other poisons began to fall each day in neighboring villages" (Mallon 1983: 226). Livestock had to be moved to higher altitude pastures. In neighboring communities many of the eucalyptus trees died and entire harvests were lost or seriously damaged. People and animals suffered from related diseases and malaise (see Espinoza 1973:347–348 and Mallon 1983:226–229).

What is also certain is that the establishment of the large mining industries in the region marked the beginning of a new phase in the lives of the population of the Mantaro Valley. The Cerro de Pasco Corporation, since its establishment in the central Andes in 1901, was directly responsible for the unprecedented expansion of internal and external markets and for the building of the Central Railroad, which arrived in Huancayo in 1908. Over a few years, the peasantry of the Mantaro Valley had encountered the possibility of maximizing their agricultural production for the market—beyond the subsistence levels—and had seen the social and geographical distance to the nation's capital dramatically shortened by the railroad.

These milestones triggered a rapid modernization of the Mantaro Valley. The city of Huancayo grew in size and in economic importance, and by the 1940s it had already achieved fame as the major urban center in the valley, to the detriment of Jauja, which remained withdrawn from the intense commercial development that affected Huancayo. Seasonal migration also brought changes in the culture and ideology of the peasant, besides providing a major cash flow into the peasant economy. The intense cultural, social, and economic exchange with Lima provided them with new alternative lifestyles, markets, and audiences and exposed the peasantry of the valley to national modernizing trends. None of these changes, however, disturbed the regional consciousness of the Mantaro Valley or inspired a massive migration of the peasantry of the valley to Lima. The reasons for this "resistance," if I may use this term only in reference to the first decades of the twentieth century in the valley, are solidly grounded in practicality. Because neither the colonial system of encomienda nor the republican hacienda (large private landholding) pattern was instituted in the Mantaro Valley, most of the peasantry were small landholders, owners of their own means of production. This access to land was the main reason for the peasants' not becoming full-time miners and not feeling the urge to emigrate permanently from the valley. Of course, access to land was an unequal privilege. For the richer peasants the land meant profit beyond subsistence levels; for the poorer it meant basic maintenance. For the land-deprived, the steady economic growth and intense commercial activity of the valley provided other means of financial support.

However, the process of *mestizaje*, which accelerated after the turn of the century, redressed ethnic inequalities in the valley and obliterated the unresolved conflicts between mestizos and Indians that pervaded life in the southern Andes. Inequality in the Mantaro Valley, through the first decades of the twentieth century, may be assessed by economic differentiation rather than ethnic and cultural considerations. Mestizaje made all Indians equal, reconstructing them into mestizos who preserved their allegiances to Andean society (Quechua language, cultural traditions) and their local and regional differences, especially in regard to the national elites.

The peasantry of the valley, therefore, confronted the impact of the mining industries, migration, new economic challenges, and the closer, yet always threatening, presence of Lima in the valley with the best of material conditions (access to land or commercial enterprises) and relatively stable cultural consciousness regarding their own regional identity and historical past. This past was colored by the Wankas' invincible resistance to Inca

A mural titled *Wanka Identity*, located inside one of the buildings of the University of Huancayo. Photo courtesy Gustavo Reyna.

dominion and even prolonged into the colonial wars and is now rescued as "Wanka identity" in their quest for maintenance of a cultural difference from the "national image" that originated from Lima's cultural media.

## Tradition and Modernity

The notion of tradition as a fixed and timeless convention has recently been subject to reformulation. Since Eric J. Hobsbawn made the indisputable observation that "traditions which appear or claim to be old are often quite recent in origin and sometimes invented" (1983:1), the term *invented tradition* has been widely used in defining perpetually changing cultural practices, in permanent states of negotiation and redefinition. It is now understood that traditions do not have to be old to be claimed by a group of people as "authentic" and part of their heritage. Traditions are invented and claimed because "they normally attempt to establish continuity with a suitable historic past" (Hobsbawn 1983:1). It does not matter whether this continuity is imaginary or based on hard facts; what matters is the structure it brings to social groups otherwise immersed in constant change and innovation (Hobsbawn 1983:2).

This conception of tradition is very useful in the inquiry into the different ways history is claimed by the people of the Mantaro Valley. They are proud of their cultural traditions, though many of them are of recent invention. The term *typical* (*típico*), itself a synonym of *tradition* in the rural areas of Peru, is applied to a type of musical ensemble considered representative of the culture of the valley (the *orquesta típica*). But in fact, this ensemble achieved its contemporary format only around the middle of the twentieth century (chapter 3). Why is it then considered típico? An ensemble that includes clarinets, which were introduced in the valley in the 1910s, is proclaimed as the more "authentic" expression of "Wanka culture" in the town of Huaripampa.[6] What mechanisms are at work when imagining "traditionality" and "authenticity" in cultural practices that are no older than one hundred years? Such a process would not be extraordinary except for the fact that the Mantaro Valley is the site of a culture more than a thousand years old (Peñaloza Jarrín 1995:5). What happened in the Mantaro Valley that made it necessary for its residents to redefine and reinvent their cultural traditions?

In recognizing the usefulness of Hobsbawn's critique of the concept of tradition, I am also aware of the problems in introducing the notion of invention into the sphere of the Mantaro Valley's cultural practices. *Invention* is a term too closely related to the idea of discovery. Novelty and originality would seem to be requirements of something "invented." But in the Mantaro Valley the traditions that we are talking about are not sudden fabrications; they are reelaborations of previously invented and reinvented cultural practices that go back as far as the pre-Inca colonial and republican periods and extend into contemporary times. The saxophone and the clarinet are reinvented traditions but only within the context of a musical ensemble that also includes the harp and the violin, which were in turn reinvented as traditions during the colonial domination, and whose main musical repertoire consists of colonial genres (like the huayno and the muliza), which have, arguably enough, perpetuated substantial elements from the pre-Hispanic past (pentatonicism, for example).

Consequently, while acknowledging that Hobsbawn's precise definition of "invented tradition," as those cultural practices that emerge "within a brief and dateable period . . . and establishing themselves with great rapidity" (1983:1) appears to match the cases under review in this book, I prefer to avoid whenever possible the notion of the invented, in favor of other terms like *construction* and *building* of traditions. These concepts better express the various and simultaneous processes that go into the making of complex and multilayered cultural practices of people who manipulate and claim different conceptions of their own past. The orquesta típica of the Mantaro Valley, for example, in its current format is indeed traceable to a "dateable period" (turn of the century), but its different components are themselves "invented" instrumental traditions that go far back in time. As far as I know, no one has ever been successful in estimating the exact dates of when the harp and the violin were accepted as Indian "traditions" in the Andes or when the huayno genre was consolidated as the most popular Andean song and social dance.

Tradition is usually challenged by modernization, a concept that assumes diverse meanings and stands for dissimilar practices. In a choice between the academic notion of modernization as a developmental stage, which all contemporary societies must go through in the context of world capitalism (mostly maintained by theoreticians and policy makers), and the more popular understanding of "modernization," I emphasize the latter. My interest falls upon what the people of the Mantaro Valley interpret to be "modern." This "modernity" is understood primarily as "progress," technological innovation, urban services (electricity, running water), global communications (trains, planes, and automobiles, fax machines, and the Internet), and, more broadly, the process of incorporation into the wider national context.

The usefulness of this approach is especially welcome since it avoids the usual preconception that modernity will inevitably bring homogenization to world cultures, bringing them all into a single process, a global system, in which local cultural differences will disappear (Comaroff and Comaroff 1993:xi). The fact is that, notwithstanding the astounding development of capitalism, world markets, mass communications, and mass migration throughout the world, local cultures and ethnic differences continue to exist, struggle, and create novel lifestyles, which are, in turn, products of both "tradition" and "modernity." What García Canclini calls "the sociocultural hybrids in which the traditional and modern are mixed" (1995:2) are indeed those societies or populations that continue to maintain their identities while at the same time keeping up with the development of world capitalism.[7]

Sociocultural hybridity certainly appears to be the case in the Mantaro Valley, but we should be aware that those "hybrid cultures" are not, in turn, all the same. Each case is the result of different historical processes, and each displays distinct ways of appropriating modernity. While I recognize that hybrid cultures is a useful concept in referring to societies that cannot be explained through the old-fashioned method of separating "authentic" culture from modern "innovations," I disagree with the "homogenizing" flavor with which it impregnates all the cultural diversity that exists in the world today. The Mantaro Valley might be categorized as a "sociocultural hybrid," but so may the Tarascan area in Mexico, which García Canclini himself studies (1993:55). Both cultural areas have, however, different histories, maintain separate identities and worldviews, and relate differently to the state. Every process of cultural mestizaje, as of hybridization, is similar in its launching stages, when the forces of tradition however invented, reinvented, or constructed—are confronted with the forces of the modern, but they arrive at very different conclusions and are posited within separate wider national contexts.

The same observation would have to be applied to the Peruvian case. The Mantaro Valley, as a regional culture, is only one of several cases of regional developments in the nation. According to Arguedas, it may be the most successful one in terms of its abilities to maintain certain cultural independence while at the same time achieving some degree of economic prosperity (1957b). But the region of Cuzco—the capital of the old Inca empire—is also a powerful area that struggles to become a cultural alternative within the nation's complex and unresolved development prospects. Cuzco's success in institutionalizing its ideological struggle (and its perennial quest for material resources from the national elites) through a strong academic movement, *indigenista* (pro-Indian) organizations, and political regional unity recently has been the subject of serious study (see Tamayo Herrera 1980, 1981, and Rénique 1991).

The rupture between the previous clear division between the traditional and the modern is also crucial to understanding that, first, both concepts are no longer useful in distinguishing different types of societies and, second, every society has a peculiar way of confronting and creating modernity. In this respect there has been a significant development in the studies of "musical change" from a structural-functionalist perspective to the recent studies that have followed Hobsbawn's critical understanding of the concept of reinvented tradition and the notion of culture as a permanently contested arena in which ethnic and class divisions permeate the way each segment of society experiences it (Clifford 1986:19). The former trend has been well summarized by John Blacking (1977) and more recently epitomized in Nettl (1985). The latter, more dynamic perspectives can be seen, for example, in recent publications in the field of ethnomusicology (Waterman 1990; Erlmann 1991; Turino 1993; Guilbault 1993, Rice 1994; and Averill 1997). The interference between tradition and modernity has been clearly established by Arjun Appadurai in stressing the consequences of mass migration and the mass media (1996a:9). Both processes have made local cultures no longer exclusively "local" and the "modern" no longer circumscribed by industrizalized countries alone. In the context of an increased globalization process, it makes no sense to think of communities existing outside of this dynamic. Tradition and modernity, as Jean and John Comaroff say, "underpin a long-standing European myth: a narrative that explores the uneven, protean relations among 'ourselves' and 'others' in world history with a single, epic story about the passage from savagery to civilization" (1993:xii).

Following the same line of thought, I would also point to the notion of Westernization as another inadequate concept in demarcating differences between industrialized societies and the "other." This is a concept that freezes in time the tangibility of Western thought and science in a fixed geographical milieu—Europe and the United States—and is blind to the fact that globalization is not a recent phenomenon but began centuries ago with colonialism (Appadurai 1990:1). Latin America, for example, has been "Westernized" since the sixteenth century, when the Spaniards stepped down from their ships, mated with Indian women, built in a few decades numerous churches, schools, and plazas, and taught the Bible, the harp, and the violin to all the available Indians. Thus, the West, just like modernity, has been appropriated and reelaborated by local cultures into newer forms and meanings for centuries ago.

This issue is particularly relevant to Latin America and the case of the Mantaro Valley. Despite the common practice of situating Latin American indigenous and mestizo cultures as part of the non-Western world, Latin America is indeed part of the Western Hemisphere. I have already mentioned the colonization of the region in the late sixteenth century. Da Matta and David Hess in trying to transcend this dichotomy have highlighted the mixture between Western and non-Western cultures that has been going on for centuries after the arrival of the colonizers. For them, "Latin America is something else": the reality of Latin America is one that combines and merges traditional and modern, precapitalistic and capitalistic systems, democracies and dictatorships, Western and non-Western worldviews, all along the same national frontiers, simultaneously or taking turns along the passage of time (see DaMatta and Hess 1995:3). The authors also observe that in the Latin American nations "the upper classes are mostly descendants of Europeans, and the language, high culture, and formal institutions are all Western." They also mention the presence of democratic constitutions and a capitalist economy as common traits. In spite of the ambiguity implicit in their phrase "[Latin America] is something else," I prefer it to the simplistic consideration that local Latin American cultures can be "Westernized," as if the distinction between the culturally fixed and the culturally invasive would be a clear-cut operation by the ethnographer working as a field surgeon.

In the Mantaro Valley the issue of Westernization is particularly applicable, since most of its popular culture is comprised of Western-derived elements, designs, objects, and organizations: the fiesta system built upon the Catholic saints and the Virgin, the orquesta típica with its harp, violins, saxophones, and clarinets, the dances that mock the French *contredanse* (Sp. *contradanza*), the clothes and hats loosely based upon sixteenth- and seventeenth-century European fashions; the political structure derived from Western models with a municipality, a mayor, police officers, national identification cards, Peruvian citizenship, schools, universities, hospitals, and a universal health care system. Who can say when and how the culture of the valley is being "Westernized" nowadays? Yet it "is something else": the Andean deity *wamani* comes to mind, the wakrapuku trumpet, the chewing of coca leafs, the huayno, pentatonicism, communal reciprocity, racial and cultural mestizaje, the Quechua language, and the vigorous claim of a unique Wanka historical past as well as a self-reliant regional politics.

## Resistance and Hegemony

The facts that residents of the Mantaro Valley are still claiming their Wanka identity over any other cultural alternative and that the participating components in this identity are reinvented cultural forms of pre-Hispanic and colonial origins suggest that some kind of "resistance" has occurred throughout the centuries of colonial domination and peripheral development within the nation-state since the nineteenth century. Certainly the Mantaro Valley has gone through many crises over time. The Incas stormed the region, subduing the Wankas and incorporating them into the Inca empire. In the process of disentangling themselves from that oppression, fierce battles were fought by the Wanka and their new Spanish allies against the Inca armies. Despite this early alliance, the region nonetheless suffered from the devastating effects of the European invasion. Previously unknown diseases like influenza, smallpox, and typhus affected the population (Stern 1982:44–45). New political systems disrupted previous social structures. Ideological struggles against indigenous religious practices were also enforced, such as the "extirpation of idolatries" campaign conducted by the Spanish clergy in the seventeenth century (Arriaga 1920). And the wars of independence of the nineteenth century, like the war with Chile

some decades later, brought the regional economy to near-destruction
(Manrique 1987:25). Early into the twentieth century, the expansion of the
North American–owned Cerro de Pasco Corporation in the region was
achieved at the cost of small local mining entrepreneurs (see Manrique
1987:250–254) and dislocated as well the political, economic, and cultural
practices upheld until then.

Despite all odds, the regional culture of the Mantaro Valley remained,
not unchanged, but unique and distinct from other cultural paradigms that
floated around within the context of the modern nation-state. How does
one explain such persistence in a context of intense changes that were
forced upon the region? As Michel Foucault reminds us, "Where there is
power, there is resistance" (1978:95), and indeed the Mantaro Valley has
experienced external power more than once (the Incas, the Spaniards, the
Chileans, and the North Americans). But *resistance* is often translated as
*passive reaction*, suggesting a portrait in which the subaltern suffers from
external pressure and defends himself clinging to his most precious cultural treasures, having lost control over his material existence. This image
corresponds to James Scott's version of "everyday forms of resistance" in
which people apparently "conform to" forms of external power but in the
way of "hidden transcripts" (1990). These "hidden transcripts," manifested
through such prosaic actions as dissimulation, false compliance, and
feigned ignorance (Scott 1985:29), constitute forms of resistance different
from the explicit social movements in which people revolt physically
against the dominant rule.[8] Thus, the former is a "passive" form while the
latter is an "active" one.

I favor, however, a broader view of resistance that does not separate
the popular reaction to domination into two different and opposed sets of
behaviors. Following Foucault's notion that resistance is not outside power
itself and that the concept broadly includes "resistances that are possible,
necessary, improbable, spontaneous, savage, solitary, concerted, violent"
(1978:96), I believe that the Mantaro Valley has not only ideologically but
also physically revolted through the more effective forms of expressive
culture such as the festival, the music, and the ritual dance. Moreover,
since these expressive forms are not only private but also public ways in
which people demonstrate openly their worldviews, opinions, and cultural
alternatives, these are not "hidden transcripts" but exposed ones. At the
same time, I suggest that the residents of the valley have opposed the
status quo through a mixture of "passive" and "active" forms of defiance,
which may be present at different moments but may also coexist in expressive culture. Underneath a public, outspoken dance-drama there is a
private, concealed oral discourse. In between the notes of regional musics
there are discourses of authenticity and identity being sorted out, and
beneath the festival's external religious organization there are meanings
and symbols that are interpreted in oppositional and alternative terms.

I am not relying exclusively, though, on the notion of resistance in interpreting the Mantaro Valley because of its strong tendency to be identified with a particular social class, sector, or ethnic group. The danger of localizing these notions in particular social groups is real: the subaltern resists; the dominant sector exercises power and hegemony. Instead, Foucault favors the blurring and omnipresent attributes of power and resistance in saying: "Just as the network of power relations ends by forming a dense web that passes through apparatuses and institutions, without being exactly localized in them, so too the swarm of points of resistance traverses social stratifications and individual unities" (1978:96). Accordingly, and as we will see in the course of this book, resistance is indeed being exercised in the Mantaro Valley but is not fully articulated into the practice of an entire social class. There is controversy, discussion, and conflict among the different attitudes toward what is to be continued or incorporated, where and when one has to resist, and where and when to concede. There is no single stance of resistance among the residents of the valley, and the current debates, at the level of everyday life, on what is culturally "authentic" and what is "modern" are a reflection of this dissension.

I could make the same observations on power and hegemony in the Mantaro Valley. In most instances in this book I will use these notions in relation to these forces that come from the elites of the modern nation-state of Peru. Elites who are centralized in Lima, the nation's capital, and who control economic resources and political systems determine the directions of the mass media and its themes, elaborate national policies (legal, educational, economic), and national symbols (the national flag, the national anthem). It is in relation to the cultural, hegemonic models generated from these locations that regional cultures like that of the Mantaro Valley emerge as alternative worldviews, as counterhegemonic endeavors. But it would be wrong to dismiss power and hegemony from this alternative model in itself. If, as Raymond Williams attests, following Gramsci, hegemony is "a culture" and countercultures imply as well the creation of "alternative hegemonies" or "counterhegemonies," Wanka identity must also be seen as the source of power and hegemony (Williams 1977:110). From this perspective, the expansion of the orquesta típicas, the main musical ensemble of the valley and the renowned emblem of Wanka presence, into neighboring areas such as the Ayacucho region in the south and Cerro de Pasco in the north is revealing.

## Ethnicity and Mestizaje

The well-known Peruvian writer José María Arguedas was captivated with the process of mestizaje that had developed in the Mantaro Valley in central

Peru, because, as he observed, the mestizos, instead of being individual outcasts caught between the worlds of Indians and whites (as the mestizo has been usually defined in anthropological literature), in the Mantaro Valley had evolved, since the turn of the century, as a social class. The mestizo of the valley was not the tormented and tortured individual many authors had presented to us as the prototype of the Andean mestizo but a proud, cheerful, and even financially successful individual, with a highly dynamic and creative popular and traditional culture (see Arguedas 1953: 122).[9]

Mestizaje is a fundamental factor in the understanding of the regional identity of the Mantaro Valley. The term itself carries strong colonial and racial connotations, but studies in the social sciences have long argued that mestizaje in the South American Andes is not a racial but a cultural process, which I introduce here as the gradual appropriation of modernity by the Andean Indian peasant.[10] In the context of the imposing and violent presence of modern capitalism in the region, I view mestizaje in the Mantaro Valley, following Arguedas, as a sovereign regional initiative, a result of the sheer determination of the peasants of the valley to integrate their local household economies into the larger national system in a creative, imaginative way, for which, as a group, they seize the necessary tools to negotiate with the market in the best of terms. Thus, the valley's peasantry embraced bilingualism, learning Spanish while maintaining Quechua, adopted the basic precepts of the state-promoted Western-oriented protocol, and enrolled their children in the public primary schools.

Around 1910, the process of mestizaje in the valley had already consolidated, and the "Indian" (that representation that consisted of the Quechua peasant), living in what Eric Wolf called an isolated closed corporate community (1966), on a subsistence economy, who could only establish ties with the external world via cultural brokers, had disappeared as such from the Mantaro Valley (see Adams 1959:85). However, what anthropological literature identifies as Indian symbols, rituals, festivals, and music did not disappear, because the mestizos of the valley, despite their solid integration into the national economy, continued carrying, developing, innovating, and re-creating regional cultural traditions, some of which were previously promulgated only by Indians.[11] Today all the mestizos of the valley celebrate archaic rituals like the branding of the animals and offering symbolic homages to the wamani, a precolonial Andean deity; maintain one of the most dynamic fiesta systems in the Andean region, displaying more than forty different ritual dances; have preserved their Quechua language in addition to Spanish; and speak openly about their Wanka identity.

In the Mantaro Valley ethnicity has gone through numerous historical transformations, the last of which has been mestizaje as a process by which Indians reelaborated their ethnic consciousness and practices in the context of the modern nation-state. Mestizaje in this sense has been the result of historical processes and of reactions to other groups that have imposed their habits through coercion, manipulation, and intimidation. But today the specific character of mestizaje, as the current ethnic configuration of the valley, distinguishes the residents of the valley from other groups in the nation, whether these are the controlling national elites or the other regional cultures that emerge in other latitudes of the national territory. Wanka identity is declared as unique and as the "natural" ethnic character of the valley, a marker for cultural difference. While specific economic and social forces have shaped the current configuration of ethnicity in the valley, mestizaje once developed takes on a life of its own and moves the regional culture of the valley into new spaces and national domains. This understanding of the nature of mestizaje, consequently, has recently caught the attention of scholars who view it as a process of ethno-genesis, as a liberating, counterhegemonic discourse, in opposition to the view of mestizaje as the political discourse that fosters the "assimilation" of the Indian as citizen of a newly built nation-state (Mallon 1996:180–181). But the debate on the issue of ethnicity and mestizaje in Andean scholarship already pervaded the literature from the 1940s until the 1970s. In all the ethnographies of this period considerable space was dedicated to locating, defining, and comparing the different ethnic categories in the Andes, particularly the main categories of Indian and mestizo. Who was and what characterized an Indian? What was the role of the mestizo in Andean society? The emergence of an intermediate group labeled as *cholo* contributed to obscuring the debate in the midst of innumerable local and regional variants and transformations. Indians were generally described as monolingual Quechua peasants, carriers of ancient traditions, and situated at the bottom of the social and economic hierarchy in the Andes. Mestizos were portrayed as bicultural, Quechua-Spanish bilingual merchants, professionals, and administrators, with links to the national culture to which Indians could never have access. The mestizos lived off of Indian production, acting as intermediaries with the regional and national markets, establishing patriarchal and sometimes exploitative relationships with the Indians. The group called cholo arrived on the scene, later defined as the Indian ex-peasants who originated from the peasant community and traveled to the urban centers, familiarizing themselves with the national culture yet never losing membership with the original village (Mayer 1970:120).

The previous passage constitutes a very condensed summary of the positions, controversies, and endless discussions on the issue since the 1940s.[12] But what seems to be the center of the debate? Mainly that the ethnic terminology used by scholars, borrowed from local usages, gives rise to a degree of variety impossible to consolidate into satisfactory generalizations. It was soon observed that ethnic terminology diverged from village to village and that the notions of Indian, mestizo and cholo were more relational concepts than discrete classifications in themselves (see de la Cadena 1995 and 1996). In a seminal article Fernando Fuenzalida reminded us that the Indian would call himself a *llajtaruna* (townsman), a *lugareño*, or a "natural" (native), but never an Indian. It is the mestizo who uses the term *Indian* or *chuto* when referring to peasants and in turn calls himself a *vecino* instead of a mestizo or *misti*, as he is called by the Indians themselves (1970:29–30). Both terms, *Indian* and *mestizo*, have been charged with pejorative attributes as well. The Indian viewed from the higher hierarchies has been depicted as a degenerated being, drunk, indolent, a liar, and a thief. The mestizo and the misti, as a *yanacona*, is viewed as a traitor to his race and an unstable individual (Fuenzalida 1970: 17). Such is the diversity of intentions and meanings suggested by the authors who deal with ethnicity in the Andes that the denotation of who is an Indian, a mestizo, or a cholo, can be said to be totally dependent on the social position of the adjudicator and the traditional criteria used to define who is an Indian become useless when we try to apply it to different cases. As Bernard Mishkin phrased it: "The same individual can be considered Indian from a certain point of view and mestizo from another" (1963:413).

This apparent ambiguity in distinguishing ethnic profiles is explained because ethnicity in Peru is not defined by ancestry but by social and cultural criteria (Kubler 1963; Fuenzalida 1970; Murra 1984). If, in fact, race has been the official indicator in census and national statistics (the population has been classified until the 1940s in terms of whites, Indians, mestizos, *raza amarilla* [Asians], and blacks), it is the cultural practice that actually defines who is "white," Indian, and mestizo in everyday life. That is, the social position of the individual affects the social perception of races. Social and cultural mobility in Peru is so intense that "the race of an individual may change throughout his lifetime" (Fuenzalida 1970:26). The concept of social race proposed by Charles Wagley for the case of Brazil is in this case highly relevant as well (1965).

In the end, ethnic concepts such as Indians, mestizos, mistis, cholos, and creoles have survived in the narratives of Andean scholars to today despite the reciprocal condemnations and self-denunciations of those involved. The consensus today is that ethnic differentiation in the South American Andes has to be assessed in each local setting, rather than attempting to search for futile and confusing generalizations. The Mantaro Valley constitutes a case that demands such a specific treatment. Through intense interviewing and revision of historical documents Richard Adams determined that at about 1880 substantial differences still existed between Indians and mestizos in the region. They were distinguished by the traits that were usually found in other areas of the Andes: language, clothing, surnames, occupation, education, economic status, and so forth. To transcend the subjectivity of the procedure of classifying peoples Adams asked four "informants" to judge the ethnic affiliation of 457 individuals of the town of Muquiyauyo. The results confirmed the volatility and inconsistent ethnic differentiation based on systematic, "scientific" methods, since nearly 40 percent of the people under review went undefined. The "informants," acting as "judges," were hesitant to categorize themselves as either Indians or mestizos (1959:83–84). But in the valley a unique process began to develop around the turn of the century: "People from both castes began to participate jointly in more affairs; together with this, there was a simultaneous borrowing of some culture traits and a merging of others. The result has been, in effect, to blend the two previously distinct subcultures of mestizos and Indians" (Adams 1959:85). The mestizo in the valley became not a group that denied its Indian heritage based on the destruction of its agents but one that blended both legacies in an uncommon mechanism for the Peruvian Andes. This unique process was the one that appealed to José María Arguedas and prompted him to view it as an alternative action to the annihilation of Indianness.

The historical construction of mestizaje in the Mantaro Valley constitutes an example that disavows the long-standing views that understood ethnicity as being "primordial" and "essential" to specific and localized social groups. More than twenty years ago Fredrik Barth criticized these postures as inadequate for the understanding of ethnic groups in the context of intense social interaction and mobility and in the presence of market pressures and an imposing and mediating nation-state (1969). Analyzing Narroll's classic definition of ethnic groups as biologically self-perpetuated, with shared cultural values, in constant interaction, and self-identified, and externally identified as "different" (Narroll 1964, cited in Barth 1969:10–11), Barth concluded that this definition was not far from the blend of race-culture-language that had permeated much of the past anthropological literature on ethnicity (1969:11). Isolation, localization, and an unproblematic reproduction of culture were taken for granted in defining ethnic groups. This ideal characterization changes, of course, in the context of modern pluriethnic nation-states, in which relationships of power, domination and subordination are sources of struggles, conflicts, and resistance. Against these "primordialist" views, which essentialized the cultural contents of ethnic "units," are those who maintain that ethnicity does not contain unique cultural essences but is historically constructed, fluid, and constantly invented.[13]

Barth's emphasis on the notion of boundaries clarifies this point further. For him the cultural contents of an exclusive group may change through time, but the ways in which this group maintains its difference ("boundaries") with other groups are what ultimately constitute the core of its ethnic consciousness or identity (1969:14). In other words, ethnicity may not be "primordial" with regard to its initial formative stages, but once it has been historically constructed it may appear, act, and function as a "natural" cultural reference of the people involved in the dynamics of that group. As the Comaroffs suitably stress, "While ethnicity is the product of specific historical processes, it tends to take on the 'natural' appearance of an autonomous force, a 'principle' capable of determining the course for social life" (1992:60). The tendency of "all discourse about culture to embrace some form of essentialism" is also relevant to my point here (Herzfeld 1996:277). If indeed the contemporary identity of the Mantaro Valley is the product of particular historical forces, the current competing discourses on identity in the valley are elaborations and presuppose the existence of "essential" traits that characterize the different conceptions of "authentic" regional cultures.

## Region and Nation

My insistence on the regional space as a site for cultural contention is related to the vision of the modern nation of Peru as an aggregate of "internally differentiated regional spaces" (Lomnitz-Adler 1992:17). That is, that the nation is divided not only into social classes, ethnic groups, and languages but also in to regions that serve as centers of cultural production. As the foremost Peruvian anthropologist José María Arguedas noted, regions in Peru commonly coincide with broad ethnic boundaries (1975). He distinguished major regional divisions, or cultural areas, in the Andean region of Peru, each of them erected upon the pre-Hispanic sites of ethnic kingdoms. Arguedas showed that in the case of the Chanka region (named after the pre-Hispanic ethnic group that lived there and encompassed by the regions of Ayacucho, Huancavelica, and Apurímac) the population still maintained a distinct cultural identity, as expressed in their architecture, arts, and language. Arguedas portrayed the Inca (currently coinciding with the department of Cuzco) and the Wanka regions (referring to the area that corresponded to the department of Junín) in similar ways, the latter including the Mantaro Valley as a major cultural center.

The region as a major culture-producing center, therefore, is a primary factor in assessing the formation and dynamics of the nation-state. In the quest for hegemony the nation-state constitutes the highest level of spatial integration, but hegemony is "modified and worked out in each local context" (Lomnitz-Adler 1992:26). This notion is particularly fitting to the case of the region of Junín and the Mantaro Valley because since the conquest of the Wankas the contemporary inhabitants of the region have maintained a unique status and cultural identity that has distinguished them not only from their neighbors (other regions, other peoples) but also from mainstream national styles (see Tschopik 1947; Hutchinson 1973; Arguedas 1975; and Long and Roberts 1978, 1984).

A particular case that illustrates the cultural distinctiveness of the inhabitants of the Mantaro Valley is conveyed by Mallon in analyzing how the peasants of the Mantaro Valley formulated a project of nationalist ideology and consciousness in the war with Chile at the end of the nineteenth century (1995:2). In the war the peasantry of the Mantaro Valley continued fighting against the invaders from another nation even when the national bourgeoisie had decided to surrender. For Mallon the idea of nationalism not only is circumscribed to bourgeois ideology and the development of an internal market in its transition to capitalism (Hobsbawn 1990; Gellner 1983) but also has to be understood as a "project for collective identity" capable of being proposed by any segment of society, not necessarily the hegemonic one. In this sense different groups within a nation (peasants as well) can present different nationalist projects that are to be understood as "competing discourses" in constant formulation and negotiation (Mallon 1995:3).[14]

Following this line of thought, I view the regional culture of the Mantaro Valley (the Wanka identity) as a "competing discourse," an "alternative hegemony" to the cultural trends practiced by the national elites. As I will explain in chapter 5, the national elites consisted until the 1970s of a small group of peoples who based their power on large landholdings (haciendas) and large-scale commerce and mining industries. Their cultural alignment was with Europe and, in recent years, with the United States. The Peruvian elites always managed to avoid "nationalist" trends (except occasional interludes during which pro-Indian policies surfaced) and failed to incorporate the political and cultural demands of Andean Peru into their agendas. The absence of a "national project," that is, the lack of concern of the elites in representing other social classes, regions, and cultures besides their own, has been recurrently mentioned by political analysts (see Cotler 1978).

The notion of "imagined community" (Anderson 1991) is only partly useful in conveying the particular case of the Mantaro Valley within the national context, since it suggest a "false," or constructed, perception of feelings of a common territory and heritage. Although this "image" of community is said to ultimately induce the formation of national units, it does not adequately explain the intricacies of regional cultures with "real" histories of war, confrontation, and resistance (Lomnitz-Adler 1992:317). Arguedas's interest in Wanka regional culture as an example of how a cultural mestizo alternative could arise forcefully from a nonelite, nonstate source, with actual chances of spreading into other spaces and locations within the nation-state, was indeed appropriate (1975).

# 2

# PERPETUATING THE
# RURAL PAST

## Ancient Rituals and
## Modern Performances

While in the Mantaro Valley the public realm seems to be the space for negotiating modernity, the private domain appears to be reserved for maintaining continuities with a rural "past." The latter is the sphere of ritual and musical expressions linked to rural productive activities, such as the *herranza* (a fertility ritual aimed at the protection of land and livestock) and the *waylarsh* (a compound of games, dances, and songs tied to the harvests of beans, peas, wheat, and barley). Also linked to agricultural labor is the music called *huauco*, played with a *tinya* (small Andean drum) and *pincullo* (vertical flute) in a pipe and tabor fashion during the communal harvest of grains. The common factor among all of these musically structured rituals is that they are performed privately: in the context of the nuclear and extended family (in the case of the herranza) or strictly by the members of the peasant community who participate in communal labor (as happens with the waylarsh and the huauco).

### Dancing with Animals: The Herranza Ritual

The herranza is often described as a fertility ritual because its main purpose is directed toward the protection of livestock and lands.[1] It is a complex ceremony that consists of several phases, involving the marking of animals, material offerings and gifts, collective play, prediction rites, music, dance, singing, and a general state of jubilation. In most cases it is a ritual in which only the nuclear and extended family that owns animals participate, but when the entire community is owner, it is a communal event. In both cases it maintains its private and secluded character. However, it does not go unnoticed in the valley, since around this time the local markets stock themselves with plenty of goods for the ritual and there is considerable commercial activity around the purchasing of gifts and materials to be used in the herranza; the fabric for the *mesa* (a ritual table), the liquor, the mountain flowers, the cigarettes, various gifts such as candy and pastries, *cuyes* (a type of rodent, a traditional Andean meal), *cancha* (toasted corn), and cheese for the generous feast to be offered during the ritual. And even in the thriving commercial city of Huancayo, hundreds of herranza musicians coming from the highland communities, with their wakrapukus (cattle horn trumpets), their violins and tinyas, gather in the vicinity of plaza La Inmaculada waiting to be hired by the heads of family households.

The central day of the herranza is July 25, which coincides with the Catholic celebration of the Saint Santiago, but contrary to the public festival, where the Mass, the Virgin, and the saint are guiding events or

Peasants gathered around a ritual *mesa* (table) during the ritual of *herranza*. Photo: Manuel Ráez Retamozo, courtesy Center for Andean Ethnomusicology, Catholic University of Peru.

*Herranza* musicians playing the *wakrapuku* and the *tinya*. Photo: Manuel Ráez Retamozo, courtesy Center for Andean Ethnomusicology, Catholic University of Peru.

images, no Catholic elements are present in this private ritual. The herranza is also called *santiago* in many villages because of the association made between the European imagery of Saint Santiago and the Andean deity called the wamani, who is believed to inhabit the mountains. In fact, the herranza ritual is celebrated as an offering to the almighty wamani, owner of the crops and cattle, who is revered as much as and feared. Santiago was for the colonizer a symbol of conquest, nicknamed Son of Thunder, a killer of Moors who in the war against them was considered an inspiration for the victorious Spanish soldiers (Silverblatt 1988:174). The Indians associated Santiago with Illapa, the god of thunder and lightning, who in time became consolidated into a single supreme being, wamani, or santiago.[2]

But on the lower slopes of the Mantaro Valley, notwithstanding the herranza's persistence, the belief in the wamani is not openly recognized or verbalized in any form, as it is in the communities most distant from the highway and railroad.[3] As one resident of the district of Huancán, in the valley, told me during a herranza, "We do not offer a *pago* [offering] to the mountain; they do it in other towns, those who live near one." Despite this denial, the herranza in the valley concludes with the *señal pampay*, in which the remains of the objects utilized during the ritual are buried in a "sacred" place. The act of burial in itself resembles the pago to the wamani as performed in the higher and more distant communities of the valley and many other areas of the Andes as well. In the highland communities of the valley the herranza begins with this pago, in which the head of the family walks unaccompanied to the mountain believed to be inhabited by the deity, buries gifts, and sings a distinctive chant. This burial is performed in total secrecy and with a feeling of sacred determination. In these "distant" communities the wamani is openly and proudly acknowledged. During one of the rest periods of a herranza in the district of Huayucachi, in the lower valley, I recorded the following description from one of the participants (my translation from Spanish):

> This [pointing to an object] is to be used in the señal [pampay] for the wamani in the night. The wamani is like a creator, who gives us animals when we ask him for them; he protects us. The *cerro* [mountain] is honored on the evening of the twenty-third [of July]; we do a señal; we take apples, fruit, all kinds of mesa [ritual food], to the power where the bravest of all bravests are, the bravest mountain; to this we call Tayta Wamani [Father Wamani], *cinta raso*; that is the major *tayta* here. He is like the chief, like any other chief; what we ask for, he gives to us. He is the chief of all the mountains. We ask for flocks; we give our pagos; incredibly, he gives that to us. That's why during santiago two, three flocks wake up on our mesa; one has to have faith. At seven A.M. we take it to the altitudes, it is the mountain where no people ever get to; we tell him, Senor Waman Raso, you are the greatest, the greatest of any other mountain.

The phases of the herranza are manifold, and they proceed over a span of two days. On the evening of the first day the initial arrangements are made, the ritual mesa (table) is put in place, the first songs are performed, and the ritual then continues into the night, during which friends and relatives are entertained or visited and the central prediction rite is accomplished (the "reading" of coca leaves). On the following day the central activity is the branding of the animals, which is interspersed with more songs, more dances, more food, and liquor. What follows is a condensed synthesis of the most important phases of the herranza in the Mantaro Valley, based on my observation of the ritual in four representative districts of the Mantaro Valley: Huanca, Huayucachi, Masmachicche, and Pariahuanca. While the musical content and style vary in each of the districts of the valley, there are consistent characteristics that I will describe here. When possible I will provide representative musical examples of some of the songs that accompany these stages.

The ritual begins with the preparation of the ritual table (*tendal mesa*), around which all the participants (nuclear family and guests) will gather and upon which the meal and drinks will be served and the gifts and all the ritual utensils displayed (ribbons or branding iron for the branding, small effigies of Saint Luke, Saint Santiago, and several animals, mountain herbs and flowers, stones, soil, and minerals). The "table" consists of a piece of fabric placed on the floor.[4] The person responsible for the building of the mesa is called a *despensera* (literally storeroom), the same designation of the cargo holder in the festival system, the person who is in charge of keeping the ceremonial or festive implements. During the *mesa* periodic rest periods, called *chaupi mesa*, take place, at which times the participants eat and drink wine and *chicha* (fermented corn). There are several *chaupi mesas* during the entire ritual that separate the different steps of the herranza.

Around midnight of the first day is the time for a general dance called *chaupi tuta*, in which everyone, without exception, takes part with more intensity than before. While there is dancing throughout all of the ritual, this phase is more intensive and longer in duration. It can proceed until dawn, at which time the entire family visits the houses of relatives at which the general dance continues. The dancing is so intense that at this point of the ritual the entire group dances through the streets of the village. Throughout, the musicians play tunes they call *zapateo* (shoe tapping), *pasacalle, paseo,* or *visitacha,* all terms that allude to the act of strolling the streets or visiting. Chaupi mesas are also performed during this phase, since rest periods are always necessary. Musical example 2.1, from the herranza in the town of Pariahuanca (as are all of that follow), features a basically tritonic song performed during this phase. The second musical phrase (B) is reiterated at will. (I will elaborate on the musical aspect of herranza later in this chapter).

The prediction rite called Koka Kintu is performed during one of the rest periods or chaupi mesas. It is a pan-Andean rite that consists of the reading or interpretation of coca leaves. A specific amount of these leaves is given to all the participants, who have to choose the "healthy" ones, that is, those that are not broken but intact and complete. Each coca leaf represents a previously designated amount of cattle, ten, one hundred, or

Example 2.1: Herranza music for the Chaupi Tuta (general dance) from Pariahuanca

one thousand animals, depending on the size of the leaf. Meanwhile, the participants chew coca leaves, as is customary, and drink and indulge in conversation, while a competent "reader," or *caporal*, interprets the signs of the selected leaves and predicts a good or a bad year for the owner of the cattle. The Koka Kintu has many variants in its "interpretative" phase. One of these is that the participants who fail to collect the adequate amount of "healthy" leaves are "punished" and those who do collect an adequate number are "rewarded." The tune for this phase (example 2.2) is built on an anhemitonic pentatonic scale, and as in all the *herranza* tunes part B is persistently reiterated.

At dawn everyone is expected to participate in a ritual chase of animals in a corral (Luci-Luci), leading them out into the place where they will be marked. This is a ritual with fire, since the participants use torches to chase the animals and even simulate frightening one another as well. The Luci-Luci marks the end of the first day, after which everyone goes to sleep for a few hours while waiting for the next day, on which the animals will be branded. Example 2.3 is the tritonic melody (with passing notes E and G) sung during this episode.

Example 2.2: Herranza music for the Koka-Kintu (prediction rite) from Pariahuanca

Example 2.3: Herranza music for the Luci-Luci (ritual chase of animals) from Pariahuanca

In the Señalacuy (branding of animals) several animals may be marked: cattle, llamas, horses, and even donkeys. The animals that were not marked the previous year are marked first, branded by ribbons being inserted in their ears with a needle. The ribbons are not merely ornamental. In the district of Masmachicche, for example, yellow ribbons mark the males, orange the females, green the "native" stallions, red the purchased stallions, and blue the mothers. Everyone collaborates in the marking, since the animals do resist and the strength of many is required to keep them still. During the process, the animals are given coca leaves to chew, and in certain districts the blood of the animals, mixed with *chicha* (fermented corn), is consumed by the participants; some may also paint their faces with the same blood (musical example 2.4).

After the branding, in the Chico-chico, all of the animals are separated according to their species and are sent back to their original locations. Special food is thrown upon the animals, a mixture of flour, candy, and cookies in animal shapes.

As a concluding act, a ceremonial offering of gifts, called señal pampay, takes place in a special location (called sacred by some) where pieces of the ears of the animals, unused ribbons, coca leaves, and liquor are buried. In some districts this burial is carried out in secrecy by a designated person. This act suggests certain similarities to the offering to the *wamani* described earlier, but in the valley it is not explicitly described as such, nor is the word *wamani* ever spoken. The ritual burial of ceremonial media is, however, a pan-Andean custom related to supernatural deities that takes place in the context of similar rituals.

There are a few variants to the general description of the herranza presented here. The branding of sheep (not including other animals) is usually enacted by some communities during Carnival, instead of on July 25. Also, when the animals are the property of a peasant community instead of a nuclear family, the herranza is performed collectively, following, nevertheless, the same phases. In the district of San Jerónimo, for example, there is a distinction between the *patrones* (the patrons) and the *pastores* (shepherds). In these cases the "patron" is the community, which appears

Example 2.4: Herranza music for the Señalacuy (branding of animals) from Pariahuanca

in the ritual personified as an individual patron, and the "shepherds" are the members of the community who are in charge of the animals during the year. Instead of the head of the nuclear family, the treasurer of the community is in charge of preparing the mesa and organizing the ritual. The herranza takes place in the communal corral, which can be located far from the town. The patrons and the shepherds engage in ritualized play in which the former may reprimand the shepherds for a supposed mishandling of the animals and the shepherds may, in turn, complain and challenge the patrons for being abusive and creating difficult conditions. These complaints are usually sung rather than verbalized and have a satirical character, often taking the form of a musically improvised contest between both parties.[5]

The music of the herranza is performed by two players of wakrapukus (spiral-shaped horn trumpets), one violinist, and a *cantora* (female singer), who sings and plays the tinya (small Andean drum) simultaneously. Herranza or santiago tunes open with an introduction by the violins and wakrapukus (playing in thirds), and the tune itself begins when the cantora sings it, while the violin continues doubling the melody in heterophony and filling in during the pauses of the singer. The wakrapukus play only during the interludes, when the cantora rests after a series of stanzas; they never play while the cantora is singing.

The music of the herranza is generally based on a tritonic scale constructed on the major triad, and only in very rare cases are other scales found, such as the pentatonic scale example shown previously. Based upon an analysis of the songs (called *tonada 3* by the musicians themselves) from four different districts, I found that all of them were designed as a two-part form (AB), with part A repeated once and part B repeated at will, numerous times. This type of binary form is common in Andean songs and, therefore, is not inherent to the herranza. What is characteristic to this ritual is the tritonic quality of its scale. This scale is solely restricted to this ritual context and to certain types of Carnival songs of southern Peru. It is also the prerogative of nonprofessional musicians.

The musical ensembles for the herranza generally come from the highland communities. There are herranza musical groups in the valley, but they are few and cannot meet the demands for the entire area. The idea of a herranza musical ensemble, however, could be misleading. Herranza music is only performed once a year, for two days, so the musicians who do play this music integrate themselves into a group only a few days before the ritual, which is during Carnival or around the end of July. Herranza musicians are not "professionals" like the members of orquesta típicas, in spite of the fact that they are paid for their services.

Herranza musicians are, however, highly specialized, since herranza is their main performance context and since none of the members perform in other "professional" ensembles of the valley (the orquesta típica and the brass band). Many of the herranza musicians who come to the valley from the higher altitude villages are peasants with scant financial resources. Their economic and social status differs greatly from that of members of the orquesta típica, who are well-paid professionals all year round. The herranza musicians are seasonal performers, and their status as "musicians" is not even that clear, since there is an identification in the valley of "music" with "professionalization." There are two factors to be considered here: first, that herranza music is so remarkably fused with the ritual as a whole that its musicians tend to be regarded as like any other participants; and second, the character of this ritual is private and secluded, a condition that favors the amalgamation of the musicians into the general group of participants.

Herranza music is considered by the people of the Mantaro Valley old and very traditional, a pre-Hispanic music from which all others have stemmed. The "indigenous" character of this music is further marked by the peasant and modest origins of performers, the use of Quechua in the lyrics of the songs, the antiquity of the wakrapuku and the tinya, the small size of its ensemble, the high-pitched female singing, the rhythmic patterns based on a steady regular beat and avoiding syncopated figures, and the tritonic scale structure, all of which are traits usually associated by the people of the Mantaro Valley with "Indian" music, which undoubtedly distinguish it from the mestizo huayno. In fact, herranza or santiago music stands as the foremost musically distinct genre in relation to the ubiquitous and dominant mestizo huayno, from which the most popular musical genres of the valley arise, genres such as the *huaylas* and dances of the *chonguinada* and *tunantada*.

### Dancing during Harvest: The Waylarsh

The nocturnal threshing of grain, or waylarsh, was enacted until the 1940s by young single men and women who sang and danced throughout the night on top of a mound of grain. While singing and dancing, they threshed the grain, separating the seeds from the husks. The participants were convened by the owner, and they gathered around the mound on the designated evening. The entire night was then spent not only singing and dancing but also playing games until dawn. Most of the dances were realized in circles and executed with a vigorous zapateo (shoe tapping). At some points men or women would leave the round to chase each other, always on top of the mound. An atmosphere of play, joyfulness, and subtle eroticism characterized the whole ceremony, and these sentiments are the first ones to be recalled by those who used to participate in the waylarsh (see Arguedas 1953).

There was a specific repertoire of songs for the waylarsh, all sung a cappella by the participants while they danced or played these games. Arguedas mentions one testimony that indicates the rendition of eleven songs during one night (1957b:241). I have been able to record nine songs from the waylarsh repertoire performed by a group of elders from the town of Huanchar and twelve songs from the town of Apata, some of which are variants of the first group of songs. In their younger years these elders used to take part in these ceremonies, and they still remembered most of the songs performed during those nights. As ceremonial labor, the waylarsh is less structurally complex than the herranza, which, as we have seen, is a highly elaborated series of rites that imply the presence of a spiritual being or emotion, in relation to which an appeal for the well-being of land and animals is dramatized. The waylarsh, on the contrary, was communal labor, realized in a ceremonial fashion, the central plan of which was the threshing of grain. While it nurtured a sense of collectivity and promoted the encounter of unmarried men and women (and in this sense was relevant to the life cycle as well), it was not an event related to the supernatural nor was it involved with or connected to any other sphere besides its own.

The initial song of the waylarsh, as performed in Huanchar, began with an introduction called the *quiyaway*, which resembled a harawi.[6] Early colonial chroniclers like Guaman Poma and Bernabé Cobo mentioned the harawi as a type of song that dealt with unrequited love (Stevenson 1960:169). One of the local testimonies provided by Arguedas corroborates the presence of a melody in the harawi style: "The melody was of an imploring character, like an old *jarawi*" (in Arguedas 1953:241). The inclusion of a harawi melody in the waylarsh repertoire is indicative of its links with Indian traditions of pre-Hispanic roots. It is a monophonic song that consists of one musical statement repeated several times, with extensive melismatic passages and long glissandos (see musical example 2.5). It is associated with specific ceremonies and rituals like farewells and marriages, as well as with agricultural labor (sowing and harvest) in the south-

Example 2.5: Song of the waylarsh from Huanchar (Quiyaway)

ern Andes. It is generally sung in a high-pitched, nasal voice by a group of elder women called *harawiq* (see Cavero 1985 and Varallanos 1989).

This introduction, transcribed in example 2.5, even when it corresponds stylistically to a harawi, was not referred to as such. The second part, repeated several times and actually the song's main theme, is of a different style, one that avoids the long glissandos that are characteristic of the harawi, although it retains the tritonic scale upon which most harawis are structured.

The rest of the songs in the waylarsh repertoire were "indigenous" huaynos. First of all, they were all sung in Quechua (in a region where Spanish is widely spoken), and consisted of a brief and plain musical phrase repeated at will, performed a cappella and in a rural, agricultural context.[7] They were also pentatonic, like the great majority of Andean huaynos. This genre, however, whether Indian or mestizo, always maintains its association with leisure and recreational contexts and occasions. Huaynos may be rendered in ritual contexts, but they will probably be sung during *mishkipas* (recesses) or used, as in this case, to accompany festive and joyous, nonsacred activities. While the first song, in a *harawi* style, was designed to "call" the participants and to launch the ceremony, the ensuing huaynos were part of the various recreational games men and women engaged in during the night. In fact, most of the huaynos were named after the games themselves, among them *el rabo* (the tail), *el carpintero* (the carpenter), *el torillo* (the little bull), and *vuelta que redonda* (a round turn). Most of these songs consisted of the repetition of one musical phrase: A, A, A, A, and so forth. But two-phrase huaynos could also be found: AA, BB, AA, BB (see the musical examples 2.6 and 2.7).

Men and women participated in the games, which were all enacted on top of the mound. A group of six elders of the town of Apata, the oldest

Example 2.6: Song of the waylarsh from Huanchar (Torillo)

Example 2.7: Song of the waylarsh from Huanchar (Carpintero)

of whom is seventy years old, described a few of the games during a meeting at which they remembered the custom and sang short renditions of the songs. In the game of the *viudita* ("little widower"):

> We all formed a circle, holding hands; someone said, "I am the little widower; I am looking for someone to marry," and she would look at the men one by one and, "no, I don't want you, I don't want you either," until she said to one, "Only with you," and they would hug each other.

In the game of "the old man and the old woman":

> We were sitting down in a circle, the *abuelito* [grandpa] sent the *abuelita* [grandma] to buy coca leaves, but the abuelita returned with her lover; the grandson would run to tell the abuelito, who would then run to punish the lover.

There was also a game in which two of them pretended to be a mouse and a cat:

> "Who is it?"
> "It is Mr. Mouse. Who are you looking for?"
> "I am looking for Mr. Cat."
> Then the cat would chase the mouse for like five times around the mound.

And in the *corrida* ("runaway"):

> We were making a round, all with our hands in our backs, someone with a whip said, "Who has an enemy?" and then he whipped one of us, the whip was then passed one by one, and we whipped one another.

All of these games were performed in an exceedingly joyful mood, and the elders in both towns, in re-creating these nights of play, song, dances, and heterosexual encounters, seemed as amused and delighted as the young people. Twice during the session in Huanchar the elders were laughing so hard that they could not even start the singing for several minutes, and in Apata they became so involved in their gratifying recollection of the games that they completely overlooked my presence and that of the tape recorder at several moments.

The waylarsh was a musical celebration of youth, communal labor, and Andean reciprocity. The young men and women who participated in them were gathered together by the owners of grain, and they gladly went during many nights with no expectations other than to spend an evening singing, dancing, and playing. But the waylarsh served an economic purpose as well in completing the grain harvest in time to meet the market demands and deadlines. When the pressures of these deadlines began to grow in intensity due to the increasing economic growth and the owners of the harvest could not wait for the youth to fulfill this task, the use of heavy and industrial machinery, already available in the valley, became an irresistible temptation. "Now the girls don't go out; they don't play; now everything is just machines in making the *trilla*," said one of the elders in Huanchar. Contrary to the herranza ritual, which did not overlap with or affect any productive task, the waylarsh custom did clash with the pressures on the peasants of the Mantaro Valley to meet market demands. Hence the demise of such a convention, which already in the 1940s had become a rare occurrence. But well before that decade, a dance with the same name had begun to develop in the festivals of the valley. It was enacted during Carnival in the province of Huancayo and was achieving increasing popularity. Its music was a variety of the huayno, with no harawi connotations, and its dance featured an energetic zapateo (shoe tapping). It was named after the waylarsh but used the Spanish pronunciation, "huaylas." The "original" rural custom had been appropriated by the mestizo population of the valley and incorporated into its main expressive showcase, the public festival, as I will explain later in this chapter.

### Working with Music: The Huauco and Communal Labor

The *faena* (also called *minga* in other regions), or communal labor, is one of the fundamental occasions of Andean solidarity. It is a task intrinsically linked to the existence of communal lands and peasant communities. In the Mantaro Valley *huauco music* refers to the music and the instruments played by a single musician during the communal faena. These instruments are the three-hole pincullo (vertical cane flute) and the tinya (small drum), which the musician plays in a pipe and tabor fashion. Communal labor in the fields is a special event reserved for specific occasions of the agricultural calendar that require total participation of the villagers: for the *barbecho* or *volteo* (turning of the soil), during the *cultivo* (first tillage of the land), and for the *siega* (harvest) of grain. Communal labor in the fields begins with a general meeting at the central plaza of the village, after which the workers walk to the field where they labor for the whole day. The musician plays during the whole faena and during the mishkipas (rest periods), during which drinking chicha and dancing may also ensue.

Different tonadas (tunes) are used during the day. They have different names in each village, but the repertoire follows a similar structure. The

Performer of pincullo and tinya during the harvest of grains. Photo: Raúl R. Romero (courtesy Center for Andean Ethnomusicology, Catholic University of Peru).

initial tune is to congregate the *comuneros* (villagers) early in the morning, and the following one, generally called the pasacalle, is performed while the workers walk to the field. For the labor itself there are several tunes, varying between faster and slower tempos according to the type of task required. Each of these tunes has a descriptive name given by the performer. At the end of the day, there is a farewell tune, or *despedida*. For the mishkipas, the performer plays huaynos, a genre that, as we have noted earlier, within these contexts fulfills recreational functions during interruptions in the ceremonial sequence.

The huauco tradition in the Mantaro Valley is not completely lost, but only a very few communities continue to observe it, and only a handful of performers continue to master the repertoire. It is a tradition in the process of being discontinued, an assessment that is not mine but a claim of the performers themselves. I was able to locate and meet performers from the districts of Paccha, San Antonio de Ocopa, Masmachicche, and Huanchar. In each of these towns only one musician knew the huauco repertoire and, without exception, all complained about the lack of disciples who could learn and continue this tradition. I found later that this was absolutely true. In one town that I visited looking for this kind of performance tradition, Llacuari, the town's sole huauco musician, had died a few months before. His only son, suddenly aware of the significance of this repertoire because of my visit from afar, dramatically expressed his grief and repentance for not having learned the complete repertoire as his father wanted him to do before his death. In the town of Paccha, the son of another huauco musician, who was not as emotionally involved since his father was still alive and well, told me that he was not interested in learning huauco music because it was "difficult" and that he had preferred instead learning the guitar in the city of Huancayo. All of the performers I met, however, expressed their pride at being the guardians of such an "ancient" repertoire, which they affirmed had remained unchanged throughout time. One of them told me that this music "was from Inca times."

One of the performers, Leoncio Miranda from the town of Huanchar, plays this music on two different occasions throughout the year, during the volteo and the cultivo. Only on special occasions is he hired to play this repertoire by private landowners who use wage labor. Normally the huauco musician plays his music during the communal labor of his own peasant village, for which he receives no payment, since he is considered just another worker performing labor tasks for his community. But there are some communities as well as private landowners that still want agricultural chores performed with huauco music and, since there are no such performers in their towns, approach a musician of another village and pay for his services. This occurrence is rare: consequently, the huauco musician does not consider these infrequent deals to be a significant source of additional income or a sign of professionalization in this area.

There are six basic tunes in the repertoire of the huauco performer in Huanchar. The musician uses a variety of musical scales in his tunes, three of them pentatonic, two tritonic, and one tetratonic. I transcribe three of these tunes (in musical examples 2.8, 2.9, and 2.10).[8] The initial one (Pasacalle) is a pentatonic melody associated with going to the fields and

Example 2.8: Music of communal labor (huauco) from Huanchar (Pasacalle)

Example 2.9: Music of communal labor (huauco) from Huanchar (Santa Catalina)

Example 2.10: Music of communal labor (huauco) from Huanchar (Punipuncho)

featuring two contrasting musical statements (ABAB). The second (Santa Catalina), is tritonic and consists of a reiterated single musical statement (AAAA). And the third (*punipuncho*), is pentatonic and similar in form to the pasacalle. The latter two melodies are performed when the labor in the fields is at its height.

The ongoing process of withdrawal from huauco music in the Mantaro Valley echoes the case of the waylarsh, since both are related to agricultural tasks. The introduction of industrial machinery in the valley to perform these tasks much faster than manual labor has obviously been a factor in this process. But since there are many peasant communities that still perform the harvest and other tasks manually, machinery alone cannot be blamed for such a demise. The explanation, then, must be related to the overall process of redefining identities within the national context. The role of the youth in this venture is crucial, and the lack of disciples, about which the huauco musicians frequently complain, is directly linked to this process. This absence breaks the learning chain of a musical tradition, which then dies with its only surviving carrier, as observed in the case of Llacuari.

### The Festival System in the Mantaro Valley

Huancayo is a city without festivals. The rapid economic and commercial growth of the city transformed it into a paradigm of modern urban life. Plenty of movie theaters, hotels, restaurants, and late-night bars provide entertainment for the locals and business travelers. But elsewhere in the valley, the festival system is so intense that hardly a day passes without a festival being enacted in one of its sixty-four rural districts. Many of these districts have an average of six to eight notable festivals during the year and from four to six festivals smaller in terms of both attendance and community significance. The communal participation in these festivals varies from event to event; however, they all involve total participation, as sooner or later all residents will be implicated. At any given moment during a festival, virtually everyone will be involved in some festival activity, whether as organizer, financial contributor, performer, or spectator. The importance of the festival can also be assessed by the volume of migrants who return to their native town to attend or perform in the main festival of their district. The public festivals, which are the core of the community life of the peasants of these districts, reflect as well the affluence of the residents in their alluring costumed and masked dances and the impressive amount of food and drinks served at the festival.

A frequently told story in the Mantaro Valley that attempts to convey the significance of the festival in the lives and struggles of the residents reports that one year the town of Acolla (one of the largest districts of the adjacent valley of Yanamarca) refused to collect a substantial sum of money to collaborate with the national government to build an energy plant for the town. The reason given was that it was too costly. But in that same year the total amount of cash spent on the main festival of the town exceeded the sum required by the government for the energy plant. Generally, the name of the town changes in variants of this story, but the message is that the festival has priority in the valley over other needs, activities, and expenses that may be considered more important from an outsider's point of view.

It is most probable that this account has some truth in it, since the cost of buying hundreds of cases of beer, providing free and abundant food, hiring professional and expensive musicians, and sponsoring games and sometimes bullfights or horse races during the festival may well match or even exceed the price of some public services for the town. But festival expenses are not secondary or optional in the valley, as festivals act as the center of community life and the events around which the town convenes to express itself as a community.[9]

Early studies of the festival in Latin America have in fact attempted to measure its impact through the calculation of its detailed costs (see Martínez 1959) but also in terms of its social consequences (see Smith 1977: 18–30). Many studies have emphasized the widely accepted notion that festivals endure in Andean peasant society because they serve two primordial functions: first, they stimulate a redistribution of wealth within the community, since the sponsors of the fiesta spend much of their yearly income in this endeavor (Wolf 1955); and second, they accrue social status since the sponsors achieve social prominence and prestige (Cancian 1965). The basic notion behind these interpretations is that the festival reinforces community bonds and strengthen institutions within the village. Other interpretations have emphasized the ideological aspects of the festival, mainly from the point of view of considering it a necessary and welcome interruption of everyday and mundane life. This viewpoint stresses the function of *communitas* (Turner 1969) within the festival as a mechanism by which conflicts and differences temporarily disappear (see Albó 1974).

While these materialist interpretations of the festival elucidate consequences that are indisputable, they fail to convey the overall cultural significance of the event for the community at large and for the individual immersed in the festival. None of these interpretations fully explains the persistence and the centrality of the festival in the Mantaro Valley. The Andean festival is a multifaceted celebration in which people are able to express and expose their ideas, creatively, critically, and even humorously, to themselves and the outside world. In this respect, I think that the role of music and dance within the festival is crucial to its continuity, even more than the organizational and economic repercussions that the festival may have a posteriori. In this sense I concur with Julian Laite and Norman Long's assertion that festivals should not be seen only as a means for reinforcement of group solidarity but also as "vehicles for reaffirming, reconstituting or reordering social relationships and networks" (1987:28). In other words, festivals not only reflect social processes but also have "generative power."

Most of the towns of the Mantaro Valley celebrate numerous festivals throughout the calendar year. As said earlier, some of these festivals are *fiestas grandes* (major festivals) attended by everyone in town, while others may be smaller celebrations with only partial participation. Usually one of the largest fiestas in terms of size, participants, and paraphernalia is the *patronal* fiesta, celebrated in honor of the Virgin or the foremost saint chosen as protector of the town. The patron, a saint or the Virgin, may change from town to town, as the importance of each festival also may vary in every town. For instance, the day of Saint John may be the occasion of large celebrations in one town but a smaller festival in another. In addition to festivals honoring the saints and the Virgin, the festivals of the Christian liturgical calendar such as Holy Week, Christmas, and the Epiphany are also widely popular around the valley and are celebrated throughout all of their districts with major or lesser productive means. Carnival is also a pervasive celebration in the valley, preceded in the previous weeks by the *jueves de comadres* (Godmother's Thursday) and *jueves de compadres* (Godfather's Thursday), celebrations which are of lesser significance than Carnival itself. Customarily included in the festival calendars of the valley is the celebration of santiago, which is not a festival in itself but, as we have seen, a family-centered ceremony that celebrates the branding of animals. Thus, it is different from the festival in that it is not public but restricted to family members, relatives, and close friends and does not follow the common structure of the festival.

The fiestas grandes in the Mantaro Valley last for several days up to a week, on those occasions when the *octava* (eighth), a conclusive reenactment of the fiesta, is celebrated on the eighth day after the central day. In most cases festive activities begin during the evening before the central day, when the musical ensemble tries out the festive tunes and meets the public in the main plaza of the town for the first time. Fireworks and festive enactments like the *toril*, in which a bull made of wooden sticks is carried around to frighten bystanders, "warm up" the public for the events to come the following day. The central day features the Mass and a procession as the main religious events in the festival, in which homage is paid to the saint or the Virgin. Dance groups, accompanied by the musical ensembles, also initiate their participation in the religious activities on the central day, paying tribute to a saint or the Virgin by saluting him or her in front of the church as well as by dancing and showing reverence to the image during the procession.

When the Mass and the procession conclude, however, music and dance continue to be the center of the festival's activities on the following days.[10] Thus, the religious facade of the festival is overtaken by a more secular, expressive, and theatrical type of performance in which music and dance are the principal ingredients.[11] The contents of the dance-drama, the oral tradition that sustains it, and the representations inherent within it are creations that fall beyond the mere devotional role that dancers and musicians manifest during the Mass and the procession. After the homages and praises to the Virgin or saint, music and dance-drama address issues relevant to the temporal world and everyday life of the people who are celebrating with the festival.

There are different types of ceremonial festivities in the Mantaro Valley. Apart from the pervasive festivals in honor of saints and the Virgin, civic occasions like Independence Day and the anniversary of the district are sometimes celebrated with a festival format. Together these occasions form the annual festival calendar of a particular district. Although each town may have its own festivals, celebrations in most of the districts include Carnival (February–March), Holy Week (March–April), Day of the Holy Cross (May 3), Saint John's Day (June 24), Independence Day (July 28), Saint Rose's Day (August 30), Saint Luke's Day (October 18), the Day of the Dead (November 2), Christmas (December 25), and New Year's Eve (December 31).

The history of festivals can be traced to the *cofradía* (brotherhood), a colonial institution that promoted and sponsored religious activities (Celestino and Meyers 1981). Richard Adams has studied the origins of this organization in the district of Muquiyauyo (province of Jauja) in the mid–

eighteenth century. Land was allocated for cofradías by the colonial administration to help them pay for the expenses of religious fiestas. By the early nineteenth century cofradías had grown in number and also in landholdings. Independence from Spain, however, changed this state of affairs, and the institution of the cofradía was abolished. The fate of cofradías' lands remained uncertain for a time, since cofradías were supposed to represent the townspeople themselves, and in time the land was sold in *remate* (at auction) to members of the community (1959:56–59).

By the beginnings of the nineteenth century a new institution, which took on the function of the cofradía, surfaced. The association or *sociedad* was a clublike society dedicated to the devotion of a specific saint and depended primarily on contributions by its members (Adams 1959:53). Adams cites records dated to 1811 that indicate that many attributes of the association resemble those of the current *comité directivo*. The association met every year to elect new officers for the following year and had a hierarchy of *cargos* similar to the current ones (*mayordomos, priostes, mayorales, alféreces*).[12] As is the case today, each of these cargos had specific responsibilities in the fiesta and was supposed to pay for particular ceremonial events, such as the *tumbamonte* (a ritual that has as its central activity the cutting of a tree) or the Mass. Many of these sociedades bought land (many of them also lost the land later on), which was administered by the higher cargo holder, the mayordomo.

Around the beginning of the twentieth century the organization of festivals began to change in the Mantaro Valley. The current system constituted by the comité directivo seems to stem from its diverse antecedents. This committee is now constituted by a president, a vice president, a secretary, an adjunct secretary, a treasurer, a prosecutor (fiscal), members-at-large, and a despensero (in charge of guarding the holdings, assets, and ceremonial objects). This committee is called together before and after the fiesta in a general assembly where relevant decisions regarding the festival are held. Each of the members of the committee has a specific function to fulfill in the festival, but there are other contributors who also collaborate, such as the *padrinos* and *madrinas* (godfathers and godmothers) and the cargo holder. These contributors are in charge of sponsoring special events at the fiesta (like the *cortamonte* or tumbamonte ritual cutting of a tree and the *cintas* game of stripes), and the cargo holder pays for the expenses of the Mass and the mishkipadas (communal rests), for which he has to provide cigarettes, liquor, coca leaves, beer, and sometimes even the fireworks. The committee also collects additional funds from general contributions of the townspeople; indeed, activities for fund-raising are organized during special sections in the same fiesta, where participants are supposed to donate useful goods or cash. There are also fixed fees that committee members and members-at-large have to pay if the committee is constituted as an association. Many committees have already constituted themselves into associations with legal status, but few maintain the significant holdings or possessions of the historical cofradías.[13]

Aside from the institutional base of the fiesta system, different barrios (sectors of a town) may participate in a single fiesta. Each barrio may take the responsibility of presenting their own dance groups and musical ensembles. Whatever the organization, however, an element of ritual competition is involved, since each barrio competes with the others to be the best at that year's fiesta. Sometimes this competitiveness is formalized when a dance competition is organized with a jury determining the best group in the festival. There are many variants in this arrangement, and each town may present diverse schema. Different barrios can take turns organizing the fiesta for all the town.

Whatever the overall organization of fiestas in the valley, the asociaciones remain open and voluntary organizations in which anyone may participate. Even the barrios are not strictly reserved for the residents of that particular sector of town; any resident may decide to participate in one or another sector according to his or her own particular feeling. The cargo system continues to be an important mechanism for social status and ensures the effectiveness of the fiesta performances. However, many festival expenses are shared and supported by other participants besides the main cargo, constituting a collective enterprise rather than a closed and strictly individual endeavor.

## The Dance-Dramas in the Mantaro Valley

Dance-dramas constitute the foremost performance setting for music in the Mantaro Valley. Given the intensity of the fiesta system in the valley and the centrality of dance-dramas within the fiesta, it is not possible to understand the significance of the popular culture of the region without conveying, however briefly, the complexity of the dramatic and expressive elements involved in these theatrical events.[14] I have observed and documented more than thirty dance-dramas, but from oral sources I can confirm the existence of nearly forty different dance-dramas (see table 2.1). It is not my intention to propose a classification of them in this work. Indeed, classification is problematic, and prior efforts have seldom achieved consensus. Luis E. Valcárcel distinguished the following thematic types in Andean dances: religious, totemic, martial, associational (guilds), satirical, regional, pantomimes, entertainment, agricultural, and strolling dances (1951:11–13). Mildred Merino de Zela has preferred a chronological model, classifying dance-dramas as pre-Hispanic, conquest, colonial, independence, and republican dances, according to the origins of the characters represented in the dance (1977:70). Deborah A. Poole, however, has called attention to the fact that the ethnic or historic external representation of

Table 2.1  Musical Ensembles and Repertoire in the Mantaro Valley

| Designation | Ensemble Type |
| --- | --- |
| DANCE-DRAMAS | |
| Tunantada | Orquesta típica |
| Chonginada | Orquesta típica |
| Carnaval Marqueño | Orquesta típica (no sax) + cacho/tinya |
| Jija | Orquesta típica (no sax) |
| Huaconada | Orquesta típica |
| Huaylas | Orquesta típica |
| Llamishada | Orquesta típica |
| Avelinos | Orquesta típica |
| Negrería (Garibaldi) | Orquesta típica |
| Negritos Decentes | Orquesta típica |
| Chacranegros | 3 violins/drum/bombo |
| Collas | Orquesta típica |
| Fajina | Orquesta típica |
| Pachahuara | Brass band |
| Huaylijia | Orquesta típica + pitos |
| Corcovados | Violin/Harp; Brass band) |
| Pastoras | Orquesta típica |
| Moscones | Accordion solo |
| Auquines | Pito/tinya |
| Vaqueros | Quena/mandolina/guitar |
| Viejitos | Brass band |
| SOCIAL DANCES | |
| Carnival | Orquesta típica |
| Cortamonte | Brass band |
| Huayno | Orquesta típica |
| Marinera | Brass band |
| Toril | Orquesta típica |
| Santiago (R) | Orquesta típica |
| Cumbia | Brass band |
| Pandillada | Brass band |
| Huaylas (R) | Orquesta típica |
| THEATRICAL DRAMATIZATIONS | |
| Maqtada | Trumpets/drums; Brass band |
| Death of The Inca | Orquesta típica |
| LIFE CYCLE CEREMONIES | |
| Zafacasa (roof building) | Orquesta típica |
| Weddings | Orquesta típica |
| FERTILITY RITUALS | |
| Herranza (branding of animals) | Violin/tinya/cacho |

characters in a dance, if in fact the most prominent trait, is not necessarily the most important factor to be taken into account in categorizing a dance-drama. The significance of local concepts of time, space, and hierarchy usually goes beyond the plain portrayal of a personage. Thus, the repre-sented character may in fact embody a different persona than the one that appears on the surface (1990:101).

Nonetheless, the representation of a particular character is a valid in-itial point of departure for a subsequent contextual analysis of the deep meanings of such a persona for the community. Moreover, the people them-selves tend to identify and verbalize the dance-dramas according to the surface image of their characters, even when these characters may in fact have different connotations. Consequently I will follow this everyday prac-tice to convey the abundance of dance-dramas in the valley. People of the valley portray in their dances a variety of personages, drawn from both their collective past and recent history. The frequently cited trend of the Andean peoples to represent the foreign and the stranger is clearly illus-trated by the various dances that portray the black slaves who are widely dispersed throughout the valley (such as the *pachahuara*, the *negrería*, the *negritos decentes*, the *chacranegro*, and the *moscones*), the noble and rich Spaniard (the *chonguinada* and the *tunantada*), the inhabitant of the Ama-zonian jungles (the *shapis*), the isolated shepherds of the valley's highland pasturelands (the *llamishada*, the *huaylijia*, and the *pastoras*), and the co-lonial Spanish or republican bureaucrats depicted as elderly characters (the *corcovados*, the *viejitos*, and the *auquines*). Other characters who are asso-ciated with the past and therefore considered "others," like the peasant guerrillas of the war with Chile in the nineteenth century (the *avelinos* and the *huaconada*) and the Inca's consorts (the *pallas*), are also common representations in the valley.

This is an arbitrary grouping, since Poole's notion of the multivalent meaning of personages in Andean dances is very germane here. Many dances are interpreted in different, sometimes ambiguous ways by towns-people themselves, like the huaconada, which is considered by some to be a representation of a peasant resistance fighter in the war against Chile and by others a representation of a pre-Hispanic mythical being. The corco-vados constitutes another example, since for some people it is just a satir-ical portrayal of the elderly, however venerable, but for others it is that of an old Spaniard. Recent studies on the meanings of masks in Andean festivals have emphasized that through masks (as a primary element of the dance-drama) the dancer appropriates the power of a foreign, sometimes threatening character, controlling, manipulating, and thereby transforming it (Cánepa-Koch 1992, 1993, 1998).

All of the dances have a solid dramatic story line, which is further enriched by oral tradition. In the pachahuara, for example, music and dance join together to narrate the drama of black slavery in the region.

The first section, the *pasión* (passion), is a slow, suspenseful segment representing slavery that ends with the advent of the pasacalle, a contrasting joyful and loud piece that, according to popular belief, stands for freedom and emancipation. The characters of the dance-drama stress the story line of the *gamonal* (the oppressive landlord) and the slaves.

Most of the dances are multisectional forms that may contain distinctive tempos and thematic contents. These sections are referred to by specific names and correspond in turn to specific choreographic figures and formations, as well as to specific moments of the fiesta. Some of the dances can consist of four to six distinctive choreographic sections (like the *carnaval marqueño*, the *shapish*, the huaylijia, and the auquines). Others may exhibit only two main sections, like the dance *la jija*, whose parts exhibit the same names as the pachahuara (the slow pasión and the faster pasacalle), although with different musics. Following these two sections, there are twenty-four *mudanzas*, which consist of huaynos (the most popular Andean song genre) to which the dancers are supposed to perform with different choreographic movements.

Some dances are only performed on specific dates of the calendar year, like the pachahuara and the huaylijía, which are used during Christmas, or the jija during the Festival of the Holy Cross (month of May). Others appear rather infrequently and erratically throughout the festival calendar. Two dances, however, are the most popular in the fiesta system and constitute the most ubiquitous dances in all the Mantaro Valley. The tunantada in the region of Jauja and the chonguinada in the area of Huancayo are performed throughout the calendar year. Both dances have many points of similarity, although each maintains its own distinctive identity, both musically and choreographically. Both are variants of the popular huayno. The chonguinada has a structured choreography and is danced in pairs and in columns.[15] Its characters come from a blending of times and circumstances: the *chonguino* wears colonial dress and a mask with European features, and his partner, the *chupaquina*, regional dress; the *chuto* represents by all accounts an Indian, who does not dance within the group but revolves around it making humorous jests and amusing the audience; while the *bolivianos* (natives of Bolivia) represent the foreign traders, an image of the old *arriero* (colonial traveling merchant) who joins the group somewhat as an outsider. The tunantada presents very similar characters: the *tunante* is the rich European; the chupaquina and the chuto remain the same characters as in the chonguinada and are joined by the *argentinos* and the *mexicanos*, who stand for the foreign traders.

Besides the dance-dramas, in which a dramatic story line unfolds with different costumed and masked characters playing distinct roles, I have also documented social couple or group dances, which are performed unrehearsed and without special attire. These dances are spontaneously realized by the participants in the fiesta. I have documented as well theatrical representations and life-cycle ceremonies. Of all of these, the tunantada and the chonginada stand out prominently (in the following chapter I will analyze the music of these two dances).

## The "Old" and the "Modern" Huaylas Dance

The case of the dance of the huaylas is one of the most suggestive among other mestizo re-creations of the peasant "past."[16] On the subject of the huaylas there has been a considerable amount of discussion in the valley, and there is still an ongoing debate. The primary topic of this discussion is the origins of the huaylas. It is an informal debate, as well as a formal one, since symposia on the origins of the huaylas have been organized even by government institutions such as the municipality of Huancayo.[17] The rise and wide popularity of *concursos* (public competitions) of the huaylas charge this ongoing debate further but emphasize the concern for "history" rather than contemporary identity. The third "official competition" of huaylas organized by the municipality was announced on a billboard as "the expression of the beauty and vigor of this Wanka land, birthplace of great people that shine in the pages of our history."

In comparison to the unofficial and sometimes hidden controversy over the "authenticity" of the orquesta típica, in which each position is grounded in specific tenets of tradition, modernity, and identity (chapter 3), the debate over the origins of the huaylas appears like a cluster of loosely founded individual opinions, frequently plagued by historical speculation and rewriting of the past. I will synthesize the general aspects of this discussion with that observation in mind.[18]

The central point of agreement in the debate is that the ritual of the waylarsh, described earlier, developed into a *carnival* dance, carnival understood as an urban and public phenomenon in the valley. Most of the accounts relate stories about how the participants of the waylarsh ended up accompanying with their dances an urban carnival parade in the outskirts of the city of Huancayo, but when the parade approached the city the waylarsh gathering returned to their villages without entering the town. In time, however, they did enter, and their songs and dances became known and widely popular among the citizens of Huancayo, being rendered or appropriated by the orquesta típica. These stories imply that, from then on, the huaylas as a carnival dance became a familiar event in the festival system of the valley. The *huaylas antiguo* (old huaylas) and the *huaylas moderno* (modern huaylas) stem from this festival dance, which has remained otherwise a part of the regional festivals to this day. Yet this is not the topic of the controversy but, rather, the recent renditions of the "old" and "modern" huaylas, both primarily performed on open stages

Dancers of the huaylas at a patronal fiesta in the village of Huanchar. Photo: Raúl R. Romero, courtesy Center for Andean Ethnomusicology, Catholic University of Peru.

(primarily in concursos) and in urban theaters. Inflamed arguments are rampant over how the "modern" huaylas deform and misrepresents the "authentic" dance by inventing new steps and choreographic figures, and how the "old" huaylas does not embody the "authentic" history of the ritual and dance despite its efforts to dramatize peasant work.

Both dances depict the Wanka peasants, men and women, and their choreography suggests the courting between the sexes. These two elements are the main identifiers of the dances: peasantry and courting. In the old huaylas, on the one hand, the dancers are portrayed as modest peasants, in attire that conveys their "humbleness." The music generally follows a moderate tempo, and its performance includes various theatrical representations of communal work in the fields (including, for instance, the manipulation of agricultural tools, dancing upon wheat, and the chewing of coca leaves). In the modern huaylas, on the other hand, dancers wear festive, "clean" dress, the music follows a very fast tempo, and the choreography is based on straight corporal movements, avoiding any literal dramatization of peasant work. In general, the modern huaylas is perceived as much faster, its choreography more "lively," and its attire more colorful and fancier than the old, which exhibits the inverse qualities. These differences provoke the fuel for this debate, which is aimed at defining not which type is the best depiction of a rural "past" but the origins of the generic dance itself.

The positions in this controversy are further obscured by the multiple meanings and "histories" assigned to the waylarsh, as an "ancient" communal harvest ritual and historical source of the huaylas. Most of the participants in the debate manipulate different versions of the "authentic" waylarsh. In the following version Agripina Castro de Aguilar describes the waylarsh as a competition between peasants working in the fields:

> A dance of competition between two men, representing two different *ayllus* [a pre-Hispanic derived kinship group], communities or localities. At the end of the harvest, when the sun went down, men challenged each other and did with their feet what they did with their hands. The steps of the waylarsh imitate the movements of agricultural work and have specific names. There was always a winner. The music was exclusively vocal, without instruments, and sung by women. They also encouraged the men to work with their chants.[19]

Other accounts offer varied and detailed descriptions of the same dance. The ascription of Quechua names to some of the dance's traits is common in their attempts to relate the "history" of the waylarsh to pre-Hispanic times. Many refer to the waylarsh as *takanacoy* (meaning "challenge" or "duel" in Quechua) and to its sung version as *taki-waylarsh* (*taki* meaning "song" in Quechua). These "historical" accounts even describe the origins of the distinctive cries and whistles that dancers employ to animate the performance, tracing them back to the "ancient" ritual, when the peasants encouraged the challengers by shouting expressions like *wayap, chayap*, and *chajajay*. Some of the discussants affirm that these shouts were the roots for the huaylas song genre, which they insist on calling by the Quechua name taki-waylarsh. The version of the waylarsh as a musical challenge between two men who represent their respective communities is sometimes mixed with an account that seems to be referring to the nocturnal harvest of grain. In this case, it is said that the duel between peasants of different villages occurred after the communal harvest, which suggests that there is no contradiction between both accounts of the "original" waylarsh. Some common elements do arise from the discussion. Everyone associates the huaylas with common emotions of joy and exhilaration, the role of women as singers, the unmarried status of the peasants involved, the communal character of the entire event, and the seasonal character of the ritual (time of harvest, usually around Carnival).

I would conclude from the examination of these accounts that the waylarsh as a nocturnal threshing of grains is not necessarily unrelated to the widely accepted notion of the waylarsh as a duel between two different communities. During my stay in the Mantaro Valley, however I was not able to gather oral testimonies of actual participants that support the dueling type of waylarsh, and Arguedas does not mention it in his study of the waylarsh as a nocturnal harvest ritual. The group of elders whom I interviewed in two different districts and who described the ritual and performed its songs also did not mention the existence of peasant and village ritual duels. I do not discard, however, the possibility of the past existence of village duels in areas located to the south of Huancayo, since many of the discussants in the huaylas polemic affirm that these duels originated in the towns of Pucará, Sapallanga, Huacrapuquio, Huancán, and Viques, all of which are located in that zone. This could suggest that the waylarsh as a ritual duel was in fact a local variation of the more widely dispersed waylarsh nocturnal communal harvest, but as far as I know, no one in this debate has connected both variations. Such an avoidance of local versions of the huaylas is not rare in this context, because the primary aim of this debate is the search for common roots of Wanka culture, thus the need for generalization and homogenization of regional "history."

The re-creation of ancient rural customs can be seen in other realms as well, if less spectacular and public than the huaylas debate and performances. The the jija, performed in communities near Jauja on the Day of the Holy Cross (May 3), is a festival mestizo dance performed by men only that also depicts peasants. They are dressed in working attire, fully ornamented in some cases or "refined" versions of working clothes in others. The dance dramatizes the work in the fields. A first, lively section, called the jija, represents the marching to the fields. Then, a second section follows called the pasión (passion) or surge, which is a slower, serious phase in which dancers are supposed to represent the actual working in the fields. The dance ends with the *doce pares* (twelve pairs) of huaynos as a festive ending to the dance. The local interpretations about the origins of this dance relate it to the harvest and to the demonstration of manliness, thus suggesting obvious points of contact with the case of the huaylas. But the jija has not achieved the regional popularity of the former, being performed only in a few communities. This dance, however, is another example of how mestizos of the valley have an irresistible urge to re-create the rural past through dramatization. In this case, unlike with the huaylas, the orquesta típica does not include saxophones but rather incorporates two clarinets, two violins, a harp, and a tinya. As in the case of Huaripampa, analyzed in chapter 3 of this book, this version of the orquesta típica is considered to be the "authentic" format but with one addition, the tinya, an "Indian" instrument that fosters the representation of the rural and the distant peasant customs that are rendered by the dancers.

A different case, although also part of the same process, is the popularization of herranza music through a song genre called santiago. This is an example of de-ritualization of a musical genre that is also aimed at remembering a distant past. But in this case it is a genre taken from a living custom, since the herranza, as we have seen before, is a widely held and dynamic ritual throughout the entire Mantaro Valley. There is no need, therefore, to dramatize the herranza through dance-dramas or to re-create the ritual through public dances performed in theaters. Hence the strategy of de-contextualizing the musical song genre for its free dissemination around the valley. This is also an attempt to remember the past on a daily basis and give it a space within the terrains of everyday life of the mestizo population of the valley.

## Conclusions

In this chapter I have argued that the people of the valley view herranza music as being in an unchanging, "timeless" realm. As ritualized music, it is conceived as part of a "past" derived from colonial and pre-Hispanic traditions that are not open to manipulation. No one wants to change, innovate, or experiment with herranza music; nor does anyone want to introduce new, "modern" instruments to its customary ensemble. Its seasonal character works as an additional "protective" shield against manipulation, and so does the fact that professionalization is not a feasible alternative here. The "antique" music of the herranza is, then, reserved for peasants from distant localities, who are tacitly assigned the roles of carriers and guardians of this tradition. I contend that herranza conceptually links the regional memory further back into time, certainly further back than the first decade of the twentieth century, which is considered by many to be the point in time at which "authenticity" was constructed (see chapter 3). It thus operates as a living museum of musical archaisms, "safe" from controversies over modernity and "authenticity" and the pressures from the public sphere. In fact, there is no argument here, simply because no one in the valley doubts the "antiquity" of herranza. The fact that herranza is or should be an unchanging tradition is not a matter of discussion, nor is the fact that the "past" to which herranza alludes is more distant in time than any other tradition in the valley.

In highlighting the protective, preservationist posture of the peasantry of the valley regarding herranza, I do not mean to propose that all rituals contribute to social cohesiveness, integration, and harmony within the group, as a structural-functionalist perspective on ritual would. Neither is the herranza a straightforward "ritual of rebellion," in the sense that it does not directly confront to modern forces, nor does it seek to impose indigenous practices (see Kelly and Kaplan 1990:134–135). In this sense, the practice of the herranza in the valley is far different from the rituals of invocation of the ancestors or ancestors' spirits in Zimbabwe during the guerrilla war of the 1970s (Lan 1985). The herranza can be conceived as a ritual of resistance only if seen within a wider historical context, in which the herranza appears as one element among others in the struggle for regional authority within a context of national cultural conflict. The historical context demonstrates that the herranza permits the regional culture to "remember" a regional history and trace its roots back to ancient times, when animals, land, and crops were dependent not so much on modern technologies but on nature, fate, and the supernatural.

It is in this sense that herranza contests national culture, displaying a "different" or "alternative" worldview. The peasants who hold this worldview are the same ones who will later produce for, confront, and negotiate the market. In view of this apparent peasant surrender to the market, it would be possible, following Maurice Bloch, to interpret the herranza as a "diabolic smoke-screen" whose main function is to "hide reality" rather than foster, in the long run, a counterhegemonic national culture. But as Stanley Tambiah affirms, in criticizing Bloch's formulations, ritual is always an "ideological and aesthetic social construction that is directly and recursively implicated in the expression, realization, and exercise of power" (see Tambiah 1979:153). So, too, I see the herranza, rather than as an event separated and disconnected from everyday practice, as one that plays a distinctive role in the reaffirmation of the regional culture of the Mantaro Valley.

However, we have seen that the valley's mestizos feel somewhat responsible for the loss of ancient rural customs, other than the herranza, and that this concern is expressed through the re-creation of these practices. The re-creation is not through modernizing strategies but through the redramatization of these conventions, which are recognized as belonging to a distant and already lost rural past.[20] Rather than blaming new technologies, we must understand the reasons for forgetting traditions in terms of the encounter between the manifestations of modern capitalism (as a complex entity that consists not only of technologies but of ideologies as well) and local cultures and customs. Both spheres have different outlooks as regards production, one linked to market demands and cost/benefit analyses and the other to communal celebration and "archaic" reciprocity practices. Following Marshall Sahlins's assertion that production is "something more and other than a practical logic of material effectiveness" (1976:169), I maintain that the "cultural intentions" of both domains derive from two different labor practices, one characterized by the absence of music and ritual and the other by the celebration of reciprocity. The claim that huauco music "is from Inca times" further discourages the younger generation from getting involved in this repertoire. They turn in droves to the orquesta típica or similar ensembles to redefine their identities in relation to modernity.

A major difference between huauco music and the waylarsh is that while the latter involves a communal event in which men and women met and courted, the former was based on individual performance. Hence the different attitudes that mestizos of the valley hold toward the demise of these two traditions. In the waylarsh everyone was involved, since it contributed to the maintenance of the life cycle in significant ways. In contrast, huauco music contributed only to productivity, attempting to enhance the workers' energy so they would produce more. This has become useless in the current industrial context, and so has its remembrance. Few people in the valley feel at a loss about the increasing disappearance of huauco music or even acknowledge its stubborn persistence. It was only after many months of fieldwork that I found out about the existence of this musical practice. When I heard accounts about the music of the valley, huauco music was never mentioned or even remembered. There is no nostalgia or sorrow concerning the departure of traditions like huauco music, as there is in the case of the waylarsh. The sense of community and the reproduction of the life cycle that the latter evokes in the memory of the valley residents are significant ingredients in the current reaffirmations of regional identity; hence the "rescuing" of the waylarsh as an "image" of what the valley really was. Rescuing traditions for the sake of collecting past events is not the purpose of this quest. Rather, it is the "rescuing" process by those who allude to a "past" that is relevant to the current constructions of identity. The claims for a cultural "past," therefore, appear as a selective task, very much in tune with the current endeavor of moving into the future.

# 3

# AUTHENTICITY AND
# MUSICAL ENSEMBLES

*The Emergence of* Orquestas Típicas

The relationship between the assimilation of the clarinet and the saxophone and the impact of modernity in the lives of the people of the Mantaro Valley can be noticed in the many legends about how the saxophone was introduced in the valley. The following story was told to me in 1985 by the widow of Teodoro Rojas Chucas, a well-known musician from the valley. This narrative tells about a North American man who accidentally hit a child with his car. He was carrying a saxophone with its case and wanted to sell it to pay for the damages. Then Teodoro Chucas, who happened to be nearby, bought the instrument for 300 soles (Peruvian currency). He brought the instrument to Acolla, where nobody had heard about the saxophone, and began to play it on June 24 at the Festival of the Tunantada. From then on, many orchestras were founded that featured the saxophone. This is similar to other stories told around the region but with different names and other variations. However, the common ground among all of them seems to be the sudden, abrupt introduction of the saxophone into the region and the responsibility for its appearance almost always attributed to a particular musician who acquired it through trade, barter, or sale from a foreign, in this case North American, source.

The fact that this story mentions a North American as the owner of the first saxophone to be used in the valley is likely related to the North American ownership of the large mining companies in the area. In the story the local musician seems to be appropriating the instrument from the agents of "modernity" in the area, the proprietors of the mines. The North Americans forfeit the instrument as a penalty for the lethal consequences they brought into the region (manifested by the hegemonic foreign presence, the car accident, and the death of the child). The saxophone, a foreign instrument, is then assimilated into the regional traditions, giving birth to a new musical style. Thus, the musicians of the valley appear to domesticate an element of modernity (the saxophone), subdue its capacities and power, and use it for its own purposes. One can further suggest that the saxophone is an interchangeable sign in this oral narrative, since the clarinet could be substituted and still maintain the same basic logic and meanings.

The orquesta típica is one of the most representative types of musical ensembles of the mestizo peasantry of the Mantaro Valley. It is an ensemble that plays a major role in the festival system and the dance-dramas of the region. The contemporary instrumental configuration of the orquestas típicas is the result of continuous processes of cultural assimilations and discontinuities, which took place during the first half of the twentieth century. These processes took as points of departure previously existent local ensembles that included the Andean harp and the violin. Indian peasants imaginatively incorporated both instruments, introduced by the Spanish colonial system, into their own cultural and aesthetical frameworks. The harp and the violin were promoted, taught, and disseminated by missionaries in their quest for evangelization early in the colonial period (Béhague 1979:3; Arguedas 1976:239).[1] Jesuits, Franciscans, and Dominicans considered these instruments, unlike the guitar, fit to be performed by Indians and thereby effective in their attempts to spread Catholicism. Over time Indians became accomplished performers on these instruments as well as skillful makers of them. While the violin preserved the basic characteristics of the European model, the harp was constructed according to different local traditions and aesthetics (see Olsen 1986–1987; also Schechter 1992). The harp and violin became an important part of Andean musical traditions and soon were regarded as "Indian" instruments, despite their European origins.[2]

In the Mantaro Valley the harp and violin also gained wide popular acceptance and soon constituted the basis of several musical ensembles that performed extensively at public festivals (Arguedas 1976:239). Even today, while the orquesta típicas are the most pervasive ensembles in the region, there are other particular dances that are still accompanied by smaller ensembles of a harp and one or two violins.[3] By the end of the nineteenth century, the ensembles based on the harp and the violin grew into larger ensembles characterized by other instruments like the guitar, the mandolin, the *charango* (small Andean guitar), the indigenous tinya (small Andean drum), and the *quena* (end-notched flute).

All of these instruments, many of which have already disappeared from the valley, were part of the dominant regional ensembles at that time, ensembles called *conjuntos* (musical groups) or orquestas—the forerunners of the orquesta típicas. Rubén Valenzuela has outlined a condensed history of the evolution of this ensemble, as well as compiled ample photographic evidence of the existence of the conjunto (1984). In one of these photographs a conjunto is shown as being constituted by two guitars, one mandolin, two quenas, two violins, and one harp. This formation is, however, only one of several options, according to other photographs of the same period. What is certain is that these instruments were neglected during the first decades of the century and displaced by new ones, first by the clarinet and subsequently by the saxophone.[4]

All of the processes of displacement and appropriation occurred throughout the twentieth century. Today the guitar, the mandolin, and the quena have been left out of popular musical practice in the Mantaro Valley, although they are well known by the people of the valley who are familiar with their popularity in other Andean regions.[5] The clarinet was the first European instrument to be incorporated by the conjuntos, by the first decade of the twentieth century, at the expense of the Andean quena, which was swiftly uprooted from the ensemble (Valenzuela 1984). The precise origins and details of the clarinet's introduction are, however, difficult to assess based exclusively on oral tradition. In the Mantaro Valley the narrative of every interviewed musician tends to attribute the introduction of musical instruments to individual performers. For example, Alberto Paucar, known professionally as Pachacho, a well-known musician who founded many conjuntos and orquestas in Huancayo during the first two decades of the century, is credited by many with the introduction of the clarinet in the area of Huancayo.[6]

This practice suggests that at this time, in the Mantaro Valley, the notions of individuality and originality had already prevailed over traits of collective creation and anonymity—traits usually ascribed to "traditional" musical creativity. This trend, which is further confirmed by the subsequent appearance in the 1930s of a song collection gathered by Jose Hidalgo of nearly 700 mulizas (a nostalgic and lyrical regional song genre), all of which had an individual author (Arguedas 1976:204). This propensity, however, does not completely obliterate the idea of collective creation in the valley, since musical composition at public festivals is to this day still accomplished cooperatively, with no individual author being signaled as responsible for the festival tunes. Thus, both creative trends (individual and collective) coexist without friction or conflict, each one in separate contexts.

It is around the 1910s, when the clarinet was incorporated into the conjunto, that the denomination of the orquesta típica emerged, as well as the popular assumption that this configuration was in fact típico (traditional) or authentic to the region of the Mantaro Valley. Why was the clarinet so swiftly accepted as típico to the region? The introduction of the clarinet in the Mantaro Valley occurred at a time during which the region experienced the impact of a national "modernization" project launched in 1895 by the government of Nicolas de Piérola, which created the conditions for unprecedented processes of economic expansion and ethnic homogenization in the valley. The de Piérola government followed a period of national crisis and economic uncertainty in the aftermath of the war with Chile (1879–1883). Andres A. Cáceres, who had been a war hero in the Mantaro Valley fighting against the Chileans and who later became president of Peru, was ousted after a series of economic and political mishandlings. Piérola, who assumed the presidency in 1895, supported a program of modernization of the country that advocated national industrialization. As a result, several improvements in urban environments took place. In Lima the first trolley cars appeared, electrification, potable water and sewage disposal systems were installed, and health services were substantially improved, and the first automobiles began circulating on the roads of Lima and the rest of the country (Dobyns and Doughty 1976:212–213).

These improvements attracted the earliest waves of Andean migrants to the cities, initiating the period during which the first Andean migrant associations in Lima were founded. For the residents of the Mantaro Valley, access to Lima and its urban facilities became even easier and more fluid than for other regions because of the construction of the railroad to Huancayo in 1908, which made the trip shorter and safer all year round. But more important, it opened the possibility for individuals to visit and maintain closer ties with Lima without abandoning their lands or occupations in the valley. This access was not possible for other Andean migrants from more distant locations.

Thus, the nation experienced a spectacular economic expansion, and the Mantaro Valley became attractive to entrepreneurs who invested heavily in mining, commerce, and agriculture (Long and Roberts 1978:5; Mallon 1983:135). The peasantry of the valley participated actively in all of these processes. Thousands engaged in temporary migration to the nearby mining centers, and others significantly increased their agricultural production for the expanded market. In the midst of these transformations the process of cultural mestizaje became accentuated. Indians and mestizos, who until the mid–nineteenth century had maintained different positions and ideologies in the Mantaro Valley, began to blend. As Richard Adams (1959: 85) concluded in his study of the district of Muquiyauyo, by the end of the nineteenth century, "people from both castes began to participate jointly in more affairs; together with this, there was a simultaneous borrowing of some culture traits and a merging of others. The result has been, in effect, to blend the two previously distinct subcultures of mestizos and Indians."

Adams also refers to significant aesthetic indicators like clothing, which has been mentioned frequently as one of the main symbols that distinguishes between Indians and mestizos. He confirmed that "by 1910 the last of the men had given up their Indian dress for mestizo clothing, and the women's dress was changing to a form which was being used by both Indians and many mestizos" (1959:85). This transition from Indian to mestizo, which occurred during a time span of one or two generations, was not a traumatic experience, nor was it perceived by the peasantry as a loss of identity; rather, it was perceived as a renewal. It was different story in the southern Andes, where interethnic conflicts between Indian and mestizos assumed other forms of tense confrontation.

The saxophone was incorporated into the orquesta típicas in the 1940s, some thirty years later than the clarinet. This was a short interval of time but one that allowed sufficient time for a new generation to have arisen in the region. For this new generation the initial impact of modern capitalism was already part of the history of the valley. They were living in an age in which temporary migration to the mining centers was a natural mode for making a living and in which the demand for their agricultural produce was considerable and dependable (Mallon 1993:310). The railroad had been the regular means of transportation to Lima for decades, and the Central Highway, finished in 1939, provided yet another improvement to their already efficient communications with the capital (Long and Roberts 1978:5). Also in the 1940s, the use of the Spanish language became almost universal among all of the peasants, although Quechua continued to be spoken widely (Adams 1959:86). This generation was responsible for the introduction of the saxophone into the orquesta típica.

But the use of the saxophone was not shared by many of the older generations who had seen the saxophones almost forcibly introduced into the orchestra. To this day, the saxophone is still a matter of controversy with regard to its "authenticity." Folklorists and laypeople in the valley ponder the size and number of saxophones in each ensemble in order to assess their quality, expertise, and, more important, fitness to the occasion. Accordingly, in some contexts the greater number of saxophones may be perceived as an advantage and a sign of musical power and prestige, but in others it may be evidence of shallow aesthetics and distasteful musical practices.[7] Both opposing contexts correspond to what roughly could be labeled as the traditionalist and the modernist points of view: the former generally embodied by the folklorists and the elders (who consider themselves carriers of the oldest and more "authentic" traditions in the valley) and the latter by festival sponsors (mayordomos), whose prestige depends on how powerful and "modern" an orchestra might be, and also by members of the younger generations who are looking for new and innovative musical sounds.

Mallon has noticed a parallel distinction but in relation to regional economic development. She perceives an "innovative" and "individualistic" group of richer peasants, mostly gathered around district capitals, and a group of poorer peasants, residing largely in hamlets or *anexos*, who rely on "traditional reciprocity" for their survival. However, I have not perceived that the division between "traditionalists" and "innovators" corresponds to strict social sectors. Rather, I have observed that this struggle involves all the peasantry of the valley regardless of their income or administrative positions. I tend to agree with Norman Long and Brian Roberts, who view these dynamics as common to all the communities of the valley, celebrating how the region has been "exceptionally successful in adapting traditions of community self-help to meet modern necessities" (1978:4).

The first saxophone to be introduced in the valley was the soon-to-be discarded C melody saxophone. It was followed shortly afterward by the alto and tenor saxophones (Valenzuela 1984). Saxophones appear to have quickly extended throughout the region, most likely provoked by the massive draft of Andean youngsters for mandatory military service and their subsequent participation in military brass bands. As in the case of the clarinet, oral accounts of musicians in the valley tend to refer to particular individual performers as responsible for the introduction of the saxophone. Often the musicians proudly declare themselves to be the initiators of the new musical practice, as in the case of the well-known musician Ascanio Robles, who alleged:

> In 1920 I introduced for the first time an alto saxophone to the orchestra "Orfeón de Huancayo," not as a permanent instrument, rather for only one performance, and I should say that the audience did not like it, neither did the sponsors of the festival, the reason for which I rarely included the saxophone in my presentations, but after the 1930s I saw a few orchestras with saxophones.[8]

Another musician, Teodoro Rojas Chucas, who played the tenor saxophone, also claimed a prominent role in the introduction of the saxophone. Valenzuela summarizes his testimony in the following passage:

> [The] tenor saxophone was introduced to the orquesta típica by the clarinet and saxophone player Teodoro Rojas Chucas in the orchestra "Centro Musical Jauja," in the 1930s, who alternated between the two instruments he played. Is interesting to note that the tenor sax-

ophone that the maestro Teodoro Rojas Chucas used was tuned in C
and not in B♭, as it is today.[9]

Oral tradition aside, the precise explanation of why these instruments
and not others were incorporated into the region's popular culture should
be linked to aesthetic and cultural factors, rather than to their dissemination or availability in the valley. The clarinet and the saxophone, along
with many others European instruments of recent introduction, have cir-
culated widely throughout all the regions of the Peruvian Andes. Notwithstanding this, the only region where they have been broadly accepted
is the Mantaro Valley. Moreover, in the valley the instruments of the ubiquitous brass band have achieved wide popularity as well, but none of them
(the trumpet or the trombone, for instance) enjoyed the destinies of the
clarinet or the saxophone. Some musicians of the valley have called attention to the similarities between the clarinet and the quena (now vanished
from popular demand in the valley) and the saxophone and the wakrapuku, thus suggesting the possibility that the modern instruments displaced the previous indigenous ones due to the similarities of their timbre.

## Aesthetics, Repertoire, and Musical Styles

From its consolidation in the mid-1940s to this day, the orquesta típica has
been constituted by one harp and a variable number of violins, clarinets,
alto saxophones, tenor saxophones, and baritone saxophones. Over time
the number of saxophones has tended to increase, while that of the clarinets and the violins has tended to decrease. According to the well-known
violinist Zenobio Dagha, from Chupuro, the configuration of the orchestra
around the 1940s consisted of one harp, two clarinets, two violins, two
alto saxophones, and one tenor saxophone.[10] This instrumentation actually
became the standard one for the orquesta típica for more than two decades,
until the pressure arose to add more saxophones to the ensemble. Today
it is not uncommon to find orquesta típicas with eight saxophones (two
baritones, two tenors, and four altos) and only one clarinet and one violin.
This trend has been further corroborated by older musicians of the valley.
One of them, Dario Curisinchi from Acolla, remembered:

> Since 1945 the sax was in use. According to the taste of the asocia-
> ción, well before the orchestra consisted of the harp and volin, noth-
> ing more. Later the clarinet joined in, afterward one sax, and from
> then on, with the passage of time, it [the orchestra] has grown to two
> alto saxes and one tenor. Before it was a sax in C; it was intermediate
> between an alto and a tenor. The soprano [saxophone] was used, but

The orquesta típica Alegría Andina in the 1960s as conducted by renowned violinist Zenobio Dahga (kneeling to the right). Photo courtesy Center for Andean Ethnomusicology, Catholic University of Peru.

it was forsaken. And one baritone [saxophone], even sometimes two baritones.[11]

The alto saxes are considered the leading voices within the orchestra, and the other instruments double their voices according to their normal ranges. When a second instrument is doubled, the second plays a line at a distance of a third from the principal melody. The clarinets play the main melody an octave higher than the altos and the violins an octave higher than the clarinets. In turn, the tenor saxophones play the melody an octave lower and the baritone saxophones an octave lower than the tenors. The harpist provides a bass line with his left hand and a harmonic accompaniment with his right hand.

This standard procedure, however, undergoes significant transformations when the instrumentation changes. Most frequently, there is the tendency today to add more saxophones to the orchestra while reducing (and sometimes even eliminating on certain occasions) the clarinets and the violins. But the overall result continues to be a musical arrangement in which some instruments play the same melody in different octaves and others double that main melody at the lower third, which then also can be doubled in different octaves. The harp remains the sole provider of the bass line and of the harmonic base, which, it should be noted, is barely audible

An orquesta típica in the town of Huanchar, province of Concepción, during the Festival of Saint John, in the month of June (1985). Photo: Raúl R. Romero, courtesy Center for Andean Ethnomusicology, Catholic University of Peru.

in festival contexts, when street noise and the sound of the saxophones tend to overpower it.

One of the most frequent reasons submitted for the expansion of saxophones to the standard formation of the orchestra is that in order to impress its audience an orchestra has to "sound more" than others, especially in formal competitions. "Sounding more," however, as explained by Rubén Valenzuela, an author, orchestra director, and clarinetist from Sicaya, is not to be understood as a matter of intensity but as a matter of density of sound.[12] That is, it is not enough to blow harder to achieve a higher volume of sound, but the orchestra must display collectively a big sound, which can only be achieved by the sheer number of instruments. To clarify his idea Valenzuela used terms like *diámetro de sonido* ("diameter of sound"), *grueso* ("thick"), *estructura gruesa* ("thick structure"), and *denso* ("dense").[13] In search of this ideal, instruments like the clarinet and the violin, which do not substantially contribute to the thickness of sound when playing live, tend to be eliminated in extreme cases.

"Sounding more" than other orchestras, however, is not to be understood as an exclusively musical achievement or as a source of pride only for the musical director or for the members of the ensemble. It is primarily a source of prestige for the comité directivo, for its president and other authorities, for the barrio that sponsored the dance that year, and for the cargo holder that paid the expenses of that orchestra. The element of competition, formal or implicit, is always present, and aesthetic ideals end up depending upon issues of status and social prestige. In this regard, it is not hard to perceive that this aesthetic ideal of sounding louder and thicker than others is a "modern" ideal, since it does not exist when smaller rural ensembles enter into the scene. "Sounding more" is not the aspiration for peasant herranza musicians, and neither is it for the harp and violin ensembles that still play around the valley. But even more significant, "sounding more" is not the aesthetic ideal for the self-proclaimed "authentic" orquestas típicas of the "traditionalist" town of Huaripampa (a case that I will elaborate further later in this chapter), where the ideal is a mellow, soothing sound and, suggestively, the sound of the saxophones is perceived as vociferous.[14]

The size of the orchestra is also a sign of prestige for its sponsors. For many residents of the valley, an orchestra of twenty musicians is more impressive and gives a better impression than a smaller ensemble. It is also going to have a better chance of beating the other orchestras in the formal competitions that may be organized during the fiesta. A resident of Sicaya who was the prioste (a festival sponsor similar to the mayordomo) of the Fiesta of Santiago told me that since the last year's prioste had hired an orchestra of sixteen musicians he had to hire a "better" orchestra the following year. Subsequently he hired one with twenty-two musicians and felt that he had "done better" than his predecessor.[15]

The tunantada and the chonguinada are the most popular dance-dramas of all those accompanied by the orquesta típica. They are also the most widely and frequently performed throughout the year, thus constituting the main source for the orquesta típicas' professional activities. In spite of their many common traits and comparable origins, both dances have distinct formal characteristic. The regional dispersion of both dances is also dissimilar; the former is exclusively danced in the Jauja region, whereas the latter is extant only in the Huancayo area. Several of the musical forms of the valley are variations of the ubiquitous huayno, the foremost popular genre in the Andes, and both of these dances display common traits that link them to this generic source. The tunantada is played in a slow tempo and is frequently performed with legato passages. Conversely, the rhythmic patterns of the chonguinada utilize a faster pace, along with the staccato playing of the saxophones and clarinets. The melodic initiative is taken in both cases by the saxophones and the clarinets and the harmonic function supported by the solitary harpist. While the violins appear to play a subordinate, supportive role overall, they lead during the compulsory introduction and during the interludes that are interpolated between the different tunes.[16] In general terms, the music of

Dancers of the chonguinada in the town of San Agustín. Photo: Raúl R. Romero, courtesy Center for Andean Ethnomusicology, Catholic University of Peru.

Dancers of the tunantada in Acolla. Photo: Raúl R. Romero, courtesy Center for Andean Ethnomusicology, Catholic University of Peru.

the tunantada is perceived as "lyrical" and "sentimental," whereas that of the chonguinada is perceived as "incisive" and more "joyful."[17]

The tunantada is customarily constituted by three different musical phrases called huaynos by the musicians.[18] Each of them consists of two musical segments, not always symmetrical, as often occurs with the Andean huayno (Roel 1959). The first musical statement is a periodic phrase, as is the second, after which both musical statements are reiterated. Then the second huayno, often longer and *mas cadencioso* (more melodic), is usually restated as necessary in relation to the dancers' requirements. The third huayno is in fact a *fuga* (fugue), a short, highly syncopated, spirited concluding section, also called zapateo (because of the shoe tapping that the dancers perform in this section). The fuga is also restated over and over according to the performance situation. Finally, all of the three tunes are recapitulated without repetitions:

huayno no. 1   /:   a + b :/

huayno no. 2   /:   c + d :/ Da Capo (no repeats)

huayno no. 3   /:   e + f :/ (fuga, repeated ad lib)

The preceding summary of the structure is, of course, an ideal one and not necessarily rendered as such at all times. The symbolic letters of this chart are not to be taken literally, since the first two musical statements and their constitutive phrases develop very similar motivic materials, thus they are not contrasting entities, and sometimes, for the unfamiliar listener, it is difficult to discern differences at a first hearing (see example 3.1).

As I noted earlier, the sound of the harp generally goes unnoticed beneath the blaring sound of the saxophones. Only those walking or standing close to the harp are able to hear it. However, in the introduction and

Example 3.1: Dance of tunantada from the town of Jauja

in the interludes the harp and the violins are much more prominent, since they are the only instruments that play. In the interludes, the harp continues providing the walking bass and harmonic chords; throughout, the violin improvises freely while adhering to the latent harmonic base of the piece.

The improvisatory interlude serves many purposes. First, it provides a necessary partition between musical sections, allowing saxophone and clarinet players to catch their breath but also allowing the dancers to rest and stroll the streets of the town while preparing themselves for the next set of huaynos. Violins and harp perform with a somewhat tenuous harmonic coordination, and to the casual listener they may seem slightly out of tune. They do in fact maintain a certain independence, but both move toward the tonic region as their main goal, establishing the harmonic area in which the orchestra will begin playing again. A middle passage in which the harp attempts a faster ostinato pattern, which is not followed closely by the improvisational melody of the violin, is further characteristic of these interludes. This type of performance freedom in ensemble playing in the Andes is common; in an extreme case it consists of heterophony.

The chonguinada has a different musical structure from the related tunantada, although it is also strictly pentatonic. The chonguinada consists of a first part called the pasacalle, a term widely used in the Andes when referring to sections when the dancers stroll the streets of the town, and a huayno. The former section is more characteristic of the dance and the one that distinguishes it from others. The pasacalle is also a huayno, generically speaking, but with specific stylistic traits that distinguish it. As in other mestizo huaynos of the valley, it consists of two musical statements, each of which consists, in turn, of a two-phrase periodic musical statement (A: a + b / B: c + d), and a closing fuga. The pasacalle's peculiarity is vested in its rhythmic arrangement, which emphasizes consecutive sixteenth-note patterns, conveying the impression of a faster, more vigorous musical pace than the tunantada. Its constituents are repeated in the same fashion as that dance; that is, the first statement is repeated once, and after the second one a recapitulation of both sections is taken. After the pasacalle, and the interlude played by the harp and violin, the orchestra plays a huayno, which is referred as to huayno de chonguinada and which concludes with a fuga de huayno as it is customary (see example 3.2).

The tunantada and the chonguinada are not only the most widely dispersed dance-dramas accompanied by the orquesta típica in the valley. They are also the cultural forms most frequently mentioned when the residents of the valley want to convey the richness of its regional culture. The fact that these dances are performed often throughout the year, considerably more than others dramatized only once annualy, reinforces their popularity. The recent mounting of concursos (formal public contests) of

Example 3.2: Dance of chonguinada from San Agustín de Cajas: pasacalle and huayno

chonguinada and tunantada in the valley is a sign of the appeal these dances hold for a wide cohort and generations in the valley. The high concentration of tunantada groups at the Festival of San Sebastián in Jauja (January 20) is, furthermore, a source of empowerment for these groups that yearly renew their affiliations and polish their performance skills in what is considered to be the most influential dance festival event in the area. At the other end of the valley, close to the city of Huancayo, numerous chonguinada groups gather in Zapallanga for the Fiesta of the Nativity of the Virgin (September 8), in what also constitutes a regional event, attracting thousands of people and visitors from adjacent areas. Both regional encounters provide new energy for the multiple performance of these dances at other festivals throughout the valley's calendar year.

## Creativity and Social Relations in Orquestas Típicas

The orquestas típicas do not perform their music according to their own preferences, nor as professionals are they able to make performance decisions without consulting with others. The member of an orquesta típica is a professional musician who is paid for his performance and who is able to earn a living from this occupation. In spite of the fact that many orchestra musicians maintain agricultural plots that they work during the planting and harvest seasons, the income they receive from their contracts is indispensable for their subsistence.[19]

In the Mantaro Valley, orquestas típicas perform predominately at the public festivals of the rural and semiurban districts, for which they are hired by a committee (asociación) that organizes, sponsors, supervises, and actively participate in festival events. The role of a committee formed by townspeople who are elected exclusively for this task is fundamental in the musical decision making of the orquestas típicas. The committee is present during prefestival rehearsals, and it explicitly expresses, in some cases, its views on the "new" tunes that the orchestra will feature that year or, in others, on the proper rendition of "old" tunes.

In the case of the festival dances that require "new" tunes every year, the committee gives its final approval upon listening to the proposed tunes performed by the orchestra during rehearsals, which take place during the evening before the central day of the festival. This endorsement, however, is not formally proclaimed; rather, it is suggested in the context of a fluid dialogue between the musicians and the committee. If the tune is not considered appropriate, another one is politely requested. The committee expects to be consulted and satisfied with the repertoire selected for the festival, and the members of the orchestra accept consultation as a professional chore. Several new tunes may be rendered during the rehearsal, until the right one or ones are chosen by the committee. The committee may also ask for changes in a particular section of a piece, in the case of multisectional dances.[20]

The entire process of rehearsal may take from one to three hours during the evening before the festival, depending on how fast the "new" melodies are composed. The orchestra may even stroll around the main plaza that same night to test the tunes and practice them in public. The following day, during breakfast, the "new" tunes will be played again, mainly to review and memorize them for the rest of the festival. The chief responsibility for bringing ideas for the "new" tunes of the dance falls on the musical director of the orchestra or, in other cases, on a member of the orchestra who is at the same time a composer.

The formal connection between the musicians and the patrons is further explained by several facts. First, the former are generally performers hired from other towns. While most of the orchestras have their operation base in the bigger towns of the valley like Huancayo and Jauja, there are numerous orchestras dispersed around smaller districts as well. When the asociaciones or organizing committees hire an orchestra, they choose from the wide array of orchestras available in the regional market (trying to find a balance between cost and aesthetic quality). This choice generally falls on out-of-town orchestras, many of which are hired one year in advance. The orchestras follow a busy work schedule, especially in the seasons when there is a concentration of festivals, which puts the best orchestras in high demand. One orchestra member expresses how his

A galería (commercial center) of orquestas típicas. Photo: Raúl R. Romero

orchestra toured the valley in one of these seasons with a high concentration of fiestas: "We played in Paca from January 1 to January 5, playing
the huaylijía; then we went to Chunán, where there is another huaylijía
on the fourteenth. Then, with the same orchestra, we went to Jauja for
the Festival of San Sebastián on the Twentieth, until January 25, but then
we had to go to Julcán, where they also dance tunantada but beginning
on January 29." William B. Hutchinson has reported that in the town of
Acolla there are seasons in which orquestas típicas are in very high demand. These include the periods from June to August and from late December to February, the latter (Carnival) one of the busiest for the orchestra
musician (see Hutchinson 1973:158).

Second, there is the perception, grounded in reality, that when the
orchestra accepts a contract with one asociación, it is also making a free
choice—similar to the one made by the organizers—from a wide range of
potential customers. The fact that musicians are independent workers capable of choosing sponsors raises them to a status equal to their benefac-
tors.

Third, the position of patrons and musicians is ethnically equivalent.
Both are part of the mestizo culture of the valley, and there are no essential
asymmetrical differences ascribed to any of them. Differences are primarily
of social class or based on the position each has in the festival. The committee or the president's committee, as carrier of the main cargo of the

festival, is playing a ritual role that is far more crucial than that of the musicians, at least during the festival.

All of these factors put the musicians in a special position. They are treated well and fairly and fed and lodged decently, and their work is regarded as respectable and at times prestigious. This case is totally different from that in other regions of Peru, where musicians are many times situated in asymmetrical relationships with their patrons. When this relationship is defined primarily in terms of ethnic inequalities in places where friction between Indian and mestizo sectors has been particularly controversial, musicians may be subject to harsher, less dignified labor conditions (see Turino 1993:26).

Within the orchestra there is also another level of musical decision making. The orchestra has a musical director, who most of the time is also the manager of the group. He is the one who generally brings the "new" tunes to the rehearsal and submits them for general approval. But it may be that other musicians of the orchestra propose "new" tunes as well, depending upon their particular qualifications as composers, beyond their skills at playing their respective instruments. When there is an open and horizontal atmosphere, precisely who proposes a "new" tune seems unimportant; rather, the goal seems to be to execute the assignment as competently as possible. As one clarinetist noted: "Within the orchestra there is a musical director. He is the one who 'knows best,' and who has the power to decide within the orchestra. He always exercises his authority considering the opinions of the other musicians. It is not like a symphonic orchestra, where the director is authoritarian and dictates what has to be done."[21]

This rigid, though courteous, discipline, which stresses the festival's guidelines rather than individual or group fulfillment, is better understood if one considers the complex and severe cargo system that supports the Andean festival at large. In the case of the Mantaro Valley, the orchestra fulfills one of the main requirements of the festival, and its own goals are subordinated to the fulfillment of the festival's success. The orchestra's musical creativity and even its longing to compete with other ensembles are subject to the festival's own tempo and needs.

In the case of dances that are supposed to be accompanied by "old" tunes, the ritual is similar although the ends may be different. In dances such as the huaconada in the area of Mito, a tune kept in collective memory as the primordial melody of the dance is expected to be repeated year after year without meaningful transformations. In the words of a violinist of an orquesta típica:

But around there, be cautious. The locals in Mito have their own customs and do not allow musicians to alter the theme, the melody.

They want the melodic line to be honored as it is; if you add an ornament, an appoggiatura, they get angry, and they are supposed to beat you. It is the only theme they revere. "No, no, play the music exactly as it is; do not change anything or add any accompaniment." That is why with that music you have to be very careful; if you are not, you will be whipped![22]

The preceding description of orchestra rehearsals and preparation of "new" and "old" tunes corresponds, however, to an ideal condition not always strictly followed in the current musical practice in the Mantaro Valley. For example, there are times at which the "new" tunes are made up during actual performance in the festival, as in the dance of the tunantada, which requires three different tunes. The second of these tunes is at times composed during rest periods in the actual festival. In other cases, the orchestra already arrives with the "new" tunes previously composed for festivals in other towns. The orchestra, however, does not disclose the tunes' former existence to the organizing committee, pretending that they are "new" tunes. Actually, they are "new" for that particular town. In the words of a professional musician of the valley: "But, a strictly confidential thing I want to tell you as a musician. I go to very different towns. I once played in one place and we performed three huaynos [of tunantada]. And then I went to another town, but we took the same huaynos and we said they were "new," then, because the public do not know . . . Do you realize how clever a musician can be?"[23]

Most of the creative and social aspects of the orquestas típicas can only be understood within the context of their relationships with the asociaciones. Composition, rehearsals, and repertoire have to be determined in close coordination with a higher organization (the asociación). However, the musicians of the orchestra manipulate a series of "clever" strategies to maintain their own decisions, many times even breaking "traditional" rules, as in the fictional rendition of supposedly new tunes or on occasions when some musicians fail to show up for rehearsals in the vespers of a festival. In other instances, "tradition" is so strictly enforced that the musician complies passively with the requirements of the hiring committee. In any case, it is a joint venture in which the members of the orchestra, the festival, and the dance-drama reveal themselves as inseparable collaborators.

## "Authenticity" in Huaripampa

In spite of the fact that clarinets and saxophones have shared the same space in orquestas típicas for more than half a century, the function of both instruments within the ensemble still provokes controversy among ordinary people in the valley. This ongoing popular debate revolves mainly around how "authentic" the sound is when the orchestra performs with clarinets only and when it also includes saxophones. The elders who witnessed the arrival of the clarinets and who grew up listening, dancing, and enjoying their sound still consider this to be the "real," "authentic" sound of the orquesta típica. Subsequent generations, however, who throughout their lives observed and participated in festivals where the orquesta típica played with saxophones, would not settle for an ensemble with clarinets only. From the contentions of both generational groups emerged two cultural models for "authenticity" and "modernity," which ultimately transcend the limits and ranks of generational cohorts and transform into two different ideologies of "traditionality." A local folk researcher and collector from Huancayo, Luis Cárdenas, who favors innovations, says: "They tell us that we have to maintain our authentic music, but time cannot be stopped; I believe that you cannot. For instance, in the late 1940s saxophones were not used in Wanka music, everything was clarinets, harp, and violin, and now we listen to it, and it seems that it was not that beautiful after all."[24] He also expressed his opinion about those who are totally against "modernizing" Wanka music:

> In the era of Zenobio [Dagha, the 1940s], the musicians themselves said that he was spoiling Wanka music with the saxophone, that it was not our instrument. . . . Today Zenobio thinks the same about the electric organ, the drum set. But I say to him that it sounds anyway, they are not out of rhythm, they are even livelier, you can't stop time . . . If we had to always preserve the autochthonous we would still be playing the quena and the tinya.[25]

What are the aesthetic and cultural implications of such a debate? The example of Huaripampa, a town that, every year for the Fiesta of the Tunantada (Epiphany, January 6) allows only an orquesta típica with clarinets to play for the dance, is very suggestive. The Asociación de Bailantes de la Tunantada (Association of Dancers of the Tunantada), which is in charge of organizing the festival, closely regulates this convention. This association overtly forbids saxophones being used in the orchestra. Thus, the orchestra that customarily plays for the tunantada consists of a harp, two violins, and two clarinets. Among the stories told in the town about how strict they are in regard the safeguarding of Huaripampa traditions is one that recounts how one year an orchestra arrived in town with saxophone players in it. The association offered to pay the wages of the saxophonists only if they left the town and would not play in the festival. Another anecdote refers to the well-known regional violin performer Zenobio Dagha, who allegedly came to the festival one year but had to leave the town, hastily and angrily, unable to accept the severe musical surveillance of the association. Zenobio Dagha himself later told me: "They themselves do the music; they arrange it; they say this has to be like this. They are the composers; I do not know any musician who has gone there with his own composition, no. Huaripampa is a town that preserves its traditional music, and even its dance is also different."[26]

Residents and authorities of Huaripampa claim that the dance of the tunantada originated in that town, a fact that not only explains why the dance is considered more "authentic" there than everywhere else but also assigns a grave responsibility to the town in maintaining such a legacy. Residents also refer to Huaripampa as "the cradle of La Tunantada," following the convention of attributing titles to towns and even larger cities in Peru after their main contribution to the national or regional heritage.[27] Both town officials and citizens share a common pride and feel accountable for sustaining the "authenticity" of the dance. In Huaripampa, the municipality has appointed its cultural office to the task of supervising the "authenticity" of the dance in the district. This assignment falls alternatively on elder residents of the town who are recognized as either *grandes bailantes* (great dancers) or devoted guardians of old traditions. The fact that the musicians are hired from other towns also explains why these mechanisms of supervision are necessary to protect the "authenticity" of the music and of the instrumentation. If it were not for the local institutions, both official (like the municipality) and civic (like the association of dancers), the prospects for innovation, alteration, and change being introduced would be certainly higher.

How do Huaripampinos assess musical "authenticity"? One of the main requirements is the constitution of the orquesta típica characterized by the absence of saxophones. In fact, the orchestra is often defined more by what is absent than by what is actually displayed in it. Thus, the absence of saxophones becomes a distinguishable trait in defining this ensemble in the Mantaro Valley, rather than the high profile that clarinets seize in this version of the orchestra. The pervasiveness of the saxophones as main components of the orquestas típicas throughout the valley explains why resistance can be considered a more effective marker for "authenticity" in Huaripampa. The opposition to saxophones in the orchestra of the Tunantada has assumed almost legendary status among musicians and ordinary people of the region. What does the resistance to the saxophones stand for? Nostalgia in Huaripampa for *lo antiguo* (the antique) is frequently verbalized and praised, and clarinet playing seems to fit well into the period of time considered primordial for the history and the identity of contemporary Huaripampinos. No one in the town questions the primordial quality of this instrument, so it appears as an integral component of the orquesta típica. A related element in defining "authenticity" is the instrumental color of the clarinet, a soft and gentle timbre that is said to reflect the aesthetic taste of older Huaripampinos and, in general, a color that is highly praised among older residents of the valley as well.

The concept of lo antiguo is also applied to past traditions (those to which contemporary dancers are trying to remain loyal), to ancient knowledge (generally perpetuated in the minds of elder townsmen), and to former dancers (who are dead or retired).[28] In any case, remaining faithful to lo antiguo is the main requirement to preserve Huaripampino identity and a fundamental stamp for distinguishing the town's traditions from those of other neighboring districts. The residents of Huaripampa are adamant that the Tunantada is only preserved in its purest form in Huaripampa. As an elder Huaripampino asserted:

> The district of Yauyos is wrong when it says that it is the place where the tunantada is danced, when who dances the tunantada is Huaripampa, and not Jauja. What they dance is the chonguinada, and the dancers are mostly homosexuals, and that is not permitted in Huaripampa. Moreover, in Huaripampa everyone [who danced] was a man, even those who danced dressed as women.[29]

What are, therefore, the "modern" elements opposed to lo antiguo? Modernity in this sense, although not referred to as such by Huaripampinos, appears to be symbolized by, among many other signs, the saxophones. The rejection of the instrument is expressed, however, in terms of aesthetics, not in ideological terms. For Huaripampinos the saxophone is too loud and too strident. Its piercing sound (as it is played in the Mantaro Valley) contrasts with the delicate and pleasing sound of the clarinet. "Modernity" is also represented by innovations in the dance, such as the participation of transvestites (men dressed as women), and in the attire (discontinuous use of ojotas or traditional sandals, for example).[30] In general, Huaripampinos reject anything considered nonauthentic by the elders of the town and thus oppose all alteration to the dance and music as it was performed in the first three decades of the century. This period in time is considered primordial to Huaripampinos, and its music and dance are considered to be a classic matrix. Hence any subsequent modification is considered nonauthentic, thus "modern."

Huaripampinos, moreover, are fully aware that use of clarinets is a twentieth-century occurrence. In fact, they even refer to the probable date on which the clarinet was introduced in the Mantaro Valley and Huaripampa. They are also fully conscious that what they consider authentic is probably more an aspiration than a historical fact. In no other way can we interpret the following account of an elder Huaripampino about how "new" authentic music is composed:

The saxophone is not used in Huaripampa, because it is too blaring, and it is also out of tune. The tune [of the dance] in Huaripampa is very exclusive. Even Muquiyauyo copies a lot from the tune of Huaripampa. The *jaujinos* come here to observe our dance. . . . It is an authentic tune that they compose during the vespers, that every year they compose during the vespers, a new one, yes, but they do it with sentiment, with the sentiment of old *tunanteros*.[31]

Musical "authenticity," therefore, is achieved in Huaripampa not through the strict repetition of archaic melodies but through the transformed rendition of melodic styles considered classical, archetypal. Stylistic homogeneity is in this regard the main goal to be fulfilled by the musicians who every year assume the duty of composing "new" dance melodies that will sound "authentic" to the ears of Huaripampinos. Thus, the knowledge of the style becomes much more important than the simple memorization of familiar tunes. In Huaripampa this musical style is constructed around a narrative that emphasizes lo antiguo; therefore, its musical parameters are presumably less flexible than in other versions of the Tunantada in other districts or in other musical genres in which variation is as well a form of composition in the valley.

## Conclusions

Authenticity, therefore, is a notion related to the state of affairs in the early twentieth century, a time of crucial change in the Mantaro Valley, in which the nearby American-owned mining centers were consolidated. These constituted powerful poles of attraction for migration, and new economic and cultural relationships with the national market were established. The railroad to Huancayo, which was built to satisfy the needs of the mining economy, enhanced the existing links among the valley, the nation, and other regional economies.[32] Huancayo had always been an intermediary space between other regional economies, a rest area for merchants from the southern Andes. The growth of Huancayo to the detriment of Jauja was evident by the middle of the nineteenth century, but the arrival of the Central Railroad and the multiplying effect of mining ventures in the area magnified its development. It is not mere coincidence that this is the period in which the orquesta típica emerged, following the arrival of clarinets in the valley and their assimilation into the former conjunto. The distinctive sound of the clarinets captured the ear of the younger generations and fit smoothly with the harp and violin, instruments that had long enjoyed the favor of the valley's residents.

The beginning of the twentieth century was also a time in which mestizaje, understood here as a process by which Indian sectors forsook

An orquesta típica in performance in Zapallanga during the Festival of the Assumption. Note the use of the harp in upright position. Photo: Raúl R. Romero.

their isolated existence in closed communities to interact fully with the regional and national markets, was consolidated. While Indian sectors were widespread at the end of the nineteenth century, it took only one or two generations turn for the majority of the population in the valley to become mestizos. By the 1920s this process was already irreversible. The passage from Indian to mestizo was not an individual journey or the lonely and tortuous cultural pilgrimage taken by rural dwellers to urban existence like that experienced by urban migrants from the southern Andes. Rather, it was a mass transformation in which the end result was not a tormented and mistreated mestizo but rather a proud, sometimes even arrogant mestizo of the Mantaro Valley. *Authenticity* hence refers to a time at which everyday life in the valley was redefined in manifold ways. Thus, it is a time considered by many a formative age, the beginning of an era. As a violinist from Huaripampa told me referring to its music, the town still lives at the "dawn of time, in 1900" ("en los albores, 1900"). In this statement he was identifying the beginnings of the century as a primordial time in which a new order emerged, a time that is a key historical reference for many and the further temporal limit to which the collective memory of the valley is inclined to reach.

# 4

# CONQUERING
# NEW SPACES

## Authenticity Is Elsewhere

When the people of the Mantaro Valley established a "presence" in Lima the search for "cultural authenticity" confronted new challenges. In a first stage (1900–1950), the migrants from the Mantaro Valley, constrained in term of its meager demographics, joined forces with other Andean communities in Lima. In a second phase (1950–present), they rediscovered their regional sovereignty and adopted new vehicles for cultural reproduction, such as the modern media.[1] Still, their quest is mediated by forces that, however concealed in the valley itself, in the nation's capital assume relevance, such as state policies and an extended interregional market. Within the processes that I will describe in this chapter, two facts are of special relevance. The first one is that music arises as the primary weapon for cultural resistance, since no other Andean artistic expression had retained the ability to propose an alternative cultural sensibility to that of the elite of Lima's coastal population, among whom were and are the dominant, wealthier, and most powerful segments of the country (see chapter 5). Andean handicrafts made by Indian and mestizo artisans were "discovered" around the 1940s by urban art collectors and since then have been ubiquitous "ornamental" pieces, some of them highly expensive, in urban homes (Arguedas 1977:27). In this process, these objects lost their subversive attributes for Limeños, who considered them art objects, museum pieces with an aesthetic quality of their own, that is, unrelated to their creators. They were viewed as symbols of an "imagined" Andean culture, disconnected from their real ethnic agents, in a process aimed to "create the illusion of adequate representation of a world by first cutting objects out of specific contexts (whether cultural, historical, or intersubjective) and making them 'stand for' abstract wholes" (Clifford 1988:220). This "assimilation," however, never happened with Andean music, and its organic function within and affiliation with Andean regional groups have always been very tight and indivisible. Andean music is no longer perceived as "inferior" as it was twenty years ago, but it is certainly still considered exotic and generally unwelcomed by people of non-Andean origins.

The second relevant point of interest is that throughout these processes in Lima the orquesta típica became, in this new context, the embodiment of Wanka musical style. It never altered its region-specific configuration and performance style to adjust to the new theater-staged performance environment or to commercial recordings or to indulge the solo "star" singer it had to "accompany." Any singer who would like to perform in a "Wanka style" would need to do it with an orquesta típica. And its sound, style, and conveyed emotions became a symbol of Wanka sensibility and character.

## Rediscovering Locality

The presence of Andean traditional music in Lima is not a recent phenomenon but has been a reality since the beginning of the twentieth century.[2] Its presence has been indicative of the growing importance of Andean migrant groups in the nation's capital and of the practices they have employed in order to organize themselves around musical activities. The role of the musicians from the Mantaro Valley was, in this context, of crucial importance, especially since the 1940s, when the presence of the orquesta típica as the main vehicle for Wanka music became pervasive. The department of Junín was, after all, one of the three regions that contributed the most migrants to Lima by the 1940s (Long and Roberts 1984:5), and according to a survey made by the Casa de la Cultura in the early 1960s, most of the registered Andean performers in Lima, who totaled nearly 6,000, were from Junín, followed by the regions of Ancash and Ayacucho (Vivanco 1973:82).

Articles and general surveys of Andean music in Lima have been written by Arguedas (1976, 1977), Alejandro Vivanco (1973), Lucy Nuñez Rebaza and José A. Lloréns (1981), Lloréns (1983), and Thomas Turino (1988). The most important process to consider in the history of Andean music in Lima throughout the twentieth century is the transition through the representation of Andean music as "Incaic" until the early 1940s, followed by the more "authentic" performances of regional Andean musics from the

1940s onward.[3] Arguedas's reactions to these processes are indications of the important transition Andean music had undergone since the late 1930s. Until then Andean musicians in Lima used to perform dressed in the regional style of Cuzco, the former Inca capital, which was identified as "Inca" and thought to represent a pre-Hispanic past. Arguedas himself describes this prospectus well in an article from 1962:

> [About] 25 or 30 years ago so-called Indian music was regarded in Lima as something exotic, picturesque, and consequently strange. It was considered—and I am referring to the populace and among them the gentlemen from Lima themselves who were acquainted with Europe but ignored Peru—"primitive," "barbaric," as "insufferable monotony," and the dances examples of backward customs and equally "primitive," certainly "shameful" for Peru. Others, better acquainted with the country, thought exactly the contrary. They argued, under the influence of a delicate romantic view of Peru, that this was the only "pure Peruvian" music and dance, and they did not call it "Peruvian," as they do not do now either, but "Incaic." (see Arguedas 1976:210 and 1977:12)

The transition from this state of affairs to one in which Andean musicians, ceasing to represent their arts as "Incaic," performed according to their own local and regional traditions is generally attributed to the significant expansion of the Andean population in Lima (Nuñez and Lloréns 1981:56; Turino 1988:134). Marking this new era from the late 1930s and the beginning of the following decade, Lima witnessed the birth of popular coliseums (coliseos), which were attended by Andean migrants en masse primarily on Sundays and holidays; the appearance of radio programs that broadcast Andean music by the late 1940s; and the rise of commercial recordings of Andean music.

The coliseos became a collective space to which migrants from diverse regions and social backgrounds came on their days off to listen to their favorite artists. The coliseos were administered by private entrepreneurs and were mostly in rustic locales, sometimes covered with a circuslike tent, humble in spirit and decor, many including naive "Incaic" figures (see Arguedas 1976:244 and 1977:28). The core of the Andean artists who performed in these locales came from the companías folklóricas (folklore companies), which were constituted by numerous performers, sometimes more than 100, most of whom were aficionados (amateurs) visiting from Andean provinces or already residents of Lima. Most of their acts were regional dances, thus there were few soloists, and all of them were dependent on the general administration of the company. Very rapidly, however, solo singers gained popularity among the audiences and became equally important to the musical and dance conjuntos (ensembles) of the company.

But the advent of the coliseo did not come easily to the migrant in Lima. Before the 1940s, as Arguedas noted, there were no spaces for local and regional Andean musical manifestations, and the companías folklóricas had to perform in movie theaters around the city, many times sharing the bill with performers of other types of urban popular music, which were preferred by the average Limeño. It is pertinent to quote at length the emotional testimony of one popular Andean singer (later to become a celebrity in her own right) who in her younger years assisted at one of these performances at a *cine de barrio* (a second-rate movie theater):

In 1938 I was married and was expecting my first child. In the market of Lince there was a kid handing out leaflets, I took one and saw [the photo of] my uncle Julio C. Vivas with the subtitle "awarded artist by President Leguía in Lima again." I took the leaflet and went home so happy, so I could go early to the theater to see my uncle. He had his orchestra Orfeón Huancayo and he was an artist, the director, he was my uncle and I loved him because he was good, he gave me candy, so I was happy to see my uncle perform. I arrived early, at 2 P.M., I bought my ticket and took a front seat, it was the front *cazuela* [first tier], the *platea* [mezzanine] was behind me. It was like this in the cines de barrio. But they had also scheduled [Latin] mambos, those exotic dances, they were very popular at that time. They had scheduled folklore as an intermission but there were very few *serranos* [Andeans] in Lima. During the first part of the other music the *criollo* audience applauded, cheered, shouted, but when they announced the awarded artist, the winner of the Pampa de Amancaes, who was going to perform huaynos, they shouted, "Go away, *serrucho*, [4] we do not want you," . . . rotten tomatoes . . . , the set was a mess and my uncle was using his harp as a shield. Then I stood up and went to the stage, I embraced my uncle and cried with all my soul, my father had already died and I told my uncle, "I am going to tame this beast, Uncle, I am going to tame them, I am going to domesticate Limeños." That was the beginning of all my work. [5]

Her aspirations became a reality with the development and popularity of the coliseos which brought together an audience of predominantly Andean origins in downtown Lima and neighboring populous districts. No longer did the Andean artist have to confront hostile urban audiences constituted chiefly of Limeños, many of whom not only were unfamiliar with Andean music but also associated it with the traits of backwardness that were also attributed by many to Andean peoples. Arguedas has asserted that the golden age of the coliseos extended from 1946 to 1950 (1969:18); however,

I believe that he was referring mostly to the formative period of the coliseo, which was probably the period during which, in the absence of commercial records, it constituted the primary performance context for Andean music and the point of reunion in Lima of Andean migrants. The coliseos continued to exist, however, fulfilling an increasingly minor role in migrant lives, until the early 1970s, when alternative spaces like sport fields and stadiums were leased for musical presentations and regional associations began to organize by themselves their own cultural activities (see Doughty 1970:37 and Nuñez and Lloréns 1981:59–60).

The importance of radio broadcasts of programs of popular Andean music, which began in the 1950s, cannot be overlooked in their supporting role for the activities of migrants in Lima. The radio played a major role in establishing an efficient means of communication among migrants in Lima and with their respective towns of origin. In between music programming the shows broadcast personal messages, thus providing an alternative to the slow and unreliable postal service between Lima and distant Andean provinces. Through the radio all kinds of musical and social activities were communicated; the radio provided, as well, the best means of advertising the latest recordings on the market. Lloréns, who has followed this development closely, attests that radio stations sold air time to Andean disc jockeys instead of incorporating them into their usual programming. Around the beginning of the 1960s it became usual for the Andean musicians themselves to buy their own broadcast time, a practice that continues to be a trend today (see Lloréns 1991). The increasing popularity of Andean radio programs in Lima is further demonstrated in a survey made by the anthropologist Paul Doughty in 1981, when he counted ninety Andean music programs on Lima stations. In a subsequent survey in 1985, the number had increased to 157. Lloréns's 1987 survey showed that 204 *programas folklóricos* (folkloric programs) existed on Lima radio stations (cited in Lloréns 1991:184).

The presence and expansion of regional musical performance in Lima within the last fifty years indicates in the end a reaffirmation of local and regional identities, instead of the ethnic and cultural homogenization that some analysts suggested in view of the supposedly equal and shared spaces in which all migrant groups would congregate and, therefore, integrate into a single Andean identity. Clearly, such a possibility would have seemed reasonable only in the period in which there was a homogenous desire to be "Incaic," when all Andeans in Lima would dress and sing "stylized" and watered-down versions of their regional repertoire. In this sense, I disagree with the notion that Andean migrants dressed in performance as "Incas" and performed interregional musical styles, concealing their own regional ones, only because the dominant criollo culture imposed those guidelines upon them. This interpretation tends to represent the

Andean migrants as a passive, dominated group unable to react, resist, and imagine new alternatives.[6] Rather than using the dominant-dominated opposition in interpreting social and cultural inequalities, I prefer to compare the process by which Andeans represented themselves as "Incas" with the conscious attempts of regional intellectual elites to reach for a "national culture" based on Andean cultural values. This was similar to the movement of peasant guerrillas who fought, voluntarily, the war with Chile (1879–1884) in the Mantaro Valley with the aspiration of fulfilling a role on the national scene (see Mallon 1995 and Manrique 1981). It is my contention that similar desires played a role during the first half of the century and, rather than implying passive subordination, the "Incaic" paradigms expressed a calculated aspiration for national unity. This illusion was abandoned as soon as the imagined national identity failed and new alternatives appeared.

The coliseos, in turn, although allowing local and regional differences to emerge, suggested to some that the possibilities for "cultural homogenization" were again viable. This prospect was proposed as the genesis of a "new" Andean identity in Lima, since migrants from all villages and regions of the country attended and intermingled in the same venues. The notion of a "new" identity had been suggested frequently in the works of social scientists who analyzed the phenomena of migrations and the "Andeanization" or "ruralization" of Lima.[7] The homogenization of Andean identities in Lima, however, did not occur at this period, either. The longing for a "new" Andean urban identity was more indebted to the anxieties of elite intellectuals than to a project of the migrants themselves. The problem with the notion of a "new" identity is that it presumes that because a mass of migrants from different regions were jammed together in a single space where different musics and dances were performed, they grew accustomed to this cultural mosaic and generated a "new" identity. This assumption, again, presupposes the inability of the Andean migrant to experience, appreciate, and savor a multiplicity of artistic and aesthetic manifestations without having to undergo a cultural metamorphosis and abandon his own identity.[8] When migration began to increase from the 1950s onward the regional memories started to reappear and the homogenizing trends were soon forgotten. As a consequence of sheer demographics a migrant internal cultural market began to surface, radio programs appeared, records were produced, live events centered around musical performance proliferated, and the mass media in general opened channels to migrant music. As a result music began to take over as the most powerful cultural drive, over the public festival, the private ritual, and regional dance-dramas, which in adapting to restrained spaces and crowded urban streets found themselves playing a less crucial role than they did in the valley.

## Arguedas, the State, and the
## Quest for "Authenticity"

The unifying factor between the search for local authenticity and the state from the late 1940 to the late 1960s was one individual, José María Arguedas (1911–1969), the renowned writer, anthropologist, and folklorist. Arguedas became the mentor, promoter, and spiritual guide of many of the Andean artists who were the protagonists of the golden age of commercial recordings of their music (1950–1980). He was a highly respected novelist and ethnologist, graduate of and professor at San Marcos University, the most prestigious institution at that time in the nation. His knowledge of Andean culture was profound and the result of not fieldwork but, rather, a vital experience since childhood, as he was raised among Indians and mestizos in Andean Ayacucho. Arguedas avoided any regional-specific specialization within Peru and preferred to show an equal aesthetic interest in all the regions of the Peruvian Andes. However, he did have a special intellectual concern for the Mantaro Valley, considering it the model for a balanced encounter between Western and Andean traditions and the most successful case of preserving a regional identity in modern Peru (see Arguedas 1957b and Flores Galindo 1992:20–21).

In his position as head of the Folklore and Popular Arts Section at the Ministry of Education since the mid-1940s and later as the director of Casa de la Cultura (the state cultural agency), Arguedas was an influential factor in the development of Andean folklore performances in Lima.[9] A widely respected and prestigious intellectual, he frequently visited the popular theaters and coliseos, expressing his views to the performers themselves. The authority that Arguedas embodied was impressive, and musicians and singers soon became followers of his views concerning musical and performance contexts and styles (dress and customs, for instance). In a time in which most of Lima was hostile to the presence of Andean peoples, the role of Arguedas became crucial. Andean artists looked and found in Arguedas their spiritual guide and a source for validation of their regional sensibilities.

The quest for "authenticity" was for Arguedas a prime objective, and he struggled most of his life against the "stylizations" and "deformations" of folklore made by some Andean artists in their quest to gain more commercial acceptance from the general public. Arguedas attempted to reinvigorate, from his position as intellectual and public servant, local and regional traditions that encouraged Andean artists to wear their "authentic" dress, and sing the songs of their own localities. In a short time, Arguedas became a father figure, their ally and mentor, while at the same time maintaining his position as an intellectual and a member of the Peruvian intelligentsia.

Arguedas was a very active writer, contributing frequently to newspapers as well as authoring his own novels and short stories. His Andean experience, as he had been born and raised in the rural Andes but educated in the city of Lima, was unique among anthropologists and literary writers at that time in Peru. This unique position gave him a degree of authority unsurpassed by other writers and scholars of his generation. His knowledge of Peruvian folklore was also impressive, since he was thoroughly familiar with the different cultural expressions of Peruvian Andean regional cultures.

It is not an easy task to conclude that Arguedas was a "purist" or that he was against change because of his quest for "authenticity." In fact, he was anything but a cultural conservative. He was indeed against extreme innovations in the performance of folklore that appeared to be the result of the pressures of the urban market, such as the operatic singing style of Ima Sumac or the Incaic stylizations that many folklore companies undertook in the early 1940s. As early as 1944, Arguedas wrote an article, "In Defense of Andean Musical Folklore," that criticized Ima Sumac, who would later achieve international prominence as a recording artist of "Inca" music. Ima Sumac became very popular in Peru singing Andean songs dressed in "Inca" attire and in an operatic style that stressed very high vocal ranges. Arguedas blamed the singer for not only "stylizing" but also "deforming" Indian music, noting that she was from Lima and had no Indian origins or knowledge of Quechua language (see reprints in Arguedas 1976:233–234 and 1977:19–20). But Arguedas was a strong supporter of the participation of Andean performers in commercial recording and the use of modern media to disseminate Andean folklore. Such was the case that he became, as explained earlier, the main promoter of the first commercial recordings of Andean music in the late 1940s.

The role of Arguedas seems more significant than ever in the passage of folklore performances as exotic representations of an Inca past to local folklore understood as simply the expression of regional cultures, each with their own traits and styles. Before Arguedas, Andean artists and folklore companies in Lima could only validate themselves through an identification with an Inca past, looking desperately into history books for sketches from which to design their costumes. Arguedas successfully attempted to give them a new sense of pride in their own local traditions, through the validation that he, as an "official" intellectual and government bureaucrat, could provide. His role as father figure was not affected by the fact that, in reality, he was not a representative of the state's cultural policies but instead as a solitary champion of folklore he happened to exploit a few breaks in the system, envisioning the possibility of the nation understood as the sum of diverse but compatible local and regional identities.[10] The nation that Arguedas imagined was one in which Andean regional identities would play a major constitutive role. In a newspaper article in 1968 he stated:

> In the same way as the *retablos* [portable altars] from Ayacucho and the *iglesias* [portable churches] from Quinua . . . are now ornamental figures of universal use and representative symbols of Peruvian culture, the huaylas and the huayno, more than those ornamental objects, are on their way of transforming themselves into cultural patrimony, in a nationalizing bond for Peruvians. (See Arguedas 1976: 243 and 1977:27)

Arguedas did not formally structure his views on the matter until 1964, when as head of the Casa de la Cultura (later the National Institute of Culture) he elaborated a set of rules and regulations for the folklore artist in Lima.[11] The document contained thirty provisions that regulated the registration of all folklore performers in Lima, the operations of the *agrupaciones folklóricas* (folklore companies), and the functions of the company directors, local musical performers in Lima, musical performers in transit (visiting from their regions of origin), and even the radio broadcasters of folklore.[12] This set of regulations was obeyed by the artists themselves, coliseos and radio stations, television stations, theaters, and recording companies to whom this legal decree was sent.

Most of the stipulations mentioned the concept of national folklore, which was a natural inclusion because this was an official document and because Arguedas believed in nation building through the unconstrained development of regional cultures. There was, therefore, no contradiction between the concept of nationality and the simultaneous concern for authenticity of local cultures and the reaffirmation of their multiple identities. The national for Arguedas is to be understood as a project, a utopian construction that did not necessarily correspond to the current state of affairs in Peru. Authenticity, a concept introduced early in Arguedas's provision number three, was to be evaluated by a regulatory commission in terms of performance, repertoire, and costumes. The director of each group had to be native to the geographical area from which the music and dance derived unless he could prove his expertise in that repertoire. To further assure compliance with this requirement the regulatory commission could ask for the personal credentials of every member of the company or group.

The director, in turn, was to be responsible for guarding that no "alterations" were made to "dances, songs, music and customs." He had also made available, at all performances, notes that described and indicated the significance of the folkloric piece to be performed. Special emphasis was placed on the dress and customs of the performers, which were to be indigenous to the geographical area of the music or dance.

The strict enforcement of these regulations and the seriousness of their aims were reflected in provisions that mandated that "artists in transit" bring with them certificates issued by their respective local municipalities or by the indigenous communities to which they belonged. These regulations were also distributed to municipalities and to all the organizations that employed folklore artists.

In spite of the "official" and bureaucratic character of this document and the apparent rigidity of its language, to this day folklore artists in Lima manifest their nostalgia for this time. Almost every performer alive today mentions Arguedas as a mentor and uses him as a reference for their accomplishments. Having met or known Arguedas is a crucial milestone in their careers, and their stories are always related to the friendly, almost patriarchal, evaluations that Arguedas provided on their performances, which were interpreted as guidance, either spiritual or aesthetic, by the performers. The testimony of the Wanka folklorist Agripina Castro de Aguilar summarize very well these feelings and is representative of how the majority of folklorists remember Arguedas:

> He used to gather us in Alfonso Ugarte School; every Sunday he used to gather us folklorists and talked to us about how positive it was to spread our culture, that folklore had to keep its roots, that we shouldn't stylize it because it was our culture. He would cheer us up; to me he was the father of folklore. I am nobody, I am not a doctor like Dr. Arguedas, but when I see the new folklorists I feel sad and nobody says anything [about it]. He used to come to our rehearsals to see if we were doing right or wrong. "I don't think this is right," he said. "This should be this way." And every Sunday he went to the coliseo to see the shows to check us out. Today there is nobody that can say anything; if Dr. Arguedas were alive this would not be happening.[13]

For the artists, the issuance of these directives meant an interest of the state, of "official" Peru, in folklore and in the authenticity of their traditions. Arguedas, whom everyone recognized as the progenitor of this edict, represented a father figure who could protect their traditions. After decades of being considered inferior, "primitive," and "barbaric," the folk artists finally saw their art officially validated and deemed worthy of being integrated into the legal system of the nation. None of the performers whom I have met and interviewed have expressed a feeling of "intrusion" or imposition in regard to these provisions, and this period has been preserved in memory as one in which the state really cared about folklore, regional identities, and the need to preserve "authenticity." In 1969 the Casa de la Cultura, the entity in charge of supervising this decree, was reorganized by the revolutionary government of Velasco Alvarado (1969–

1980) and transformed into the National Institute of Culture, also dependent on the Ministry of Education. But Arguedas, in an unrelated tragic event, had committed suicide in that same year, and everybody forgot about the safeguarding of "authenticity," except of course, the folklore performers themselves, who, once again, went on to continue performing without any interference of the state.

Did Arguedas overstate the value of "authenticity" over the dynamics of change in folklore? An evaluation of his achievements and writings proves that was certainly not the case. As we have seen, Arguedas promoted the first commercial recordings of Andean music, was a frequent patron of coliseos, and in his anthropological writings stressed the relevance of mestizo culture as an example of how Indianness could achieve success and survival in contemporary Peru by controlling and appropriating the tools of modernity and harmonizing both legacies into a coherent culture, still Indian, though "modern" (see Arguedas 1957b). "Authenticity" was for Arguedas, therefore, and in the context of his tenure as a state official, equivalent to the right of self-determination, that is, to express local cultures as they developed in time within their own contexts. "Authenticity" was not a claim of the past for Arguedas, like in Huaripampa in the Mantaro Valley, for example, but instead a quest for the present, as counterculture and resistance—processes that this time, for a change, were dramatized in a foreign, not at all neutral, sometimes even hostile territory for Andean peoples.

I disagree, therefore, with the viewpoints that impute to Arguedas the stigma of "romanticism" and even portrait him as an agent of "Westernization."[14] Arguedas' position toward folklore was not "romantic" at all, since he never attempted to "invent" or "idealize" new folkloric forms but merely followed popular processes already in progress. Moreover, as we have shown, he was one of the foremost opponents to the "romantic," Inca-style representations of Andean folklore. I must also reiterate that Arguedas was, and many other Peruvianist intellectuals still are, involved in a long-range nation-building project that involves the development of mestizo regional cultures as key segments of a democratic and multicultural nation (see Flores Galindo 1986; Burga 1988; and de la Cadena 1990). This project presupposes the role of the intellectual as political as well but mostly, and justly, the appropriation of "urban-Western values" and even new technologies by mestizo local and regional communities, following the notion that "resistance" is not merely passive but active. In this regard I agree with William Rowe, who states:

> Arguedas imagines the future on the basis of a process of modernization. The issue is not to preserve the voice of subaltern groups for the use of other social groups, but to join a modernization process within which Andean music creates a privileged channel that tra-

verses rigid stratifications. It is not, definitely, an indigenista stance. Arguedas takes side with an emergent mestizo culture: the cultural practice that conveys it and the resultant emblematic material are Andean. (1996:38)

This is, in effect, the process that is developing now in Peru, however not consistent in its popular base or fully appreciated by hegemonic groups but certainly one that Arguedas would have wanted to witness.

## Musical De-territorialization: Coming to, and from, Lima

Andean migrants who came to Lima from distant Indian villages and hamlets lacked the advantages of the peasants from the Mantaro Valley, who had long enjoyed the benefits of the flow of communications between their hometowns and the nation's capital. The Central Railroad, since the dawn of the century, and the Central Highway, since the mid-1930s, had provided rapid transportation to and from Lima, a journey that can be completed in eight hours by bus or *colectivo* (a motor vehicle that carries many passengers) and in twelve hours by train. Notable, too, was the frequency of this service: numerous colectivos commuted back and forth along the Central Highway, standing in line for most of the day waiting for passengers to arrive in order to depart. Similarly, the train provided a round-trip daily service to and from Huancayo from the Desamparados (the Helpless) station in downtown Lima. The conditions were ideal for constant communication between the valley and Lima. The cases of more distant regions were substantially different. The migrants from the southern areas of Ayacucho, Cuzco, and Puno could not afford daily travel or exchange with their towns of origin, which required air travel or a journey of several days in an overcrowded bus. The consequences of this geographically determined constraint on the cultural development of migrant life in Lima were significant. Given rare opportunities to return home, possibly only once a year, migrants forfeited considerable material connections with their original communities. In the remote southern town of Conima, for instance, the situation became more marked. This led to a tendency to idealize the original community (Turino 1993:169).

The migrants from the Mantaro Valley, on the contrary, maintain a close dialogue with their primary cultural space, not "idealized" but firmly based in concrete and practical exchanges. Jurgen Golte and Norma Adams (1987:94) and Teófilo Altamirano (1984b:59) have also observed the same process in the two different communities they have studied, in which migrants do not break their ties with the home community, maintaining ownership of their land while they are away and returning frequently to attend personal and family affairs. This type of interaction has enabled migrant individuals and regional associations to hire orquesta típicas from the valley for the festivals that are performed in Lima and has also permitted musicians who play in orquesta típicas formed in Lima to travel to the valley to perform during the festival seasons, when there is a high demand for additional musicians. It is in this sense that the fundamental role of migrants in the festivals of the Mantaro Valley should be understood as well. Going back every year to the village or capital district for the patronal festival not only is facilitated by the geographical distance but also implies a greater role of the migrant in the festival system. The participation of return migrants in town festivals is not viewed as a sign for potential conflict, as it is in other Andean regions, since there are no striking class or ethnic differences that mark the experiences of the valley resident and the migrant. In many towns, migrants' participation is eagerly anticipated, since many form their own dance groups and are active members of the asociaciones that sponsor the dances. As noted earlier, migrant participation is already a familiar phenomenon in the festival system of the valley, since it has been occurring since the beginning of the century, when thousands of peasants began to migrate to the nearby mining centers but always came back for the patronal festivals of their towns not only to observe but also to contribute economically in significant ways (see Hutchinson 1973:49–50; and Mendoza-Walker 1989).

As a result of such constant dynamic exchange and communication, no drastic stylistic differences exist between the orquesta típicas of the valley and those that reside in Lima. The description provided by a singer who resided in Lima and had to rehearse on the weekend with an orquesta típica from Huancayo presents a vivid image of this dynamic around the late 1940s:

> All Saturdays the orchestra Juventud Huancaína of Huancayo traveled to Lima by train, they lost all Saturday because they took the train at 7 in the morning and they would arrive downtown [Lima] at 6 in the afternoon. Then they would come to my home, where I would cook for the 10 or 12 musicians, dinner on Saturday, breakfast, lunch and dinner on Sunday. They would leave on Monday after breakfast back to Huancayo.[15]

This continuity did not prevent migrants from the Mantaro Valley from sharing the wider venues that Andean migrants held in Lima (popular theaters, media channels, commercial recordings) or following similar social processes. I do want to stress, however, the substantial differences among cultural practices of migrant groups in Lima and among the types of relationships that each of them establish with their towns of origin.[16] Altamirano, in comparing the migrant experiences of residents from Matahuasi (a district of the Mantaro Valley) with those of the district of Onqoy (in the southern department of Apurímac), has observed substantial differences between the two. While migrants from Matahuasi settled in middle-class neighborhoods in Lima, displayed a regional identity, and expressed their differences more in terms of economic than ethnic differentiation, those from Onqoy lived in squatter settlements, were more involved in the local affairs of their original Andean locality, and engaged in interethnic quarrels (Indian versus mestizo) at some of their meetings (see Altamirano 1984a and 1984b). Golte and Adams, who have documented specific cases of migration, also note that while the ethnic conflict is absent from the districts of the Mantaro Valley they studied (Sacsa and Mantaro), it is a major issue in migrant voluntary associations from southern Andean regions, like Sanka, Apurímac, Asillo, and Puno (1987). The distinctive traits of the Mantaro Valley migrant will help to illuminate, I hope, the vast current acceptance of the orquesta típica as the main representative of the Wanka musical style among migrants from diverse Andean regions.

Following this line of thought, generalizations on the migrant's traumatic experiences in adapting to city life must be carefully examined.[17] This was not necessarily the case for the migrants of the Mantaro Valley, for whom Lima was a less "strange" environment than for others and certainly far more accessible; thus, while it is always difficult for anyone to move away from home, people from the valley did not experience a cultural shock in adjusting to Lima. Altamirano has also observed this process in the specific case of Matahuasinos, saying that "they represent a relatively prosperous, well-established urban population that has experienced little difficulty in coping with life in the metropolis" (1984b:211). I do not intend to "idealize" the migrant experience of the Mantaro Valley's people as exempt from significant difficulties, but I do endorse progressive outlooks on migration such as those of José Matos Mar (1984) and Altamirano (1984b, 1988), which rather than accentuating the miseries of "assimilating" into the new urban context highlight migrant contributions to city life. Paul L. Doughty has argued that migrants establish regional associations to maintain their "key social institutions and relationships" and to "slow down the stressful pace of social and cultural changes" that affect the migrant in cities. As a result, regional associations contribute significantly to "the social and political integration" of the nation at large (1970: 30).[18] Thus, voluntary associations, for Doughty, arise to ease the pains of adjusting to the cities and to permit the migrants to "retain their integrative structures or to reorganize their lives in meaningful ways" (1970:32). The importance of these associations was corroborated by the sheer number of them that existed in Lima. By the time Doughty wrote this article, a total of 1,050 regional associations existed in Lima (1970:33). William Mangin, in affirming that "one of the most important aspects of the clubs is the role they play in acculturating the serrano to life in Lima," agrees with Doughty's overall outlook on the crucial role of voluntary association for the Andean migrant (Mangin 1959:28). But Mangin has also focused on the *barriadas* (shantytowns) as another site for migrant experience (1959, 1970, 1973). Speaking about the squatter settlements around large cities, Mangin says:

> The residents are mainly migrants from rural areas who have lived for several years in the city and who organized together to invade land, usually public, and usually against the armed opposition of the police. They have constructed their own houses and developed their own social organizations. These settlements constitute a remarkable example of popular initiative and creativity, as well as courage and involvement. (1970:55)

These approaches oppose those that portray the lives of migrants as frustrated attempts to adapt to the new urban environment, ending necessarily in poverty, depersonalization, and the lack of adaptability to consolidate themselves in organized groups. This negative view of migrants in cities has been frequent in the studies that focus on the "culture of poverty" (Doughty 1970:31).

The vital distinction between the character of the mestizos from the Mantaro Valley and those of other regions needs to be raised once again within a new space of cultural confrontation. I stated earlier that the widely popular definition of the mestizos as abused outcasts, equally repudiated by Indians on the one hand and the "whites" on the other, did not correspond with the position of the mestizos of the Mantaro Valley. Instead, they exhibited a great pride and assurance in their own regional culture and identity, identifying themselves as a social group rather than as "culturally expatriated" individuals.[19] Wanka sensibilities are, therefore, constituted by solid feelings of pride, self-respect, and dignity toward their cultural heritage.[20] When these passions are displayed in characteristic expressive and outspoken fashions, these mestizos are frequently perceived as "arrogant" by migrants from other region, and I myself, from a Limeño perspective, have had that impression many times. There are other migrant communities that may have these affirmative attributes as well, but the Wanka migrant is the one who is often referred as "arrogant" and recognized as the one with the highest degree of self-esteem. In fact, this trait is usually compared to the supposedly "ostentatious" quality of their regional music. As one recording artist from the neighboring region of Ayacucho told me, "The inhabitant of the Mantaro Valley is a very flashy person. They like to express themselves through strident sounds, so these instruments [saxophones and clarinets] were perfect for them. For the Ayacuchano [native of Ayacucho], for example, these instruments did not go along with their 'style.' "[21]

The wide dissemination of Wanka regional music in Lima has further bolstered this popular impression. Many migrants feel that the presence (in terms of live performances, broadcasting hours, and records) of Wanka music in Lima is excessive, even detrimental to other regional musics. The building of regional stereotypes is not limited to the figure of the brave and arrogant Wanka. A similar process has been observed by Deborah A. Poole in regard to the Qorilazos in the department of Cuzco, who are considered "indomitable, vaguely criminal people who nevertheless have an altogether admirable penchant for fine horses, romance, and the sad, nostalgic poetry of traditional Andean huayno music" (1994:97–100). Poole observes, however, that this perception is grounded in true historical facts such as geographical isolation, banditry, and rebellion and, furthermore, that this perception has been reaffirmed by the widely popular folkloric traditions that depict the figure of the now mythical Qorilazo. It is important to clarify that in suggesting specific psychological and behavioral attributes of the Wanka as a means for understanding identity and resistance, I am not referring to the "stereotyping" of cultural types that appear as a result of "essentializing" ethnicities but, rather, to the dominant ideological traits that the group members themselves identify with and which they many times use to define their own cultural presence, thus being perceived by other groups in those terms. In this line of analysis, in addition to Poole's article on the "indomitable" nature of the Qorilazo in Andean Peru, are Abu-Lughod's inquiry into the "moral excellence" of a Bedouin tribe, which defines itself according to the values of honor, sincerity, honesty, and generosity (1986), and Michael Herzfeld's exploration into the "fearsome mountain people" of a hamlet in Greece, for whom the "celebration of the self" and "manliness" become primary properties of the group's social ideology or identity (1985).

In similar ways, the rough image of the Wanka in Lima is further reinforced by their generally solid economic background, their proven abilities as entrepreneurs, and the confidence and self-esteem they brought from their hometowns, which they certainly do not lose in the nation's capital. Rather than reflecting the submissive quality that is often attributed to migrants of other regions, these attributes indicate the extent of the Wanka self-confidence.

The migrants of the valley gather around departmental, provincial, and district associations or clubs but also around private and familiar events such as weddings and the cortamonte (a widely popular carnival-related ritual that involves the cutting of a tree).[22] The access to these activities, or fiestas, is open, and even the Club Huancayo, considered the most selective of the associations of the valley, provides ticketed admission to its festive meetings. Migrants from the valley also gather at events in locales of public access along the Central Highway, which anyone may attend as long as a ticket is purchased.[23] The portion of the Central Highway closest to the city of Lima is the principal area where these public places are located. Most of these venues are soccer fields specially reserved for these occasions during the weekends and also restaurant-*peñas*, eateries where staged musical performances are presented (the term *peña* alludes to the performance aspect of the venue).

The Central Highway is the most convenient location for these gatherings because it is the main route through which the Mantaro Valley communicates with Lima and around which most of the migrants from the valley have settled. It is, however, only throughout the initial strip of eight miles of the highway (closer to Lima), in the populous and industrial Vitarte District, that the numerous sport fields, transformed into musical arenas, are evenly dispersed. Each of them presents a different program of Wanka artists on weekends, primarily on Sundays and holidays. Each program can involve more than ten soloists or musical groups per day, even more on special occasions. The music begins in the afternoon and proceeds into the night. The entire area is heavily populated, not only because Vitarte is one of the fastest-growing and more commercial districts in greater Lima but also because there is a Sunday market in the area that attracts thousands of customers and other visitors.

The most popular of these venues is the Hatunhuasi, located just at the border of the Central Highway. It is a soccer field with a large elevated stage on one side. Along the sides of the stage are drawings that depict a variety of Andean dances (the *diablada* from Puno, the huaylas from Huancayo) mixed with "Incaic" motifs, in this case the "Inca" himself and stone walls that imitate Inca fortresses in Cusco. The back wall of the stage is full of "Incaic" motifs in a naive style (just as Arguedas described for the coliseo). The image of the Macchu Picchu ruins is at the center of the wall; on its left side appear the mythical figures of Manco Capac and Mama Ocllo emerging from Lake Titicaca (to found the Inca empire, as the legend claims) and on its right side a "typical" Andean village by a river with high mountains on the horizon. The Hatunhuasi is surrounded by residential houses, and the Sunday market is located right in front of it. In front of the soccer field, which is closed off by a cement wall, there are street vendors; the whole area is very crowded during market days. Loudspeakers located at the main entrance of the soccer field, which are strictly guarded by private security, let everyone outside hear the music from inside.

The program consists mainly of the presentation of soloists with the accompaniment of orquesta típicas. Most of the time the orchestras are from Lima, and only on special occasions do orchestras from the Mantaro Valley come to perform. In the latter circumstance, they are announced as special guests and receive greater publicity than usual. The orchestras present a configuration that follows the current trend (1996), featuring an impressive number of saxophones, to the detriment of clarinets and violins. The big-

gest orchestra I have seen in the Hatunhuasi performed with nine saxophones (five altos and four tenors) and only one clarinet, one violin, and
a harp. There are, however, orchestras with up to twelve saxophones, like
the best-selling orchestra Los Super Mañaneros de Huancayo (the Super
"Daylight Risers" of Huancayo). The repertoire of the singers consists of
huaynos, huaylas, and mulizas, which have been the dominant forms of
the Wanka repertoire in Lima for decades. As in the times of the coliseos,
the women singers dress in their local festive costumes, of which there are
a wide variety in the valley. The men tend to dress in a more homogeneous
fashion, following the "typical" attire of the Mantaro Valley peasant, which
was further popularized by the legendary singer the Picaflor de los Andes
in the 1960s. This attire is used in the huaylas, which depicts peasants
working in the fields; it is not a working outfit, however, but rather a
colorful festive costume that consists of black trousers, a white shirt, a
bright and fully ornamented vest, a light scarf, and a hat.

These venues on the Central Highway are attended by a working-class
audience. Anyone who can purchase a ticket gets in, and many buy tickets
at the market outside.[24] Most of the people are from the Mantaro Valley,
first- or second-generation migrants, and visitors from the valley, but there
also are spouses born in other regions who accompany their entire family,
and visitors from other regions of the country who just enjoy Wanka
music. These spaces, however similar to the coliseos in terms of programming (a large list of performers) and visual aspects ("Incaic" figures, rustic
facilities, open or closed venues), play a different role. The sport fields are
only one of several alternatives where the migrants can gather and listen
to their musics today. Besides the public events, private events are pervasive around the capital and are preferred by the migrants. A friend from
the Mantaro Valley once said to me, "Why should I go to the Hatunhuasi
[with you]? Anyone can go there. I have been invited to a family reunion
. . . [a wedding]."[25] The sport field, in fact, is a place for the working-class
migrants of the valley, people of lesser economic resources than the migrants from the clubs at the department or provincial level. The Club
Huancayo, for example, is attended by the more affluent high-level professionals. In spite of the fact that the events organized by the Club Huancayo are also open to the public, class barriers remain dominant in determining the constituency of both organizations and venues. Wanka music,
therefore, reflects the same trends present among other Andean communities in Lima: the diversification of musical contexts. Today there are
many choices to be made: several settings, many neighborhoods, hundreds
of radio programs, a catalog of thousands of cassettes to select from. Each
migrant community follows its own musical groups and attends its own
venues. The same phenomenon found on the Central Highway occurs in
the northern sectors of the Panamerican Highway, where migrants from
the northern department of Ancash have settled and established markets

and "folklore" venues. Rather than promulgating the blending and homogenizing of identities that the coliseo culture suggested, today each community has taken over new spaces for the reaffirmation of its own local and regional differences.

## Andean "Folklore" and the Recording Industry

Since the beginning of the twentieth century, records in the 78 RPM formats have became familiar in Lima, concurrently with other "modern" inventions that were to become indispensable tools in everyday life for the rest of the century: automobiles, typewriters, movie, and the radio. Photography and the railroad had, as we have seen, been introduced at the end of the previous century. Lima, as well as other major coastal cities with important seaports, was always the first point of entrance for these "devices," and from there they were distributed to the rest of the nation, to the departmental, provincial, and district capitals, in that order. But these gadgets of "modernity" were of uncertain utility and sometimes irrelevant in many outlying places, especially where there was no electricity. In remote, smaller peasant hamlets there was no cash to buy items (a typewriter, for example) that otherwise could have been highly valuable for local dealings with the central provincial administration.

Peruvian elites, however, had the means to acquire those expensive imports and enjoy their advantages. Upper classes and the incipient middle class danced the tango, the Mexican ranchera, and popular rhythmic North American dances such as the Charleston and the fox-trot. The main vehicle for the popularity of these genres was the 78 RPM record, which until the late 1940s popularized foreign musics almost exclusively. There were, however, rare exceptions. In 1911 a duo that performed *música criolla* (creole music) from the coast traveled to New York City to make for the Columbia Phonograph Company a series of records to be forwarded to Peru later (Basadre 1968). It has also been reported that RCA Victor sent recording teams to Peru to record traditional ensembles (see Vivanco 1973:127). One of these recordings seems to be from the well-known Andean harpist from Ayacucho, Tani Medina (cited in Arguedas 1969:18).

It was only around midcentury that Andean music began to be intensively recorded and disseminated commercially.[26] Around that time, the RCA Victor and Odeon record companies had opened local offices in Lima, mainly to supervise the distribution and commercialization of their records in Peru. There are two versions, which actually complement each other, of the circumstances that surrounded the launching of the first commercial records of Andean music in the late 1940s. One version has been provided by José María Arguedas, the well-known anthropologist, author, and vigorous supporter of Andean folklore in Lima, who stated that when he was head of the Folklore and Popular Arts Section of the Ministry of Education he was able to obtain funds for purchasing a "Pesto" disc-recording machine. George Kubler, an American art historian from Yale University who was at that time a visiting professor at San Marcos University, donated 100 twelve-inch acetate discs to the Folklore and Popular Arts Section to be used for recording purposes. With those resources Arguedas realized the first recordings of Andean music, which were then given to the branch of Odeon Records in Lima, at the time operated jointly with the Philco Corporation under the management of Carlos Vich (Arguedas 1969:18, 1953: 124).

The second version was given by one of the performers who participated in those recordings: Agripina Castro de Aguilar, a singer from the Mantaro Valley. Quoting at length her passionate account of how she insisted that Mr. Vich record Andean music seems relevant here:

> He must have been Limeño because he was horrible to me. I couldn't restrain my tears because he rejected me so many times, he said the huayno is *huesería* [a nonselling item].
>
> After a month I would return to his office.
>
> "You again?"
> "Yes, I want you to reconsider, it is an orchestra with harps, violins, clarinets . . . a well-formed orchestra."
> "But, señora, it is huayno!"
> "Yes, huayno, muliza, we are going to record huaynos and mulizas!"
> "Of course, but that is serrano [Andean] and that does not sell, don't come back, please."
>
> After one, two months I would return again.
>
> "You again?"
> "Yes, it is because the orchestra is a good one. Why don't you go to the coliseo on Sunday to see them? I invite you, here are the tickets."
>
> He never went. After a while I came back.
>
> "Please, señora! I have told you that we are not going to record huaynos, they don't sell! Who is going to buy them? Go away and don't come back!"
>
> And he slammed the door . . .
>
> I then cried as I never cried before, because there have been so many times [he rejected me]. I was walking by the Jirón de la Unión crying, I cried and cried, and cried, why does he treat me this way? He doesn't know this music. I walked to Puno Street and said to

myself, "I am going to see Dr. Arguedas to tell him that this man almost hit me." When the doctor saw me:

"What happened señora? [after the story is told:] I am not going to allow him to treat you like that, a woman like you . . ."

He stood up and we went together to Mr. Vich's office. We arrived; he announced himself with his business card; Mr. Vich opened the door and invited him to go in, first the lady.

"You know who this lady is? She is a lady that Sunday after Sunday sparks the coliseos, she brings an orchestra from Huancayo with her own money for an audience that follows her Sunday after Sunday. I sit in first row, and everyone cheers. You don't know what she wants to do, to record a Wanka record—it has never been recorded; it's the first time. How is it possible that you treated her so badly? She is crying because she has never been abused in that way. You will do me a favor, you are going to produce the first Wanka record. I need it for the Ministry of Education."[27]

The recordings were made by Arguedas on the recording machine acquired by the Ministry of Education and the masters supplied to Odeon Records for their manufacture at the regional branches in Santiago de Chile or Buenos Aires. Afterward, the records were sent back to Peru for their distribution. Arguedas sent several recordings to Odeon, however, not just the recordings that Agripina Castro de Aguilar wanted to release. For the first set of recordings to be submitted to Odeon, Arguedas selected music from different regions of the Andes, four selections from Cuzco, sung by Julia Peralta, four from Ancash, played by the renowned regional composer Jacinto Palacios, and four from the Mantaro Valley by the renowned regional composer Tiburcio Mallaupoma and his orquesta típica, the Lira Jaujina. Arguedas somehow convinced Odeon executives to release all of these recordings.[28]

The commercial success of these recordings was overwhelming, and from then on records of Andean music became a major source of income for the record companies. For the musicians, however, releasing records was more a matter of prestige than of income, which they continued to earn primarily from their live performances. The market for Andean records was comprised primarily of Andean migrants, who purchased recorded music from their own regions of origin. Since there was considerable regional diversity and presence in Lima, many professional performers still encountered harsh financial requirements when attempting to release commercial recordings. A frequent strategy of the record companies was to demand a down payment as a form of a deposit in case the records did not sell. The down payment was returned only if a certain amount of units were sold. Despite these obstacles, commercial recordings of Andean music became frequent and abundant.

The largest record companies were founded in Lima during the 1950s and 1960s. Odeon Records merged with the national company IEMPSA (an acronym for the Spanish translation of Peruvian Electric and Musical Industries S.A.) and became a major producer, followed by Virrey (in association with Philips), FTA (which became a subsidiary of RCA Victor), Sono-Radio (an affiliate of Columbia Records), MAG Records, and Smith Records. Until the 1980s these were the dominant record companies in Peru. However, only one of them, IEMPSA, has survived until the present. The golden age of commercial Andean music developed around the mid-1950s and continued until the 1980s, comprising a time span of thirty years, during which the LP was the dominant vehicle.[29] During this period, almost 50 percent of the total sales of the record companies fell into the "folklore" category (meaning Andean music), signaling the importance of this market. By the late 1980s "folklore" had dropped to 20 percent of total sales, primarily due to changes in market demand and the increasing cassette piracy.[30]

By the 1970s smaller independent companies took a share of the market, but they had to do it following specific strategies. Most of these independents concentrated on what the recording industry called *música costumbrista* (customary music), a loose term borrowed from colloquial Spanish, referring to more traditional music of rural origins, in contrast to the music disseminated by the larger companies, which concentrated on the more professional and well known urban singers and regional ensembles. The independent companies that appeared all over the country in this decade returned to the types of music featured in the first recordings of the late 1940s, which were made by local groups and were mostly instrumental. The small companies did not have recording facilities, nor the equipment that the largest companies had; consequently, they had to rent recording studios and even contract the largest companies to press their records for a fee. With the records finally in hand, the small company would impress or add its own label and logo and proceed to distribute them commercially. Using this system, numerous record companies appeared not only in Lima but also in many departments and provinces of the country. Since the music they recorded was of regional significance, most of their records were sold in their respective geographical areas, and many times they relied on seasonal sales, providing, for example, Carnival music during the Carnival season, or santiago music during the months of July and August in the case of the central Andes.

By the late 1980s the LP format began to slowly disappear, not because of the advent of the digital CD technology but because of the increasing popularity and affordability of the cassette, against which the LP format could not compete. In the early 1980s cassette piracy had made it more difficult for Andean performers to release LPs, since most of the consumers preferred to buy extremely cheap cassette copies of the LPs rather than the original. Cassette piracy expanded without limits because it was not controlled at all by local or national governments. This predicament accelerated the disappearance of many of the larger companies, while the smaller ones found their way to transfer their production to cassette.

Today the entire market of Andean commercial recordings in Peru is dominated by the cassette format, with an overwhelming majority of pirated cassettes. Compact discs are being increasingly manufactured and distributed, but they are still far from being a massive commodity because of their expensive price. The golden age (1950–1980) of commercial recordings is, therefore, already part of the history of popular culture in Peru. The younger generations of Andean descent are not aware of the manner in which this period shaped the current one, still active and constituted by a new generation of popular Andean vocalists and instrumentalists.

The impact of the recording industry on Andean musical creative processes and performance is not restricted solely to the migrant world in Lima. Since the early 1950s, when the record production in Peru took off, many orquesta típicas that resided in the Mantaro Valley have issued several commercial 78 RPM recordings, among them the regionally renowned Lira Jaujina, which was directed by the now legendary composer Tiburcio Mallaupoma, and the San Jerónimo de Tunán from the district of Tunán. The distribution of these commercial recordings was not limited to Lima, but they were made available in the provinces as well, just as occurs now with contemporary recordings. Internal regional markets have been, therefore, an important part of the commercialization of records since the beginning of the industry in Peru. In that sense, the "new" process of recording música costumbrista by independent labels for regional markets is in a way a return to the initial stages of commercial recordings. It seemed inevitable, however, that the migrant market in Lima, more numerous and economically dominant, would become the largest one for the record industry and the central point for the production and distribution of commercial recordings.

## Wanka Music on Records

The solo Andean singer is a figure who slowly yet steadily emerged throughout the twentieth century, primarily in the popular theaters and coliseos of Lima. Thanks to the new electronic audio amplification systems, the solo singer could sing with an orchestra whose level of sonority was, obviously, higher than that of his unamplified voice. The solo singer was the natural continuation of a trend that was already developing in the Andean regions by the 1940s, even before the advent of commercial recordings of Andean music. The soloist represented the individualized performer and creator, which grew in opposition to the notion of the anonymous traditional creator as well as of that of collective composition as the main means of creative process in the Andes.

The previously cited song collection gathered by José Hidalgo of nearly 700 mulizas, each of which had an individual author, was a clear indication of the rise of the individual composer in the valley (Arguedas 1976:204). In the early 1940s several of these composers had already achieved fame in the Mantaro Valley, like Tiburcio Mallaupoma, Juan Bolívar, and Zenobio Dagha. In other regions of Peru, such as Cuzco, other composers, including Kilko Waraka, Gabriel Aragón, Pancho Gomez Negrón, Edmundo Delgado Vivanco, and Alfredo Macedo, also became acclaimed authors in their own right (Arguedas 1977:7). When the recording industry launched its first productions, these composers, many of whom were directors of performance groups, became leading songwriters of a repertoire that mainly consisted of mestizo huaynos.

Solo singers became pivotal figures in the dissemination of Andean music in Lima and from the capital saw their influence spread throughout the entire nation. Solo singers developed a new urban popular style, with roots in their own regional musical traditions, a style characterized primarily by the theater-staged performance context, the leading figure of the solo vocalist, the use of audio amplification, and an orchestral accompaniment. This type of performance became the most popular but not the exclusive one, since instrumental soloists, duos, trios, and orchestras also achieved popularity in their own right. However, the solo singer with orchestra format was most admired and also the most dependent on electronic amplification for live performances. This urban popular style of Andean singing did not replace any previous "traditional" performance style; instead it added a new form. The singing style was definitely based on Andean mestizo patterns, favoring the middle vocal range rather than the extremely high-pitched performances of rural Andean contexts (as well as other traits to which I will return later). This is a natural development, since as we have seen, many of the musical processes developed by the migrant in Lima were already in progress in regions where mestizaje was in the working. Because of this, I would be reluctant to suggest that the singing style of Andean recording stars was essentially shaped by "urban-Western" aesthetics. As noted earlier, Andean performers may be better served when acknowledged as appropriators of aesthetic forms that were and are available in the global world. Rather than being portrayed as compliant artists, they can be seen to reorder these forms for their own use in the national context. This is still an ongoing process, further indicating that the seizure of "urban-Western" forms and technologies (singing with a microphone, using loudspeakers, using and displaying "global" styles of popular music) does not stand for de-Andeanization or "cultural assimilation." The music of Andean soloists of the golden age of commercial recordings is to this day distinguishably Andean, aesthetically contentious, still underestimated, and consequently largely ignored by Peruvians who favor a Euro-American cultural model for national formation.

The solo singers, as we have seen, had developed from the companías folklóricas, in which they had attained wide popular endorsement of the presentation of regional dances, popular comedians of Andean heritage (who entertained the public in between acts), and strictly instrumental ensembles. By the time of the golden age of the coliseos the solo singers were on their way to becoming "stars," and commercial records simply precipitated this dominant role and furthered the fame of these artists. There were hundreds of solo singers performing in the coliseos of Lima, Huancayo, and other cities of Peru, but only a few of them became prominent celebrities and best-selling recording stars. Each of them followed his or her own regional styles, and the core of their supporters were migrants and residents of their own regions. However, due to the intense media exposure (mainly the radio and commercial records) and the novelty of these media, these singers acquired recognition and fame beyond their own organic regional publics. For example, the Pastorita Huaracina (the Shepherdess from Huaraz) and the Jilguero del Huascarán (the Goldfinch of the Huascarán) were linked to the regional styles of the northern department of Ancash, and the Picaflor de los Andes (the Hummingbird of the Andes) and the Flor Pucarina (the flower from Pucara) to Wanka folklore. There were many others recording stars, but according to the popular perception and the testimonies of the own record executives, these four were among the ones who sold more records and whose names have remained in the memory of the people more.[31]

The main song genre disseminated in this new Andean urban popular style, and in Andean commercial records, was, by far, the mestizo huayno. In the case of the Mantaro Valley, the song genre that followed the huayno in frequency of performances and recordings was the huaylas, in turn followed by the muliza. This ranking can be observed by examining the jackets of LPs of the period and inferred from the writings of Alejandro Vivanco (1973) and Arguedas (1976, 1977, 1985). The supremacy of the huayno, however, asended during the 1960s, since the first recordings of the 1950s also featured music from dance-dramas such as the huaconada from Mito, the huaylijía, the pachahuara, Carnival music, toriles from Acolla, and chonguinada from Huancayo.[32] In fact, even at some moments during the 1960s, at the height of the golden age of Andean commercial recordings, the records of Andean orchestras matched or even surpassed in number of releases those of Andean soloists. In 1967 Arguedas published a catalog of 45 RPM Andean records sold in the market of Chosica, a district bordering the Central Highway twenty-five miles from the city of Lima, where thousands of migrants of the Mantaro Valley had settled since midcentury.[33] He found sixty-two records of orquesta típicas and brass bands being sold at the Chosica market and thirty-one records of soloist singers (1969:25–27). The higher profile of the Andean singer, therefore, has concealed the continuous popularity of the purely instrumental orquesta típica, at least in the case of the Mantaro Valley.

The two most famed singers of the valley were the aforementioned Picaflor de los Andes (Víctor Alberto Gil Malma) and Flor Pucarina (Leonor Chávez). When they died, thousands of followers mourned them and attended their funerals. When Picaflor (1929–1975) died while touring in La Oroya, the central mining town near Huancayo, the vehicle bringing his remains to Lima had to stop in every town along the way. Everyone near the Central Highway, a geographical strip strongly influenced by the regional culture of the valley, wanted to see him and pay their respects. His body lay in state at the Coliseo Nacional (National Coliseum) in Lima, which had been one of his frequent performance venues. Picaflor was a hardworking man who had left Huancayo as a teenager to work in the mines, following the seasonal migration patterns that have been a source of additional income in the valley since the development of the mining industries. In 1959, when he was thirty years old, he went to Lima to participate in a contest promoted by Radio Excelsior. It took him only a few years to record his first hit song, in 1963, "Aguas del Río Rímac" (Waters of Rímac River), which sold thousands of copies then and still is included in every anthology of his music. His records are still widely available, in cassette format, and his popularity is such, twenty-seven years after his death, that a CD with a selection of twenty-four of his best-selling songs was been released by El Virrey, a major record company (CD-VIR 00001403). Picaflor had a brief career as a recording artist: from the release of his first hit song in 1963 to the day he died at the peak of his popularity of a heart attack, only twelve years passed. During that time, he recorded fourteen LPs (see discography in appendix) and numerous 45 RPM discs.

The Flor Pucarina (1940–1987) had a similar working-class background. She was born in the town of Pucará, south of Huancayo, and moved to Lima at the age of nine. In Lima she worked at the La Parada market, at the time the largest outdoor food outlet located at the margins of the city of Lima and mostly reserved for migrants from all places. But she also auditioned in the coliseos and soon became a professional singer. Stories are told of how she used to sing Mexican corridos and rancheras before turning to signing huaynos and mulizas. She died of kidney failure in 1987 after spending an entire year in a public hospital. The Flor Pucarina recorded thirteen LPs throughout her career (see discography in appendix).

The repertoire of both singers from the Mantaro Valley was overwhelmingly comprised of huaynos. In this respect they followed the trend of most regional commercial musics. In the survey elaborated by Arguedas in Chosica, the predominance of the huayno by the late 1960s is confirmed.

The Flor Pucarina singing in the Coliseo Cerrado near downtown Lima in 1969. Photo courtesy Revista Caretas.

Cover of an LP from the Picaflor de los Andes.

Of 2,668 45 RPM records he compiled, 2,245 were huaynos, 209 huaylas, and only 51 mulizas (followed by other regional genres; see Arguedas 1969: 31). The commercial huayno was not very different in musical form from the regional one. However, it goes without saying that the performers had to adapt their renditions to the two- or three-minute duration allowed by the record.

In terms of huayno form in its recorded format, the long introduction by the harp and violin became much shorter on records, as did the concluding bars. Picaflor's singing style was tense and edgy, utilizing his middle range, with no attempt to explore lower or higher vocal tessituras. Regarding the problem of how "Westernized" this vocal style is, I can only say that one can hear a similar middle-ranged and tense vocal style in rural peasant male choral music in the southern highlands. In any event, this question remains a highly speculative one, since there are no extant field recordings of Andean vocal music before the early 1950s and the only sources for recognizing aesthetic trends in Andean vocal singing are purely ethnographic ones. In terms of Andean rural contemporary vocal style, the only characteristic trait that I am familiar with is with the high-pitched female style, but there is not a similar common pattern for male singing. That high-pitched female singing is perceived as definitely Andean by the urban non-Andean Peruvian is doubtless the case. Traits such as the use of a strong vibrato, predominant staccato singing, the intensive use of slight ascending and descending glissandos to attack a note, and the use of non-standard Spanish further contribute to identifying the style. Certain common features shared with the orquesta típica further emphasize the unity of the overall performance style. The clarinets and the saxophones also alternate vibrato and staccato and use the same type of swift glissando to strike notes.[34]

The huaynos of the Picaflor de los Andes are similar in form to the regional ones but express at the same time a relative flexibility in terms of their rendition. The huayno consists primarily of a musical phrase exposed in a periodic form, with clear, not necessarily symmetrical, antecedent and consequent phrases. A huayno can consist of only one periodic phrase, which in this case is repeated also in the way of antecedent—consequent. For example: AA1/AA1. But other huaynos may consist of two periodic phrases, the second one being a contrasting unit. In this case they may be two variations; the first phrase (A) may be repeated, and then the piece may proceed to the second phrase (B), giving the following result: AA/BB. Also, the second phrase (B) may be directly rendered after the first phrase (A): AB/AB.

These patterns are, it goes without saying, repeated at will, but on commercial records repetitions are usually determined by the constraints of time (between two and three minutes). Example 4.1, "Aguas del Río Rímac," demonstrates the first variation pattern, musical example 4.2,

Example 4.1: Song from the Picaflor de los Andes ("Aguas del Río Rímac")

Aguaquecorre porelrí - o Rí-mac    en tu corriente  llevastris-te fe - cha    cha

la huar-cho-ri-na    la hua-ro - chi-ra-na    son bue-nas mo-zas    pe-ro de    mal ge - nio

Example 4.2: Song from the Picaflor de los Andes ("Gorrioncito")

Gorrionci - to can-ta pe - ro no llo-res    el a-mor es la fuer - za  más su-bli - me

bas-ta ya    zor-za-li - to    que tus llan - tos  me en-tris-te - cen

has-ta los puquiales    se-cos — suelen bro-tar al    ver-te muy tris-te

"Gorrioncito," demonstrates the second. The lyrics of most huaynos interpreted by the Picaflor were related to romantic love. They were highly
nostalgic, even tragic, and most of the time referred to a lost relationship,
rejection or abandonment. Some of them were harsher than others. In "For
You, Ungrateful," he sang:

> You might have heard of my life, ungrateful,
> that I am suffering because of your false love,
> for sure you are laughing and singing,
> but you do not know the pain that you cause.

Of the few huaynos that did not correspond to this theme, some were
dedicated to fostering regional identities, with lyrics that spoke of the
native land, the town, or the region, such as "I Am from Huancayo" or
"Huancayo feeling." The mulizas tended to be less ruthless when singing
about lost loves, as in "I Will Always Remember You":

I want to follow your path,
that you left for my comfort.
I want to travel through your smile
that lighted like you always wanted.
You were for me my heaven,
shooting star that goes away.
I will never forget your words,
nor the look of those eyes.

The huaylas, in contrast, tended to bring more optimistic messages, corresponding to the cheerful character of the genre. The song "Green Corn" also spoke about love but from a positive perspective[35]:

I want to eat corn,
with the girl that I like,
so I can steal her heart,
so that she can also give me her love.

The orquesta típica not only provides the "accompaniment" but also influences and shapes the entire performance style. In a way, instead of conceiving the orchestra as a mere "accompaniment" to the solo singer, both should be considered as elements of the same grouping. In this sense, it should be considered that the singer's repertoire is determined by the orquestas típicas and that the performance technique and style of the orchestras have not changed significantly from their role in the regional festival system, since they continue to play the huayno or the huaylas as they would do in the valley. The only difference in the urban popular style is that a vocalist is now the leading voice, instead of the alto saxophones. Otherwise, and notwithstanding the presence of the singer, all the musicians of the orchestra play the same melody (some instruments doubling in parallel thirds as usual) following the customary performance technique. While the song is being rendered by the singer, the orchestra plays more softly, allowing him or her to reaffirm a leading role and to convey the lyrics accordingly. The reduced volume of the orchestra is not so much a technical requirement, since the singer has a microphone and loudspeakers at his or her disposal, but more a stylistic gesture, a matter of musical courtesy. But when the singer finishes a stanza, the orchestra plays by itself the song theme with renewed intensity, although excluding time-consuming repetitions.

The soloist is not, therefore, such an independent performer after all, nor does he or she represent the opposite of the notion of group integration, which for many depicts a peasant egalitarian style. The fact that the orquesta típica has not abandoned its routine performance practice when "accompanying" soloists and that everyone, "soloist" and instrumentalist alike, plays the same melodic theme continues to emphasize collective performance as well as provides a distinguishable Andean quality. The orquesta típica also represents the embodiment of the Wanka style. Any singer who wants to sing in Wanka style must hire an orquesta típica. The unique musical identity that the orquestas típicas of the valley achieved for themselves, within the whole process of Wanka folklore, permitted many orchestras to become recording artists in their own right. Since their performance style and techniques did not vary at all when "accompanying" a soloist, the orchestras continued to be valid performers of huaynos, the huaylas, and mulizas.

The close identification between orquesta típicas and Wanka musical folklore is also highlighted by the fact that the most renowned regional composers who provided songs to Wanka singers were directors of orquesta típicas. Such was the case with the highly acclaimed Tiburcio Mallaupoma, from Acolla, and Zenobio Dagha, from Chupuro. The role of the orquesta típica was, therefore, crucial and determinant. For instance, Zenobio Dagha, who still lives in his native Chupuro, an hour from the city of Huancayo, is credited with the introduction of the saxophones in the Huancayo area. He has made hundreds of commercial recordings, composed "more than 600 hundred songs," and "accompanied" the most famed Andean singers. The municipality of Huancayo has recently dedicated a statue of Dagha in the new Park of Wanka Identity. There the image of him posing with his violin appears, standing by two wakrapukus (the colonial and rural cattle-horn trumpets), looking out upon the mountains that surround the valley. Nonetheless, and despite his enormous commercial success, Zenobio Dagha never stopped performing in the festival system of the valley, reminding us of the main function of the orchestra. No orquesta típica has ever been dedicated solely to the accompaniment of singers. On the contrary, the soloists and their entrepreneurs approached already existing orchestras for their services. That is why Zenobio Dagha never left his rural house in Chupuro and his small plantation that overlooked the Mantaro River. For him, the orquesta típica is more alive than ever.

## Conclusions

In this chapter we have seen how the search for authenticity in territories beyond the Mantaro Valley compelled its people to long for an archaic Inca past. This past was not to be found in their local memories; it was an imagined past that was already represented in the nation's capital and which was ready to be assimilated by and shared with other strangers from other regions. This ideal had become a common reference for a national past that was supposed to represent all "Peruvians," regardless of local or regional differences. But this (rather vague) notion of a collective

past was lost when Andean migrants, empowered by their increasing numbers, found ways to express themselves in the coliseos, spaces that were
out of reach of the dominant sectors of Lima society. I suggest that the
expressive freedom found in the coliseos was a natural choice for Andean
migrants, because of their disenchantment with the "official culture" and
their discouragement concerning the possibility of integrating into a single
"national culture." When the imagined nation, disguised as "Incaic," became an impossible dream, local and regional identities began to reaffirm
themselves thanks to the advent of new technologies. The idea of authenticity grew closer to contemporary local archetypes, rather than to an un-
specific historical remembrance (as when the Inca past was presented as
the cornerstone of the "national soul"). If this was clearly the case in the
discourses of everyday life, Arguedas contributed to the "officialization"
of these texts, acting as a mediator between the agents of popular culture
and the state. The nascent recording industry, radio broadcasting, and
regional associations in Lima created the conditions for Andean migrants
to gather together by themselves, to establish their own markets, and to
"be authentic" in their own local terms. As a disc jockey of Radio San
Isidro who maintains a daily program of Wanka music observed, "Radio
San Isidro identifies itself with Wanka music and all the Huancaínos listen
to us. The Ayacuchano is identified with Radio Exito, 'Harp music' [from
the highlands of the department of Lima] are identified with Radio Agricultura, the Cuzqueños with Radio Oriente . . . it is not that rigid, but
generally it is." Peruvian anthropologist Rodrigo Montoya has expressed
a similar view in saying: "The localism, characteristic of the colonial structure of Andean society, is reproduced in the cities. The migrants of Puquio
attend the theater piece presented by the group Challco of Puquio, in La
Cabaña Theater. Residents of the neighboring provinces do not go because
they are not interested" (1987a:19). Rather than giving birth to a "new"
global Andean identity, each community persisted in maintaining its own.
Thus, it is no surprise that today the music of each region is produced for,
distributed among, and ultimately valued by its own constituency.

# 5

# OFFICIAL,
# POPULAR, AND
# MUSICAL MEMORIES

In previous chapters I have explored the realm of ritual, festival, and dance-dramas (chapter 2), the emergence of the orquesta típica in the context of the festival (chapter 3), and the Wanka presence in Lima (chapter 4). Throughout all of these spheres I have explained how the search for authenticity, the dispute over the past, and the role of modernity have been instrumental in shaping and building the regional culture of the Mantaro Valley. In this last chapter, I will reflect on the ways in which the inhabitants of the Mantaro Valley—especially those of the younger generations—see themselves moving into the future in relation to the nation-state and its hegemonic ideologies. In doing so I intend to first survey how the nation-state has rationalized Andean culture and identity. The distinct relation that Andean regional cultures have to the nation-state suggests an interesting example of how an alternative "nationalism" (understood as a "project of collective identity"; see Mallon 1995:3) to that of the established national elites may develop and how musical practices may play an influential part within this process.

## The National Context

Since independence (1821) Peruvian national elites have embraced European ideals of the liberal state. Influenced by the ideals of the French

Revolution (liberty, equality, and fraternity), the political leaders envisioned a nation-state that consisted of individual and equal citizens (Maybury-Lewis 1984:222). Within this framework, Indians, ethnic minorities, and regional ethnic cultures were accepted only insofar as they could integrate and blend into the larger national culture. Notions like private property and the concept of progress prompted the political leaders of the Independence period to view the Indian sectors as "obstacles" to development. This was especially the case since most of these leaders depended on large landholdings and their expansion at the expense of Indian lands. The "liberator" of Peru Gen. José de San Martín's first act in 1821 was to abolish Indian tribute and replace the term *Indian* with *ciudadanos* (citizens).[1] This new status, however, rather than assisting Indian rights, jeopardized the previous legal protection of their properties.

Along the same line, in the 1820s Gen. Simón Bolívar, who inflicted the final defeat on the Spanish armies and took over the political rule of the new nation—conferred land titles to the Indians, allowing them to sell the property if they preferred to do so (Davies 1974:20). The real consequence of this measure was the massive sale of Indian lands. It is not difficult to speculate that most of the Indian population, who lacked the means (language, literacy, access to lawyers and political officials) to adequately negotiate financial deals with local authorities, would be at the mercy of these authorities. Another provision stipulated by the decree contended that the communal lands were to be measured and distributed among Indians without land. But who would make this distribution? It was to be special functionaries (*visitadores*) named by the central government who would travel to the different provinces of Peru "so to make sure that everything is done with exactitude, impartiality and justice."[2]

The next year, Bolívar retreated from this extreme liberal legislation and signed another decree that acknowledged the abuse and the usurpation that the first decree had caused. Accordingly, on July 4, 1825, Bolívar recognized that the distribution of the land ordered in his 1824 decree was not adequately verified and that Indians had been usurped from their land by the *caciques* (local leaders) and the *recaudadores* (tax collectors). He then ordered that these lands should be redistributed and remeasured. Unfortunately, Bolívar insisted on the same provision of designating the supervisors of these new measurements, the Prefecto (governor) and the Junta Departamental (departmental bureau), both of which had habitually abused the Indians in Peru. But Bolívar also included a very important provision to prevent the definitive evaporation of Indian property, establishing that until 1850 Indians could not sell their lands.

In fact, this second decree demonstrated that these measures were not blatantly against Indian property and rights. A great degree of protectionism of the Indian primary right to land remained, as it can be deduced from an analysis of the decrees themselves. There were protective clauses in the law and an implied preoccupation of the state in the subsequent land usurpation that was taking place. Why did the liberal state bother to give the impression that the Indians were being protected? If religious reasons had been instrumental in understanding de las Casas's plea during the colony, were there only humanitarian reasons in this type of concern in the Indian fate in the nineteenth century? Benedict Anderson proposes the hypothesis that "the fear of lower-class political mobilizations" was one of the key factors in inciting the urge for independence in South America (1991:48). Could this fear also explain continuous protectionism of the Indian under liberal governments?

A close examination of Bolívar's decrees show clearly this concern—at least on the formal level—for Indian rights. As mentioned, in the decree from 1825 Bolívar explicitly denounced and recognized that "a great portion of the lands attributed to the so-called *indios* have been usurped, for a variety of reasons, by the *caciques* and *recaudadores*." In attempting to resolve this situation, he suspended all trade of Indian lands until 1850 to prevent further usurption. Furthermore, in a follow-up decree a year later (signed by his Ministro de Hacienda Jose María Pando on September 1, 1826), Bolívar reinforced the orders of previous decrees, but this time stating clearly his philosophy beneath: "I don't need to explain the importance of this measure because you know how urgent it is to increase the number of owners and producers; to alleviate Indian fate; to circulate a sterile and stagnated wealth" (Bustamante 1918:45). In spite of this official preoccupation, usurption was so rampant that on August 2, 1827, the congress suspended all sale of indigenous lands (Romero 1949:276).

With the Ley de Tierras (Land Law) of 1829 (May 28), also known as "Ley 43," the liberal state would again insist on similar grounds. Indians and mestizos were recognized as the legal owners of the land they had occupied at the time, and those who did not have any property would be assigned land by the departmental bureau. These new owners, however, would not be able to sell their land until they learned to read and write (Romero 1949:277). This law was easily transgressed by local authorities and lawyers in coordination with land owners—so easily, in fact, that, as Romero describes, the only requirement was to maliciously include a simple sentence in the verified sale contract saying that the Indian who sold the land was proficient in the Spanish language (Romero 1949:278). The impact of these decrees, especially of Ley 43, was enormous. By the mid-1850s the hacienda expansion had already achieved its maximum stage due to the massive usurption of Indian lands previously owned by Indian communities (Romero 1949:281).

Notwithstanding these "integrationist" policies, the institution of the *comunidad indígena* (indigenous community) did not disappear but resisted until its legal recognition in 1920, when Leguía came into power with a pro-Indian platform.[3] Leguía embraced the ideals of *indigenismo*, a political, artistic, and intellectual movement devoted to the defense of Indian society and culture that spread in Peru in the 1920s.[4] One of Leguía's most important actions in support of the indigenous community was the official registration of all indigenous communities in 1925. After four years the Ministry of Development had registered a total of 321 comunidades indígenas, and several other dispositions were given in favor of them such as irrigation, access to water, and independence from district councils (Davies 1974:90–91).

The government of Leguía (1919–1930) reminded the Peruvian elites that the Indian community, the cornerstone of Andean culture, was not and could not be dissolved.[5] Late into his mandate, however, Leguía deserted the indigenismo he supported earlier and turned to conservative politics. Notwithstanding this shift, the degree of autonomy of the comunidad has persisted to today. Unlike the Mexican *ejido*, which was closely and strictly monitored by an "agrarian code," a law that regulated its internal organization (Erasmus 1978:14–15), the Indian community in Peru enjoyed great autonomy. They could elect their own local authorities, as well as allocate communal land for particular uses, reserve land for the *mayordomos* or for the festivals, and dispose terrains for communal use (Bustamante 1918:60).

After Leguía, the constitution of 1933, which remained valid until 1979, also recognized the legal existence of the indigenous community and guaranteed the integrity of its lands with autonomy from the municipal councils (Chavez Molina 1954:39).[6] The Civil Code from 1936 also ruled on the legal status of the comunidad and established its mandatory official registration, as well as prohibited the renting of its property (Chavez Molina 1954).

The law was, however, full of ambiguities, in the way in which Bolívar's decrees in the 1820s were. As had occurred then, these legal ambiguities were exploited by more powerful social groups. For example, the law required as sole documentation for the recognition of the land of the comunidad indígena a map and the title of original possession. It is easy to infer that such documentation could be forged quite simply and that few if any indigenous communities could submit original titles as proof of actual possession (Chavez Molina 1954:41).[7]

Outside the strictly legal debate concerning the role of the Indian in the modern nation-state, in the twentieth century heated intellectual controversies arose as well. Distinguished advocates of the liberal state envisioned a nation in which there was no room for Indians, nor for "regional Andean identities." Arguedas has characterized these intellectuals under the label of *hispanistas*, as fervent defenders of Hispanic and mestizo culture in the Americas, only insofar as they were embedded with Hispanic ideals (Arguedas 1977:120).

Among those who proposed the abolition of the indigenous community was Francisco Tudela y Varela. In 1905 he envisioned it as a communist institution that kept the Indians in a state of lethargy and alcoholism and their lands below decent production levels.[8] Leguía y Martínez also proposed the abolition of the indigenous community, a measure which, in his view, in the end would benefit the Indians, transforming them into private owners.[9] In *La Cultura Nacional* (Lima, 1937) Alejandro Deustua professed that "the malice of this country is indebted to the Indian race, which has developed to a point of psychological decomposition, . . . [a race] which has been unable to transmit to the mestizo the virtues which they once had in its phase of progress." And Manuel V. Villarán in 1907 affirmed that indigenous communities were incompatible with a civilized life and the concept of "progress," adding, however, that they should continue under protective laws.[10] This last concern for the fate of the Indian, expressed through the proposals of various protective laws based on humanitarian reasons, was not uncommon. Ricardo Bustamante Cisneros conducted a survey in 1918 that collected different opinions about the comunidad indígena, many of which voiced this anxiety.[11]

These voices were from other intellectuals who disputed the disappearance of the institution of the Indian community. Among them was Francisco García Calderón, who in his book *Le Pérou Contemporain* (Paris, 1907) called for a return to the protective laws of the colonial period. For him, the Indian culture would dissolve without the basic communal spirit that the indigenous community provided as a social and legal institution. For Alejandro Maguiña the indigenous community stood for Indian tradition and custom. It had endured throughout the Inca empire and the colonial period, and the republic should not destroy it. Individual Indian property, for Maguiña, was not adequately protected, and the community was the only collective force that could protect Indian rights. For Juan de Lavalle, if the republic destroyed the indigenous community, the Indian family and property would be obliterated, too. Perhaps better than anyone else, de Lavalle verbalized this position in the following way:

> During the Republic, the community has been, and it is, an institution
> that has had the function to protect, to guarantee and to shelter the
> Indian race; it is a respectable form of association and cooperation
> that should not be destroyed; in view of the exploitation of the ga
> monal and the cacique, the community has been, and it is, a form of
> resistance and defense. (in Bustamante 1918:89)

From a socialist perspective, José Carlos Mariátegui, in the 1920s, was also an eager guardian of the comunidad. He attacked the liberals in the Republic who sought to abolish the indigenous communities, noting that *latifundismo* (large landholdings) had not only continued but also grown (1971:32). For Mariátegui, the indigenous community had to resist because it was basic to the survival of the Indian in the first place and—faithful to his own ideological position—because there were elements of socialism embedded in the community. For Mariátegui the problem of the Indian in Peru was primarily the problem of land, that is, of ownership of land (1971: 32–33).[12]

Both movements, one supporting the annihilation and the other the continuity of the comunidad indígena, carried the implication of different projects for nation building. The liberals and the *hispanistas* expressed the ideals of the national elites, who based their power on the large landowners (haciendas), mining, commerce, and banking (see Manuel Burga and Flores Galindo 1979:88). The indigenistas contemplated a nation with Indian prototypes as the basis of Peruvian society. However, as in Mexico, this indigenismo was a "white/mestizo construct" (Knight 1990:77), a non-Indian movement set forward by Andean intellectual elites and a few distinguished men of letters settled in Lima. Unlike in Mexico, their indigenistas' pleas never became part of an official platform,[13] the exception to this being Leguía's second regime, when he came into the government with an indigenista project.[14] Another attempt within the nation-state to reappraise the place of the Indian occurred during the revolutionary regime of Velasco Alvarado (1969–1975), but it followed the same path as Leguía's frustrated attempt.[15]

It is in this context that Andean regional cultures in Peru have strived to develop. Hispanistas represented the voice of the national elites, who also expressed their beliefs through prodigal lifestyles and a fascination with European culture and values. The foremost historian Jorge Basadre has described the customs of what François Bourricaud has labeled "creole liberalism" (1971:149), noting that they always remained a numerically reduced social group in relation to the Andean ("Indian") majority:

> The ruling classes consisted of gentlemen from the cities . . . something like the local adaptation of the English gentleman. They gathered in clubs, resided in houses decorated with sumptuous "imperial" furniture and abundant carpets and curtains; they had a life proper to a time in which fresh air was not loved, and they dressed in black outfits fashioned by the French tailors of the capital. They lived in a content world consisting of marriages between closed groups; childhood friends continued together in school, and once in the university they would easily win the best chairs in literature, history or philosophy.[16]

Despite the reduced numbers of the ruling classes in Peru, they did exert complete dominion over the political and economic destinies of the nation during most of the Republic. Urban proletarians, rural Indians, and mestizos remained on the periphery of power and decision making. Peruvian elites have been generally blamed for the absence of a "national project" (Cotler 1978); in other words, there was a lack of interest in extending their ideology to the other social classes that formed the nation as well. Peruvian political centralism, based in Lima, symbolized the attitudes of the national elites toward maintaining power and resources in a few hands. Throughout the republican period regional governments and cultures have attempted in vain to struggle against centralism and the elite mentality, which routinely refused to incorporate the demands of regional cultures into their vague notion of nation (see Romero 1969, Mariátegui 1971, and Deustua and Rénique 1984).

## The Local Context

In the introduction to this book I described the Park of Wanka Identity, in which the statues of three regional musicians have been erected by the municipality of Huancayo. By building these statues the municipality wanted to pay homage to those outstanding individuals who had made substantial contributions to Wanka culture. This initiative takes us from the realm of everyday life to the domain of the local government and public policies. It was the local government that built this sanctuary and embarked on a mission of erecting monuments that represented Wanka identity. In a way, it constitutes a position regarding the past in addition to the ones already discussed here. It constitutes a past and a notion of time that differs from those manifested in the spontaneous and active discussions about what is the legitimate identity of the valley, the "old" or the "new." The mere existence of these physical sanctuaries takes the "past" of the valley into a new status. As Herzfeld attests: "Monumental time, by contrast [to social time], is reductive and generic. It encounters events as realizations of supreme destiny and it reduces social experience to collective predictability. Its main focus is on the past—a past constituted by categories and stereotypes" (1991:10).

Cultural monuments, therefore, as the result of the initiatives of a local branch of the state, attempt to inscribe permanently a preconceived notion of a regional past, leaving no space for further social negotiation. In this case, however, we cannot speak of a clash between the goals of the local state bureaucracy and the ordinary people of the valley, because apparently they coincide. Regional elites and political authorities seemed in agreement in the effort to highlight the identity symbols of the valley, strongly opposed to the symbols of the nation-state, which mainly consist of national war heroes. Yet the statue of Francisco Pizarro, the Spanish conqueror of Peru, still stands in the main plaza of the nation's capital.

And the parks of Lima are bursting with statues of military men who fought in the independence battles and the national wars with Chile and Ecuador. In contrast, the images of the Park of Wanka Identity are not those of national heroes but regional humanitarians, folklorists, and, most important, musicians. As far as I know, this is the only region in Peru that has raised statues in honor of musicians, one of whom is still alive. This is a clear indication that independence and the national wars are of relative importance to the collective identity of the inhabitants of the Mantaro Valley when it comes to assessing their own position in the national context.[17] Popular culture takes its place as the main domain in which identity is constructed and defined, and the recent past (twentieth century) takes predominance over the republican past (nineteenth century). The presence of the wakrapukus functions as a reminder of a distant past that has never been forgotten because, in fact, the annual reenactment of the ritual of the herranza serves that purpose as well. The orquesta típica and Zenobio Dagha are only possible because of the permanence of the ritual.

Concurrently with the symposia on the "authenticity" of the huaylas, also organized by the municipality, the official politics of remembrance seemed determined to capture the aspirations of the people themselves. An interview in August 1996 with the head of the cultural section of the municipality, who wished to remain anonymous, confirmed some of these views:

> People talk so much about Huancayo being a kind of Phoenicia, that people here do not like, preserve, or promote their own cultural values. [The municipality] since 1991 within its government plan contemplated a complete rescue process of its identity and customs of the Wanka dweller, through the rescue of its cultural arts, like the Carnival festivals three years ago, like the huaylas contest five years ago. We have been doing this for over six years now; we have institutionalized this here in Huancayo, and also in Lima two years ago, because the huaylas is indigenous to Huancayo. And the fiesta of Santiago, we have been organizing a meeting of Santiago here in the city; we have been trying to rescue our identity.

The official also told us that their aims are directed to enhancing the memories of children and the youth about *lo nuestro* ("our own") and that the embellishment of the city follows a conscious plan "through works that speak out our identity," citing as examples the use of the *laja* stone (slab stone) found in the valley, open theaters, tourist peñas (folk music bars), a chapel for the celebration of the Festival of the Holy Cross, and the restoration of the first railroad that arrived in Huancayo.

The cultural policy toward the reinforcement of the regional identity of the valley incorporates several levels of history: the Wanka pre-Hispanic heritage stressed through the use of the term *Wanka* ascribed to many of their monumental buildings (the coliseum, the park); an agricultural past, which may be colonial or republican, which surfaces in the "institution-alized" symposiums of the huaylas; and the contemporary past as present, in the monumental homage to Zenobio Dahga and the singers the Picaflor de los Andes and the Flor Pucarina, who always performed with the ac-companiment and within the style of the orquesta típica. It is highly sug-gestive in this regard that the municipality of Huancayo renders equal tribute to the ritual wakrapuku as a regional cultural symbol and to the railroad that signaled the economic incorporation of the valley into the larger national system.

At the district level, municipalities advocated the rescue of local iden-tities as well. In Huaripampa the municipality still takes an active part in tunantada contests and explicitly does it to reinforce the "authenticity" of a dance that is claimed to be indigenous to the district (see chapter 3). During one of the recent concursos the municipality invited a member of the national congress (Teodoro Castro Villareal), a native of Huaripampa, to give a speech from the atrium of the municipality:

> May folklore continue to live on, but do not distort the authenticity of the tunantada in Huaripampa. That is why I have given my un-conditional support to the mayor so that next year two entire days will be dedicated to this concurso, and I have offered a first prize of one thousand [American] dollars, so that people can see what is the national folklore from Huaripampa, not distorted. I, as a Huaripam-pino, am rescuing the values of this town of Huaripampa . . . three cheers for Huaripampa! The cradle of the tunantada!

Monuments, "authenticity" symposiums, restoration projects, and folk contests are the means by which local branches of the state attempt to assume the leadership in reinforcing the Wanka identity in the valley. In these efforts they call upon the collaboration of local intellectuals, local philosophers, and "folklorists." Officials and ordinary people engage in heated controversies over "authenticity," but everybody—residents, per-formers, and "folklorists"—seems excited about the cyclic occurrence of these disputes, being enacted in the homes, in the streets, or in the mu-nicipalities. The monuments that the visitor to the valley will view as remembrances of the regional dances, musical instruments, and famous musicians are only physical testimonies of the "intimate culture" of the valley, a contested one but one in constant awareness of its subordinate position within the national context.

## De-essentializing the Andean Mestizo

The competing discourses about the past and "cultural authenticity" should not let us believe that people in the valley feel forced to endorse a single specific option. If, in fact, there are individuals who are definitely and organically "traditionalists" or "innovators," there are others who profess mobile, multiple, and portable identities that they change in relation to their age or position in society. The shifting quality of ethnic identities in the Andes permits cultural identities to change even throughout the course of a lifetime. The mobility of the cholo, the Indian peasant who migrates to the city and returns as an urban dweller, with new values and manners, is an example of the identity switching that characterizes Andean ethnicity. Essentializing the Indian and the mestizo into rigid categories in which the global, the cosmopolitan, and the international appear as disrupting elements seems an outdated practice.

In the same way that the limits between tradition and modernity have vanished to a large extent, the differences between the agents of such paradigms have also became blurred. The crux of the matter, in this case, is that Andean mestizos in the Mantaro Valley may switch positions within the debate over the past and authenticity and even cross cultural lines whenever they feel like it, in the name of Andean cosmopolitism and globalism. Notwithstanding, I do not want to suggest that mestizo identity is multiple, therefore undefinable, or that its destiny is to cross frontiers endlessly, rather, to suggest that mobile identities are a search mechanism but also a means of cultural reaffirmation. As Ulf Hannerz has noted, "The cosmopolitan may embrace the alien culture, but he does not become submitted to it. All the time he knows where the exit is" (1996:104). Here I must assert that the regional identity of the Mantaro Valley makes no claims for a bucolic ethos and that modernity is one of the principal traits of "being Wanka." Modernity in no sense is seen as a threat to a distinct regional identity but an assurance that the region will be able to stand with equal pride in the context of the national and international trends.

An important element to consider in this endeavor is the notion of "space" in relation to cultural identity. While I firmly believe that territoriality is one the main forces behind the regional identity of the Mantaro Valley (notwithstanding the massive migration to Lima, "the valley" still is the motherland), I recognize that if one assumes that space and culture are inevitably linked, the risk of essentializing and fixing the regional culture of the valley "in" the valley, as well as decoding other cultural influences as "belonging" to other spaces, becomes greater and perhaps unavoidable. As Akhil Gupta and James Ferguson (1992:6) have attested:

> Representations of space in the social sciences are remarkably dependent on images of break, rupture and disjunction. The distinc-

tiveness of societies, nations and cultures is based upon a seemingly unproblematic division of space, on the fact that they occupy "naturally" discontinuous spaces. The premise of discontinuity forms the starting point from which to theorize contact, conflict, and contradiction between cultures and societies.

I find the breaking of this "isomorphism of space, place, and culture" useful in explaining how external cultural influences may play a role in the Mantaro Valley without rupturing the ongoing construction of a distinctive regional identity and, moreover, how the younger generations, following the paths of the older, may experiment and assume other cultural practices from other places without necessarily giving up their Wanka identity.

Among the extreme cases in this sense are the "experimental identities" assumed by the younger generations in their efforts to assess their own collective cultural identities and their own private differences from older generations. I am referring to the capacity of the younger residents of the Mantaro Valley to sample different musical sounds, musical conducts, and musical philosophies of different cultures on their way to rediscovering their own regional identity.[18] I am also alluding to their capacity to absorb equally from regional ritual and festival musics as well as from external urban cosmopolitan musics—that is, to cross lines freely, back and forth, between tradition and modernity. In the end, all of these cases—which I am going to illustrate in this and the next two sections—contradict the romantic vision by which many scholars have essentialized the Andean Indian and mestizo as following rigid, fixed, traditional patterns, segregated from the global trends that have affected the rest of the world, as if all the communities in the Peruvian Andes had remained isolated from modernity and insulated from the mass-media culture in their own closed corporate Indian spaces.

Almost all the Andean performers of the Mantaro Valley whom I have interviewed have admitted experimenting with different musical styles before assuming the regional mestizo musical repertoire. The radio and the movies arrived in the capitals of the Andean provinces at the beginning of the twentieth century, and the transnational "rhythms" that were popular in New York, London, and Paris were known and contemplated by the regional elites sophisticated city dwellers, Indians, and mestizos alike, although to different degrees. All of those who at some point would have access to a movie theater or a radio were immersed into the global media at some point in their lives.

"Mario" is a violin player who plays in several orquestas típicas of the valley.[19] He lives in Lima, where he is also in high demand by the orquestas típicas of the nation's capital. But he is also a second violinist in the National Symphony Orchestra. Thus, he switches from Beethoven and

Mozart to the regional huaylas, from the solemn and unemotional com-
posure of the symphonic performer to the drinking and convivial moods
of the public festival. Is he a mestizo musician from the valley or a cosmopolitan symphonic violinist? An outstanding bicultural performer or a
Westernized mestizo? How does he construct his own cultural identity?
Mario loves the Mantaro Valley and especially his particular district, Huaripampa. He is from the valley and is proud to be part of the Wanka
culture. But being part of a regional mestizo culture does not mean that
he cannot transcend his own space and cultural origins and wander into
other cultural universes:

> I was twelve years old when I learned the violin. My father danced
> the tunantada very nicely. I saw that the musicians were good; I
> would sit down close to them. My father hired a music professor for
> me, and I learned a little bit, but then a music teacher arrived at my
> school. I started playing in the school band; I played the soprano
> sax, the alto sax. But in my senior year I saw my violin in the corner
> of my bedroom, and I applied to the Conservatory; then I went into
> the Symphony Orchestra. I started very different things, other fields,
> then I gave myself completely . . .

Mario's cultural journey started in his youth in the valley and ended
up in the National Symphony Orchestra in the nation's capital. But Mario
continues playing in orquestas típicas: some days he plays in the morning
a program that includes works of Schubert and Ravel and at night he plays
tunantadas, the dance that his father danced "very nicely." Mario's story
is representative of the mestizo of the Mantaro Valley and is meaningful
because it disputes not only the "essentializing" images of Indians and
mestizos in the Peruvian Andes but also the compartmentalizing representations of Westeners, creoles, Indians, cholos, and mestizos as disconnected
and irreconciliables identities within the nation of Peru.

In fact, globalization has influenced Andean peoples, in variable degrees, since the sixteenth century, when the Spaniards brought ships,
horses, cannons, rifles, swords, and diseases, along with music and cultural
conventions. Andean Indians were already performing xácaras, cantatas,
and villancicos and playing the harp and the violin by the early sixteenth
century (Stevenson 1968:313–21). The process of globalization, therefore,
is not new (Jameson 1998:54). The current globalization process is only
different inasmuch as it is characterized by the role of the mass media.
Indians and mestizos in the Andes have had contact and have been familiar
with Western high and popular culture for centuries and perhaps more
intensively than ever now with television and the battery-powered radio-
cassette players. I argue that the reason for sticking with their own ethnic

and regional identities is choice, not destiny or "primordialism." The story of Mario serves to illustrate this matter further:

> When I went to the town of Parco to take my violin classes I was ashamed, because the violinist was sometimes thought of as a drunk, a beggar who played for money. The youngsters like me were listening to the "new wave" [pop music] and I felt ashamed of playing vernacular music on my violin. I studied at junior high school in La Oroya, where my father worked [in the mines]. There was everything there, movie theaters, films with Gary Cooper and John Wayne. Later, in Huancayo, I studied violin at the Institute of Culture. Soon I began playing in orquestas típicas in Tarma.

Mario's story does not differ very much from the stories of many of the recording artists who were stars in the golden age of commercial discs (chapter 4). As noted earlier, most of them began singing Mexican rancheras, very popular in Peru, and the Argentinian tango. Both genres were popularized through films in Peru, during times when the film industries of Mexico and Argentina were thriving and Peru and all other Latin American nations were important markets. Since the first decade of the twentieth century, the silent film arrived at the capitals of the Andean provinces, thus American and later Latin American films were accessible to all Andean residents who visited the provincial capital.[20] I can only speculate that this influence was more important among the provincial elites with access to cash economy than among the poorer Indian peasants who probably did not have the money to pay for a ticket. But wherever the point of entrance existed, dissemination of "global music" did occur early in the century.

The elder and great violinist Zenobio Dagha, one of the founders of the orquesta típica with saxophones in the 1940s and probably the most representative composer of regional huaynos, huaylas, and mulizas, is proud to declare that his compositions also include creole waltzes and polkas, Cuban *guarachas*, and Spanish *pasodobles*. In the same manner that some indigenistas rejected the term because they felt limited in their scope and purposes (and because they pushed themselves into a role that was viewed with prejudice by hegemonic sectors), Zenobio Dagha reacted with amazement when I told him that I thought he had only composed regional Wanka music. He corrected me, saying proudly that he had composed much more than regional music. I was essentializing him as a regional composer, while his aims were much larger than that.

This single fact, which some scholars would be too keen to interpret as a sign of Westernization or as the proof of the supremacy of urban creole values over the precious "Indianness" of an imagined pristine Andean group, to me is just the evidence that not only is Andean mestizo culture aware of what is happening in the outside, in the global world, but also incorporating modernity has been and still is one of its fundamental features. The essentialization of the Andean Indian and mestizo as individuals with primordial identities that they may never transcend has been rampant within ethnography. And one of the main consequences of this has been the antimodern attribute ascribed to primordial groups; that is, any trait of modernism, which will be of course recreated by the essentialized group in a unconventional way, will be considered irrational (Appadurai 1996b:140). But being modern has been the main goal for the mestizo culture of the Mantaro Valley and for many Andean peoples in other regional cultures in the nation. Confronting national hegemonies in equal standing not only must be played out in the formal arena of national politics but also in culture and ideology.

A young disc jockey from a radio station in Lima, which broadcasts music from the Mantaro Valley, suggested to me how some issues like cosmopolitism and internationalization become higher missions within a regional cultural framework. It is not an irrational aspiration or a sign of a process of Westernization that threatens in the long run to leave the anthropologist without a job (hence the professional need to denounce and fight it, see Bennoune 1985) but the simple right of a regional culture with aspirations of developing a "nationalist" project to encounter on equal terms the hegemonic ideologies of the larger national context:

> They say that the folk singer is provincial; they are mean in saying this, right? But now it has been demonstrated that the artist can travel to other countries to disseminate our own folklore and that they even pay their own airfare or they are invited by other countries, but it has been already established that they only travel by donkeys or horses but also can travel by plane, that they not only play their quenas but also can play other instruments.

In fact, in all the presentations of staged folklore performances of Wanka music (and in all other Andean musics as well), one of the principal honors to be given to a performer is to mention his or her "international" reputation. This credential comes after the national fame and is the final and higher sign of esteem that can be given to a public performer. Regional fame is never mentioned as such, so it is the goal of all mestizo performers of the valley to achieve extraregional renown. I do not want, however, to romanticize Wanka identity through the assumption that "alienation," "exoticism," or "sensationalism" does not exist in the valley. When the members of an orquesta típica are forced to enter the stage dancing as Cuban *salseros* and one sees on their faces humiliation rather than just fun, it seems obvious to me that ethnicities and identities are, despite the pre-

vailing emphasis on notions such as cultural negotiation, still prey to alienation and rupture. I do not think, however that this is the case with
the thriving popular culture of the Mantaro Valley, since the concursos are
enacted separately from the ritual and the fiesta, and I see no possibility
of this type of concursos (some are well organized and play a positive role)
influencing the popular culture of the Mantaro Valley.

## Traditionalists, Modernists and Radicals

I mentioned earlier that cultural debates over authenticity could be viewed
as a dispute between "traditionalists" and "modernists" in the valley. I
also mentioned that I did not see any economic or social differentiation
that could determine the ascription of one or the other into any specific
category. If, in fact, generational positions do sometimes affect views on
authenticity, these determine an attitude that I could label as radical, for
lack of a better term. None of these positions, however, should be taken
as fixed or irreconcilable postures. Shifting from one position to another
can be completely normal in the context of an ongoing debate in which a
basic consensus is taken for granted: the existence of a Wanka identity. I
will illustrate these positions with three brief examples: a local intellectual
who lives in a district near Jauja, a musician from a town close to Huancayo, and disc jockeys at a radio station in Lima that airs Wanka music in
daily programs.[21]

The first example, the "traditionalist," longs for a "pure" authenticity
and regrets the recent innovations that are "distorting" the genuine Wanka
folklore. The roots of this folklore are part of a distant past, one of which
religion and magic were part, concurrent with notions and practices of
reciprocity and ritual. For the "purist," invaded by a deep nostalgia for
this lost past, television and the radio are considered responsible for the
breakdown of tradition. He sees the dissemination of newly arrived musical
genres (the *cumbia*, the Latin *balada*) as threats to Wanka identity. Accordingly, in distant and isolated communities with no electricity the "purist" sees the survival of the "authentic" regional folklore. The local intellectual, an artist who lived in Europe for many years, offers his own
version:

> Unfortunately, now with the radio and the TV, everything is being
> distorted; here in the valley it is difficult to find something autoch-
> thonous or pure, because the truth is that tradition has gone away.
> But mostly it is the people who go away from the valley to other
> latitudes; they go to Lima, and come back with some attitudes that I
> sincerely deeply regret, because they come with a sense of those
> musics that come from Puerto Rico, Central America, the United

States. They bring that influence back here and they ask the musicians of this region for a cumbia, a balada, and all of those things, which are distorted. The religious and magical sense is already lost.

He longs for a past that is now far from the contemporary configuration of the valley. He blames the mass media and is sure that the younger generations are going to continue to distort the traditions. Commercialization and prostitution are analogous for him: for example, he believes if the beer company Cristal, the biggest distributor in the nation, sponsors a town festival, that is a sign of degradation. For the past twenty years, since he returned from Europe, he has been dedicated to rescuing the "authentic" folklore of the region, which for him is found in the distant rural areas, for example, the ceremonial music of the huauco and the ritual music of the herranza. Religion, ritual, myth, and the rural past are for him essential ingredients of authenticity. To a certain degree, however, his position is mostly philosophical, since he actively participates in the festival system of the valley and has been a member of many concursos, which he abhors in principle. Moreover, he has been trained at national and international academies, and he continues to create as an artist, alone and secluded in his home in the valley. His paintings are abstract works, based on pre-Hispanic motifs, which he sees as representing the Wanka presence. An artist, a collector, a local intellectual, he is philosophically a "purist" but also an active participant in the contemporary Wanka festival and ritual systems. Thus, he is not far from the youngsters in Paccha who engage equally in *bailes chicha* and as well as in the the "old" festivals of their parents (see later in this chapter).

The second example is a clarinet player and music teacher. He is in favor of modernizing tradition but within controlled parameters. While he is proud of the "authenticity" of the orquesta típica with only clarinets, he sees no conflict with developing at the same time orchestras with saxophones. Both types of ensembles may coexist in different "times" and "places." He sees modernity as something positive and useful for the development of Wanka identity. If something "modern" demonstrate better qualifications than something "traditional," he sees no problems in choosing the former over the latter. He explains this in the case of musical instruments: "The clarinet has more technical resources than the quena, and the people like it, and it stays because of that . . . and it sounds better. . . . Moreover, it has a register of three octaves and the quena only two octaves. But people are not thinking of 'modernity'; they are thinking of what works better for the performance of their music."

Thus, tradition and modernity may coexist, mingle, and blend in a variety of forms and meanings. He disagrees with the local intellectual's melancholy view of the mass media and the presence of advanced communication technology in the valley. The clarinetist does not see in them "cultural penetration" or "alienation": "I, for example, have Internet, cable TV; I have a fax machine, I have everything you might want, but I go to my [town], I put on my white poncho and join the crowd, I drink, I take my kids so they can watch and learn. That is the same thing that happened to me; I left [my town] when I was eight years old, and I went back when I was sixteen." He is one of the most active promoters of the orquesta típica in Lima and organizes festivals of these ensembles, always featuring orchestras with large numbers of saxophones. He admires Zenobio Dahga and favors formal academic training for regional musicians. At the same time, he advocates "authenticity," but for him, authenticity is in many places at the same time, in the clarinet-based orquesta típica of Huaripampa and in the orchestras that take part in his festivals. Thus, he believes the saxophone-based orchestra should not replace the clarinet-based ensemble. Both may and should exist as part of the different pasts that constitute the cultural heritage of the Wankas. He observes rituals, celebrates festivals, and possesses modernity without ceasing to be an active member of his local district.

A different level in the debate between cultural conservatism and liberalism appears when considering the new musical styles that are breaking into the scene of Wanka music. These new developments are too recent and innovative for the middle-aged to see reflexively. New instruments are replacing old ones; new regional genres are taking predominance over old ones. Behind these changes are youngsters from fifteen to twenty-five years of age. The colonial harp has been supplanted by an electric bass in some orquestas típicas "because it sounds louder," and the sounds of the colonial violins are being imitated by a synthesizer, because one keyboard player can fulfill the role of two violinists. This is not yet a massive trend, but it is certainly a notable one, which worries "traditionalists" and "modernists" alike and makes them suspicious about the aspirations of the younger generations (in Lima or in the valley).

The mechanism at work is, however, parallel to the replacement of the quena by the clarinet and comparable to the addition of the saxophones to the clarinet-based orchestra, which muffled the previously unclouded sounds of the violins and the clarinets themselves. "Traditionalists" and "modernists" concur in impugning this practice, accusing it of ruining the customary sounds of the orquesta típica. But the younger generations speak out in favor of innovation, while also assuring the basics of Wanka identity, with which they feel strongly associated:

> We cannot fight just because the organ, the electric bass, are being used instead of the típico instruments, right? But there is nothing típico; you know that. All the instruments come from abroad. We are the ones who make the combinations. Were the violin and the harp indigenous instruments? And people like it; we do not lose authen-

ticity. The organ, the bass, give more weight to our music. People perceive this and they enjoy it; they dance to it.

The sudden popularity of huaylas-techno among the youth, so-called because of the use of electronic instrumentation, has added further heat to the polemic. The disc jockeys whom I interviewed, both students at national universities, were clear in their views on the validity of these changes. The relative loss of popularity of the huayno (and the muliza for that matter) to huaylas-techno among the younger generations is due to a change of aspirations. The huayno is a genre of nostalgia, which speaks of incurable love, while the huaylas is joyful and may have witty and humorous lyrics. The disc jockeys saw these changes as superficial not as a threat to Wanka identity, and after all, for them the huaylas is still an "old" regional genre and representative of Wanka regional culture.

## The Case of Paccha: Local and Global in Action

Chicha music has been enormously popular among the younger generations of the Mantaro Valley since the late 1960s. It is considered one of the most recent consequences of modernity and as such is the center of the same type of controversies that we have seen in other areas of this regional popular culture. These debates ultimately raise issues of how modern they can allow tradition to be. The difference here is that chicha music is a cultural property exclusively of the younger generations, one that the elders merely judge but do not engage with. The influence of global currents on chicha music is unequivocal. It is played with electric guitars and bass, electric organ, and Latin percussion instruments (congas and timbales). But the music derives from two of the most important traditional genres of South America: the *cumbia* from Colombia and the huayno from Peru. Since chicha music became very popular in the city of Lima, it has been subject of a great deal of attention as an urban phenomenon, and a substantial literature already exists (see Turino 1990 and Hurtado Suárez 1995). In this section I will focus, however, on chicha music as a rural or semirural musical and ritual genre. Cases like this one illustrate how the different postures on tradition and modernity, like the ones examined in the previous chapter, may not only be postulated by independent individual but be embodied by a single person as well. That is, these "experimental identities" may coexist and breathe almost simultaneously. During the time span of a single day, it is possible for a young man or woman "act traditional" during daylight and "perform modernity" during nighttime. How can this be possible?

Paccha is a highland town located in the province of Jauja. It has 2,200 inhabitants, who work primarily in agriculture and livestock. Some combine these activities with wage labor in nearby localities, or they might migrate to Lima and the nearby mining centers like Morococha. Most of its inhabitants are small landholders, but communal property still survives in the town. Being located in the highland sector of the valley, Paccha does not show the signs of increasing urbanization of most of the other towns located along the river and the Central Highway. An element that contributes to this relative isolation is that despite its closeness to Jauja, only one bus runs between Paccha and Jauja per day—and only on work days.

The festive and ritual calendar in Paccha is very full during the year.[22] Rituals of communal work like faenas are performed during harvest season (June, July, and August), with the musical accompaniment of the pincullo and the tinya (see the description of huauco music in chapter 2). The ritual of herranza (marking of the sheep) is also carried out during Carnival and the santiago festival (marking of cattle) during the month of July. Public festivals, however, are the ones that mark the main moments of the annual calendar. The actuality of these festivals and dances is a sign of the strong presence of an urban-mestizo identity that coexists with peasant ceremonies such as those already mentioned. The following is a chart of the main festivals in Paccha:

| Festival | Dance | Main Date |
|----------|-------|-----------|
| Christmas | Chacranegros | December 25 |
| Carnival | | February (March) |
| Festival of the Holy Cross | Jija | May 3 |
| Santiago | | August 1 |
| Festival of Saint Catherine | Tunantada | November 25 |

In Paccha chicha music could be heard through the radio airwaves of a local station from the nearby city of Jauja. Most of the peasants owned portable radios that were always accessible during their everyday chores. Moreover, in Paccha there were several performers and even composers of chicha. But the main social contexts in which young men and women of Paccha and neighboring hamlets participated intensively in chicha music was the *bailes* (balls.) The bailes took place during the nights of the central days of the traditional festival. By doing this, the organizers assured that sufficient people would gather in town from the neighboring villages and fill their locale. According to the organizers, had it not been for this, the bailes would not likely have such large attendance. They were scheduled from 10:00 P.M. to 5:00 A.M., and the purchase of a ticket was required for admission. The venue where the baile was held was a communal building originally designed to make local handicrafts but also used for communal gatherings.

The baile that I went to in Paccha featured a group from Jauja that consisted of two electric guitars, an electric organ, an electric bass, congas and a vocalist. The women had abandoned their daily dresses to adopt urban dresses, and most men were wearing formal coats. Both genders remained separated in different and opposite spaces. Women sat down in the seats that surrounded the locale, while men were standing up and talking in small groups at the center of it. When the music started, most men approached the women of their choice and asked them to dance, but after some time I noticed that the spatial separation between men and women remained the same throughout the night. The age group of the participants ranged from sixteen to twenty-three. It is, therefore, reasonable to confirm my view that the baile in Paccha is, among other things, an occasion designed to gather unmarried men and women and to create a space and conditions in which they may interact and establish the basis for future relationships.

Two chicha groups existed in Paccha. The founder of one of them, the group Genial (Superb), presented a suggestive case. He was the son of the only local performer of huauco (the traditional three-hole pincullo accompanied by the tinya) but chose to learn the guitar in the city of Huancayo instead of his father's instrument. He considered huauco agricultural music extremely difficult. The chicha music that he had heard in Huancayo in the early 1980s influenced him greatly. There was, as well, another factor. To him, the bailes had various advantages over the traditional fiesta: he did not need to drink alcohol and did not have to meet certain expenses of the festival. However, the bailes permitted him to interact with members of his own generation and at the same time secure additional income. Also, chicha music could be performed throughout the year, while traditional ritual and festival music was constricted to a rigid annual calendar. In his own words:

> I also like the jija, but I don't really like it that much, because to that festival I have to go with money, because I meet fellow townsmen who tell me "we have to toast." . . . Instead I go to bailes for hire; we earn money; we get everything. Traditional musics have a season, only once a year, and we learn [to just wait] until next year. Also, at the festival you cannot play the huayno, and there are very few who can afford to hire someone who plays the huayno, the orchestra, for example. They have to wait their season to be hired, while we can play anytime, anywhere.

However, the young members of these chicha groups also participated in the rural lifestyle of the community. They took part in the communal labor in the fields when required, and many of them had at some point in time joined in a traditional dance-drama in Paccha.

A similar case is provided by two young women residents of Paccha, vocalists of the chicha group Los Sauces from Jauja. They were daughters of two members of orquestas típicas. In this case, they did not even have the chance to follow in their fathers' footsteps because women do not play in these orchestras. But these women had chosen, anyhow, to identify with the newly introduced chicha music. However, they had also joined in dance-dramas in their hometowns and had even participated actively in the ritual of the marking of animals (herranza). Along the same lines as the chicha musician mentioned earlier, these women acknowledged their emotional attachment to traditional festivals and rituals but at the same time confessed that chicha music allowed them to mingle with her own generational group, obtain additional income, travel abroad, and have hopes of entering the commercial recording industry. This last possibility implied getting out of the community and into the nation's capital.

The chicha composer Carlos Condezo is yet another example that confirms the trend of the previous ones. Before migrating with his parents to Lima when he was fourteen years of age, he had danced the traditional jija at the Festival of the Holy Cross. After Lima, he returned to Huancayo, where, like the aforementioned musician, he turned to chicha music. He is now a public relations executive of two record companies in Lima but always returns to Paccha for the patronal festival.

Chicha music and the bailes in Paccha do not displace the traditional fiesta and ritual, which still persist as a nucleus and reference to a mestizo identity for all the members of the community. The younger generation separate themselves from their elders in the baile but integrate with them again in the critical periods of the festival. Chicha music allows them to be part, in a particular space and time, of the consequences of globalization processes without breaking with their local mestizo heritage. It also permits them to maintain links with members of their own generation elsewhere, because chicha music is a national phenomenon. The complementarity of the festival, the ritual, and the baile suggests the coexistence of different patterns of time and memory, which displays once more the enormous capacity of Andean peoples to adopt and redefine foreign cultural elements and ascribe to them new local and regional significance. The mestizos of Paccha maneuver with diverse cultural and musical "identities" in order to fulfill different practical and ideological needs. Indigenous traditions such as ritual music of the pincullo and the tinya, festival mestizo music with the orquesta típica and the brass band, and chicha music among the younger generations of the town, which blends transnational musical styles with the regional huayno, appear as different means to measure, explore, and problematize their regional identities.

## The Debated Pasts: Music and Social Memory

Appadurai has called attention to what Clifford Geertz refers to as a "ritualized" past, which denies duration, and a nonritual, mundane past in which duration is a noncontested fact (Geertz 1973). Appadurai calls for a third kind of past, the debated past, "whose essential purpose is to debate other pasts. It generally partakes of both ritual and everyday kinds of discourse and indeed makes it possible for people to pass from one to the other" (1981:202). This is indeed the kind of process that has been developing in the Mantaro Valley since the beginning of the twentieth century. The ritual of the herranza, which I have categorized as a timeless ceremony, a reenactment of a noncontested past in which authenticity is not even discussed and innovations not even timidly suggested, is the realm of nostalgia. But rather than mourning a cultural loss, this nostalgia brings memories into the present and links everyday life in the Mantaro Valley to archaic and supernatural beliefs as expressed, for example, in the ritual of the herranza.

The debate over the dance of the huaylas is something else. In this realm people argue openly and bluntly about the old and the modern, in a variety of contexts, from official symposia to everyday conversations. What are the "historical" origins of the huaylas, which should determine the current performance of the dance? Should it be the dramatization of the precapitalist rural agricultural past or its "modern" urban version? Which one should be adopted as the regional dance of the valley?

The debate over the nature, configuration, and role of the orquesta típica takes the dispute further. This is not an official debate; it develops in the context of everyday life, conversations, informal arguments, and aesthetic discussions. The pasts in dispute are part of the very recent history of the valley, and the notion of authenticity mingles with the notions of the antique and the typical. In the orquesta típica, the guardians of authenticity claim that only clarinets should be considered typical whereas the more progressive individuals prefer to move on and introduce all kinds of saxophones into the "typicalness" of the most popular regional orchestra. The past pertains to the advent of mining capitalism around the beginning of the twentieth century, when the valley was still beginning the process of transformation of its ethnic, social, and economic formations. This past is actually a "contemporary" past, situated around the 1940s, when the valley had already arrived at its current state of affairs. The debate about the orquesta típica is, therefore, not about the notion of the typical but about how typical the most prestigious ensemble of the region should be. No one questions the validity of and the right to appropriate European instruments to play regional musics and to adopt them as "typical"; the debate is over the degree to which this modernizing trend should develop in the future.

In summarizing the disputed claims of history in the Mantaro Valley I recognize the following: a ritual, noncontested past, a precapitalist agricultural past, and a "modern" past. In my analysis I have correlated these debated pasts with the following performance contexts:

| Noncontested Past | Precapitalist Agricultural Past | Modern Past |
|---|---|---|
| Herranza ritual | Waylarsh ritual/huaylas dance | Orquesta típica |

But in acknowledging such a disparity of local and contested "histories" I do not want to suggest cultural anarchy or the presence of "subcultures" in the valley. To the contrary, I have systematically affirmed that Wanka identity is one of the most self-assured regional personalities in the nation. In transcending the external aspects of the dispute, I argue that it is precisely this cultural dialectic that provides strength and self-confidence to the regional identity of the valley. The ongoing discussions, which imply analysis and reflection, of what is Wanka identity and the simultaneous manipulation of different discourses of "authenticity" provide an answer to all the sectors involved in this cultural debate: cultural conservatives, innovators, and modernizers. I contend that the solid ground that protects the regional culture of the Mantaro Valley from serious internal confrontation is the consensual belief that its cultural difference must be maintained at all costs, with ritual, music, and drama as the main vehicles of cultural expression. In this sense, disputed claims of the past remain an internal affair, insofar as the modern nation-state has not been interested in enforcing a cultural policy in the valley, with the only exceptions being the national political and educational systems. The reason for this lack of concern is the failure of the national elites to elaborate a "national project" in the terms I discussed at the beginning of this chapter. This absence has permitted regional cultures in Peru to develop with few confrontations with the state-endorsed ideological projects.

My contention of how modernity is constructed, redefined, and contested in the realm of music and popular culture in the Mantaro Valley is analogous to the notion of progressiveness that has prevailed in the anthropological literature of the Mantaro Valley since the early report of Harry Tschopik (1947:4), echoed by Richard Adams (1959), Arguedas (1975), Long and Brian Roberts (1978), and most of the authors who have attempted to characterize the attitude of the resident of the valley toward modernity in the domains of economic and political action. Such "progressiveness" has been opposed to the "conservative" postures of other Andean communities in the southern Andes, which have been less inclined to, less successful at incorporating modernity into their usual cultural practices. Many of the initiatives labeled as progressive in this literature, however, have been localized at the level of the villages, using specific cases of communitarian enterprises as examples of this outlook. In analyzing the musical practice and contexts of the Mantaro Valley I hope to have shown how this notion of progressiveness, previously understood as a fixed and homogenizing attribute, is in fact a highly debated and challenging cultural issue at the regional level.

Musical practice and musically organized rituals and festivals serve a primary purpose in the realization of the Wanka identity, basically because they contributed to the construction of social memory in the valley in the absence of other more effective mechanisms. Rowe and Vivian Schelling have called attention to the process by which nation-states attempt to suppress histories different from the official one. They create their own homogenizing histories, with their own national heroes, which tend to disregard particular memories of struggles, resistance, and oppression (1991: 228–229). The maintenance of social memories distinct from the narratives of "national history" is fundamental to the reaffirmation of the regional identity of the Mantaro Valley. And in this endeavor, the cultural debates on musical authenticity have played a major role in the process of questioning how deep in the past the Wanka identity must see itself and how long into the future it can go without being abandoned. There are, indeed, different social memories in the valley, as there are different kinds of orquestas típicas and other musical ensembles. All of them are discussed in a historical framework, but one different from the formal and "scientific" frame of the "official historiography."

In the particular case of Peru the accomplishment of asserting a distinct regional social memory over the pressures of the "national culture" seems to have been facilitated by the fact that the ruling elites never demonstrated a systematic or sincere interest in spreading ideologies beyond certain social sectors. Their failure to build an efficient and truly democratic nation-state as well as a "national culture" that represented or embraced all of its constituent sectors has been acknowledged among liberal and nationalist intellectuals alike. In this sense, the major cultural forces against which a Wanka identity had to struggle fell in many ways in the domain of the homogenizing mass media (as producers of "mass culture") rather than in that of specific governmental cultural policies.[23] In fact, what the valley's inhabitants protest most is the Peruvian federal government's obliviousness to the needs of the regions and cultures. That is why most of the complaints of the cultural conservatives of the valley allude to the power of television and the radio and its role of propagator of foreign images and sounds rather than to any official cultural plan. And even in the realm of mass media Wanka musical culture has conquered new spaces.

The importance of music in these processes is, as I have attempted to demonstrate in this book, of great significance. Without music, Wanka identity would lose its main frame of reference, its most valuable stronghold. But as I anticipated in the introduction, I am hesitant to close this work with the usual suggestion that music by itself is capable of changing some aspects of society under certain circumstances. In the Mantaro Valley I have examined musical practices only insofar as they have become part of the larger popular culture (festivals, rituals, dances, social memories, and oral traditions) that has captured the imagination of the people of the valley. But I do believe that music in the valley is "something more" than sound itself. It is indeed the organizing force behind the private ritual, the public festival, the dance-drama, the intimate listening experience, the hopes of local bureaucracies, and everyday negotiations of the past, the present, and the future of the people of the Mantaro Valley.

# *Appendix*

## Discographies

### *The Picaflor de los Andes*

1. Aguas del río Rímac. Virrey Vir-542. No date (n/d).
2. Yo soy huancaíno. Virrey Vir-567. N/d.
3. Picaflor de los Andes y su conjunto. Virrey DV-620. 1967.
4. Santísima Virgen de Cocharcas. Philips P 6032434. N/d.
5. Sangre huanca. Philips P 632431. N/d.
6. El proletario. Philips P 632437. N/d.
7. Por las rutas del recuerdo. Philips 6442001. N/d.
8. Siempre Huancayo. Philips 6350 004. N/d.
9. El obrero. Philips 6350 010. N/d.
10. Un pasajero en el camino. Philips 6350 0121. N/d.
11. El genio del Huaytapallana. Philips 6350 014. N/d.
12. Un paso más en la vida. Philips PHI 6350 020. N/d.
13. Bodas de plata (double album). Philips 6350 021 CN-PHN 7599375. 1975.
14. Para Huanca . . . Yo. Philips 6350 022. N/d.

### *The Flor Pucarina*

1. Exitos de Flor Pucarina. Virrey DV-535. N/d.
2. Trozos de mi vida. Virrey Vir-603. N/d.
3. Corazón de piedra. Polydor 2403 002. N/d.
4. Manchaste mi vida. Polydor 2403 004. N/d.
5. Ho! Licor maldito. Polydor 2403 005. 1973.
6. Pasión del alma. Polydor Pol-2403 010. 1975.
7. Flor Pucarina y sus canciones. Polydor LV-007214. N/d.
8. Siempre te recordaré. Polydor 2403 018.6. 1977.

9. Sola siempre sola (double album). Polydor A20-PON 2669065.6. N/d.
10. La única. Polydor. N/d.
11. Acuérdate de mi. Polydor. N/d.
12. Flor de mis ilusiones. Estrella Record LER-1045. N/d.
13. Incomparable y única. Estrella Record. LER-1075.1983.

# Notes

## Introduction

1. In his study on the Huancayo market of 1957 the renowned Peruvian author José María Arguedas included an acute analysis of the recent urban development of the city. He noticed that the enormous urban growth of Huancayo was clear in the sheer number of factories, workshops, hotels, restaurants, and bus lines that had appeared in the last decades. Arguedas also noted that Huancayo's growth in the 1950s had been greater than that of urban centers on the coast such as the cities of Chiclayo and Piura (1957a:48).

2. The term *Wanka* alludes to the pre-Hispanic ethnic group that inhabited the territory of the Mantaro Valley. This term is used by the contemporary population of the valley to claim its cultural heritage with the past.

3. During a recent visit in the year 2000 I observed that a total of eleven statues had been built. Among them, the images of five additional folk music performers had been added: Angélica Quintana, Francisco Leyth Moreno, Francisco Rivera Jiménez, Néstor Chávez Calderón, and Emilio Alanya. Other personalities depicted in the park were the following: Teófilo Hinostroza (photographer and *quena* player), Sergio Quijada Jara (*folklorista* and historian), and Armando Ugarte Ríos (community leader).

4. It is understood that I have relied mainly on oral and ethnographic sources and emphasized those related to issues of popular culture at the regional level. For a different treatment on the study of a social memory in Latin America based largely on written sources of "indigenous historians" see Rappaport 1998.

5. I prefer to use the term *popular* instead of *traditional* or *folk* to designate the cultural expressions of the subaltern social sectors. These sectors stand in opposition to the "official" values endorsed by those who control the politics of the nation-state. I concur with Néstor García Canclini's query: "Why talk of popular cultures? We prefer this term to others used in anthropology, sociology and folklore—oral, traditional, or subordinate culture—which assume to some extent the possibility of reducing the popular to an essential characteristic" (1993:27). I may also use the related terms *mestizo culture* and *regional*

*culture* in referring to the specific cultural expressions of the people of the Mantaro Valley.

6. In this sense, I sympathize with Martin Stokes's perception that "the response [of ethnomusicologists] has been to overstate, to overargue the significance of music," in view of the recurrent misconception by social scientists that music is an autonomous manifestation (1994:1).

7. As has been demonstrated by the seminal studies of Steven Feld (1982) and Anthony Seeger (1987).

8. In this same line of thought, Kofi Agawu has argued that "an ideology of difference must be replaced by an ideology of sameness" in order to transcend essentializing notions of "otherness" fixed upon non-European worlds (1995:393).

9. How, then, could Latin American "insiders" be expected in the 1970s to produce what Delmos J. Jones called native anthropology: "a set of theories based on non-Western precepts and assumptions in the same sense that modern anthropology is based on and has supported Western beliefs and values" (1970: 251)?

10. For the importance of the "audience," that is, "who reads our texts and why," see David E. Sutton's "Is Anybody Out There? Anthropology and the Question of Audience" (1991).

11. This separation between researcher and subjects of research is not limited to the First World–Third World problematic. American anthropologist Sherry B. Ortner recently declared that "when I was in graduate school in the sixties, it was virtually unheard of to get the blessings of the department (not to mention a grant) to do American fieldwork" (1991:163).

12. The activities of the Shining Path in the Mantaro Valley from 1987 to 1992 do not seem to have affected significantly the festival, ritual, and musical system in the region, at least not in the towns on the margins of the Mantaro River. The Shining Path did provoke significant migratory movement from the neighboring departments of Huancavelica and Ayacucho, where political violence had cruel social and cultural repercussions, to the Mantaro Valley. The outgrowth of this phenomenon is still to be seen (for more information on Shining Path's activities in Huancayo and the region of the Mantaro Valley see Manrique 1998).

13. The Spanish word *típico* ("typical") in Andean Peru is similar to terms such as *traditional, native,* and *autochthonous.* It is mostly used to refer to objects or phenomena that are representative of a social group or culture and only rarely applied to individuals. Thus, the adequate translation for the term *orquesta típica* should be "traditional orchestra."

## Chapter 1

1. These colonial sources have been summarized effectively in Arguedas 1975:80–85. Waldemar Espinoza Soriano, however, affirms that well before the arrival of the Spaniards in the valley, the Wanka leaders had sent their emis-

saries—with promises of alliance and support—to Cajamarca upon learning that the Inca had been captured (1973:74–80).

2. From the *Relación de Hernando Pizarro acerca de la conquista (Crónicas de 1535 a 1537)*, (Arguedas 1975:83). This and other texts originally in Spanish are my translations.

3. The Mantaro Valley has been one of the most studied Andean regions. Its cultural homogeneity and its peculiar historical development have encouraged many authors to treat the valley as a whole. Colonial chroniclers and nineteenth-century travelers have left their impressions of their visits to the region in sections of larger works on Peru. Most of these have been meritoriously synthesized in Waldemar Espinoza's *Historia del Departamento de Junín* (History of the Department of Junín, 1973). Local researchers in the nineteenth century, such as Nemesio Ráez, have left us with important observations on the valley in its previous stages, before the advent of the mining industries and early capitalism (1889). One of the first modern ethnographic reports on the Mantaro Valley was made by Harry Tschopik (1947). More recent ethnographies on the valley have been furnished by Richard Adams in his seminal community report on the area of Muquiyauyo, first reported by Tschopik (Adams 1959). Another large ethnography of a district in the valley was written by Gabriel Escobar on Sicaya (1974). The district of Acolla has also been subject of a large ethnography in an unpublished doctoral dissertation by William B. Hutchinson (1973). Huasicancha has also been studied by Gavin Smith with emphasis on "how peasants make a living and how they engage in political resistance" (1989:1). In the early seventies Norman Long and Brian Roberts undertook an ambitious long-term research project on the Mantaro Valley and its modernization, which results have been exposed in two books with case studies (1978, 1984). Power relations in the valley from the nineteenth century to the present have been analyzed by Giorgio Alberti and Rodrigo Sanchez, focusing on the "traditional" elite groups of the valley (authorities and rich peasants) and the character of capitalist accumulation in the valley (1974). Larger and most documented study on the history of the Mantaro Valley with emphasis on the nature of capitalist accumulation and the mining industry has been written by historian Florencia E. Mallon (1983). Nelson Manrique has discussed in depth the effects of the war with Chile on the Mantaro Valley in the book *Campesinado y Nación: Las Guerrillas Indígenas en la Guerra con Chile* (Peasants and Nation: Indigenous Guerrilla in the War with Chile; Manrique 1981) and the development of the internal market in the valley (covering much the same ground as Mallon) in *Mercado Interno y Región: La Sierra Central 1820–1930* (Internal Market and Region; Manrique 1987). Also relevant to the Mantaro Valley are the studies by Heraclio Bonilla (1974) and Alberto Flores Galindo (1974) on the Cerro de Pasco Corporation (Bonilla 1974). Both studies stress labor relations and relations of exploitation in the mines. Most of these titles have largely ignored the cultural dynamics of the peasantry of the Mantaro Valley or have dealt with the subject briefly and as a subordinate topic. Arguedas has filled this

void in several of his publications on the Mantaro Valley (1953, 1957a, 1957b). Literature on festivals, rituals, and dances of the valley has been largely left to local scholars (see for example Orellana 1972a, 1972b, 1976; and Quijada Jara 1957). More recently Zoila Mendoza-Walker (1989), Romero (1990), and José Carlos Vilcapoma (1995) have undertaken the study of music and dance-drama.

4. In "El Estado Actual de la Industria Minera de Morococha," *Boletín del Cuerpo de Ingenieros de Minas* 25:25 65, (Bonilla 1974:34).

5. Few, if any, personal testimonies or references to particular destructive effects in the lives and existences of the valley's peasantry can be found in the literature. The only one who provides ethnographic evidence is Bonilla (song texts), although he omitted his sources. The reader is informed that the songs are from the 1930s, but no other reference is available (see Bonilla 1974: 28–32). Since Bonilla dedicates his book to his father ("whose life in the mines was my major source of learning") it is legitimate to speculate that the songs were remembered by him.

6. The terms *Wanka culture, Wanka folklore*, and *Wanka identity* are widely used in the Mantaro Valley in everyday life. It is in this sense that I will use these expressions, unless otherwise indicated.

7. For a discussion on how this struggle provokes a sense of nostalgia for the loss of the past and generates an anxiety to seek continuity with "tradition" see Marilyn Ivy's *Discourses of the Vanishing: Modernity, Phantasm, Japan* (1995) and Partha Chaterjee's *The Nation and Its Fragments* (1993), where he discusses how Indian nationalism attempts to fashion a modern national culture different from Western models. For Latin America, see Roberto DaMatta and David Hess's *The Brazilian Puzzle: Culture on the Borderlands of the Western World*, which presents a set of cases that suggest how a nation like Brazil can be neither "traditional" nor "modern" but both at the same time (1995). García Canclini himself explores similar territory for the case of Mexico and Latin America in general in *Hybrid Cultures: Strategies for Entering and Leaving Modernity*, (1993), as William Rowe and Vivian Schelling do in *Memory and Modernity: Popular Culture in Latin America* (1991). In *Exits from the Labyrinth: Culture and Ideology in the Mexican National Space* (1992), Claudio Lomnitz-Adler addresses the question of how regional cultures may preserve their own spaces and ideologies within a modern nation-state.

8. Jean Comaroff has also emphasized the habitual "apolitical," "implicit," and "unselfconscious" character of resistance in a variety of cases (1985:261). These and other recent views on resistance conform to what Abu-Lughod has described as "a concern with unlikely forms of resistance, subversions rather than large-scale collective insurrections, small or local resistances not tied to overthrown of systems or even to ideologies of emancipation. Scholars seem to be trying to rescue for the record and to restore to our respect such previously devalued or neglected forms of resistance" (1990:41).

9. Such a view of the mestizo of the Mantaro Valley is opposed to views such as that of the renowned "indigenista" intellectual Luis E. Valcárcel, who wrote that "mestizaje of cultures only produces deformations. From the womb

of America a new hybrid being is born. It does not inherit the virtues of its predecessors, but its vices and depravities" (1927:108).

10. *Mestizaje*, in this sense, should not be confused by the official discourse by certain nation-states in which it stands for a constrained cultural homogenization in which the "Indian" is largely ignored, assimilated, or, in the worst cases, even exterminated (Mallon 1996:171).

11. The discussion over the nature and prospects of interethnic conflicts in Andean Peru has been very productive but is still an ongoing debate. Many of the still influential studies on Indian–mestizo relationships in Peru appeared in the 1970s (see Fuenzalida 1970; Mayer 1970; van den Bergue 1974; Bourricaud 1975; Cotler 1968, 1995; Flores Ochoa 1974; and Ossio 1978). Most of these studies, however, were primarily dedicated to the search for definitions of ethnic terms rather than examining the prospects for ethno-genesis in a changing nation. In this sense I am particularly influenced by the positive outlook for mestizaje as a cultural project by Arguedas (1957b), John Murra (1984), and Marisol de la Cadena (1990) and the ethnographic evidence in this respect for the Mantaro Valley provided by Adams (1959) and corroborated more recently by Mallon (1983:11).

12. In addition to Fernando Fuenzalida's (1970) and Enrique Mayer's (1970) surveys of ethnic theories as applied to Andean studies, see also Pierre van den Bergue's "The Use of Ethnic Terms in the Peruvian Social Science Literature" (1974). For an interesting exposition on how ethnic analysis has changed through time see Degregori 1995.

13. See for example Jean and John Comaroff's "Of Totemism and Ethnicity" (1992), Aria María Alonso's "The Politics of Space, Time, and Substance: State Formation, Nationalism, and Ethnicity" (1994), and Appadurai's "Life after Primordialism" (1996b). For a reliable discussion of theories of ethnicity within ethnomusicology see Schramm (1979) and Stokes (1994).

14. In regard to the war with Chile, as it developed in the Mantaro Valley, and the role of the peasantry within it, there is a current debate among Florencia E. Mallon, Nelson Manrique, and Heraclio Bonilla (see Mallon 1995; Manrique 1981; and Bonilla 1978, 1987). While Mallon sustains that the participation of the peasantry suggests the presence of a "national" project, Bonilla dismisses such participation on the grounds that Peru lost the war because of the lack of a national consciousness of its constituents. Manrique, while agreeing with Mallon somewhat, assumes a more intermediary position, asserting that while the peasantry did take part in the "national" war their demands continued to be centered on local and regional issues. In synthesizing these debates Steve Stern says that Manrique and Mallon "argue that under some circumstances, Andean peasants proved quite willing to join a multiethnic and multi-class nationalist coalition, and actually forged an authentic, yet distinctive form of peasant nationalism" (1987:215).

*Chapter 2*

1. In referring to the herranza as ritual I am following the classic definition of ritual as "prescribed formal behavior for occasions not given over to
technological routine, having reference to beliefs in mystical beings or powers"
(Turner 1967:19).

2. The *herranza* ritual, as it is performed in the southern Andes, has been
thoroughly described by Fuenzalida (1980) for Huancavelica and Isbell (1978)
and Quispe (1969) for different communities in Ayacucho. Arguedas (1953) has
reproduced brief testimonies of the herranza in the Mantaro Valley as described
by schoolteachers. The structures of the ritual at all of the sites investigated
by these authors exhibit a remarkable similarity, and the herranzas that I have
observed in the Mantaro Valley follow similar patterns as well.

3. Because rather than being located on the edges of the Mantaro River,
they rise on its tributaries, in areas of higher altitude, relatively "distant" from
the central highway and railroad.

4. For information about the use of the *mesa* as an Andean tradition see
Schechter 1982:793–819.

5. Anthologies of herranza lyrics have been published by Arguedas (1953)
and Sergio Quijada Jara (1957).

6. The songs transcribed in this section were sung by the elders Alberto
Mayta Barzola, Felipa Mayta Puynes, and María Contreras Maldonado. I recorded these examples in July 1985 in the district of Huanchar.

7. The difference between an indigenous and a mestizo *huayno* is one of
musical and social style rather than form and structure. For example, Arguedas,
writing in 1938, stressed the fundamental importance of the Quechua texts in
the indigenous case, which in the mestizo huayno became diluted as Spanish
words were, in time, incorporated into the text, eventually leading to a completely Spanish version of the song. Arguedas in trying to define the character
of both types of *huaynos* wrote: "The indigenous huayno is epic and simple,
and the mestizo makes the same huayno more melodic and smooth." (See Arguedas 1989:14).

8. As performed by Leoncio Miranda from the town of Huanchar on January 21, 1985.

9. Formal communal assemblies (*asambleas comunales*) to discuss politics
and administrative affairs, as well as communal faenas to work in the fields or
to build public housing, are also areas of communal interaction. However, the
intensively ceremonial and dramatic attributes of the festival make it a more
efficient vehicle for social relations than the other intimate and closed gatherings. In many of the districts of the Mantaro Valley, participation in faenas
and asambleas comunales has tended to decrease, unlike participation in the
festival.

10. Music is also present in the Mass and the procession, but it consists
primarily of instrumental Catholic hymns. In these cases the music has no
relation to the dances of the festival. On other occasions the procession is

accompanied by the dance groups and their musical ensembles. They perform as a tribute to the Virgin.

11. The recognition that the religious aspect of fiestas occupied a different space from that of other nonreligious facets is reflected in a 1902 provision of the district council of Muquiyauyo that declared that only religious events could be paid for with the income produced by cofradía lands and not the "ancient customs" of the community, which were also enacted in the fiesta (Adams 1959:59).

12. *Cargo* is a Spanish word adopted in the Andes to designate community or ritual offices and responsibilities. The holder of a cargo assumes the obligation to sponsor all or part of the festival events.

13. This description is based on data collected from *asociaciones* such as the Sociedad Cultural Santa Cruz de Mayo (founded in 1890), Centro Social Acolla (founded in 1925), and Institucion Folklorica Pacarina Acolla (founded in 1921), all located in Acolla.

14. There are very few systematic studies on the dances of the Mantaro Valley. Among these few are Simeon Orellana's articles about the *huaconada*, the *pachahuara*, and the character of the *huatrilas* (1972a, 1972b, 1976), Michael F. Brown's short piece on the *chonguinada* (1976), Jose Carlos Vilcapoma's recent book on the huaylas (1995), and Mendoza-Walker's article on the *avelinos* (1989).

15. It is believed by many people in the valley that the choreography of the chonguinada originates from a local indigenous version of the European minuet that was danced among the Spanish colonizers in the area. The formation in columns and the coordinated movements among the couples seem to suggest such a process. Other stories relate the name of the dance to the district of Chongos, which had a strong Spanish presence in colonial times, an account that seem to complement the former.

16. The term *huaylas* is a Spanish derivation of *waylarsh* (Quechua). Following Arguedas (1953), I will use the former as the name of a festival dance and the latter in reference to the previously explained nocturnal threshing of grain (chapter 2).

17. The first National Congress of Huaylas was organized by the municipality of Huancayo in April 1995 and a First Workshop on the Historical Process and Authenticity of the Wanka Huaylas was convoked by the Municipal Library the year after.

18. I base my synthesis on my own interviews and on the testimonies reproduced by José Carlos Vilcapoma in *Waylarsh: Amor y Violencia de Carnaval* (1995).

19. Agripina Castro de Aguilar, interview in Lima, August 1985.

20. Lomnitz-Adler, in recalling Roland Barthes's concept of "mythification," defines it as "a social class's appropriation, recontextualization, refunctionalization, and resignification of a sign or of statements" (Lomnitz-Adler 1992:29). There is a substantial difference, however, between the mestizo appropriation of Indianness in Mexico with that of the Mantaro Valley, since

in the former mestizos "mythify," "share," or plainly "steal" peasant symbols in order to reaffirm their dominating role, while in the Mantaro Valley mestizos mythify their own rural past to reaffirm their own contemporary identity.

*Chapter 3*

1. For a careful account of the historical background of the European harp in Andean countries and Latin America in general see Schechter 1992. For a detailed study of the harp tradition in Peru see Olsen 1986–1987.

2. Conversely, the guitar was forbidden to the Indians, as the Spanish clergy considered it a sensual instrument. The guitar became an instrument of "mestizos" who in turn became proficient constructors of and performers on the instrument (Arguedas 1976:239). Those interested in a more comprehensive treatment of the history and ethnography of musical genres and instruments of the Andes can see Romero 1988, 1993, 1998, and 1999b and Turino 1998.

3. These types of ensembles perform on rare occasions around the valley, and impoverished peasants from the upper valley usually play in them. They accompany dance-dramas like the auquines, the corcovados, and the chacra-negros and constitute the last vestiges of the colonial type of musical ensemble that dominated the valley until the nineteenth century. Harp and violin ensembles are locally considered more traditional than the orquestas típicas, but they do not play a role in the local narratives and discussions of authenticity.

4. Instruments like the charango, the guitar, and the mandolin continued to be immensely popular in other regions of the Andes. The current geographical dispersion of the guitar and the mandolin covers most of the northern and southern Andean regions in Peru, but they are absent from the Mantaro Valley, in the central Andes (see the musical atlas *Mapa de los Instrumentos de Uso Popular en el Perú* [Instituto Nacional de Cultura 1978]). Similarly, the dispersion of the charango covers the entire southern Andes but stops just south of the border of the Mantaro Valley.

5. The charango and guitar are also sold in stores and played privately by many, but they are no longer performed in musical groups or at public occasions. I should remind the reader that the city of Huancayo is a flourishing urban center and maintains an active and cosmopolitan musical life. Urban dwellers have access to a variety of international musical styles, which are disseminated through the radio, television, and commercial recording, including various popular music styles, rock and roll, Latin-Caribbean rhythms, and Latin American *nueva canción*. Thus, when I refer to processes of displacement of musical instruments, I primarily allude to massive popular musical practices. In the Mantaro Valley popular music corresponds to regional mestizo musical traditions that are primarily performed outside the city of Huancayo.

6. Valenzuela presents a photograph from the beginning of the century that shows Pachacho with his clarinet as a member of a group that consists of three violins and a harp (1984:35). Among other legendary musicians who are also frequently cited as the pioneers or innovators of clarinet performance in the valley is Ascanio Robles, who performed with his orchestra, Orfeón de

Huancayo (Valenzuela 1984:66). Since most of the musicians who witnessed these events—and, furthermore, were actually their main protagonists—were active until recent times and even made commercial records in the 1950s, their names are well known in the valley and are constantly remembered when people attempt to reconstruct the history of the orquesta típica in the valley.

7. I will document this controversy later in this chapter, in analyzing the case of the district of Huaripampa.

8. Ascanio Robles, interview given to Rubén Valenzuela in Lima, November 18, 1976 (see Valenzuela 1984:42).

9. Based on an interview given by Teodoro Rojas Chucas in the district of Acolla, March 15, 1976 (see Valenzuela 1984:43).

10. Zenobio Dagha, interview in the district of Chupuro, September 10, 1996.

11. Dario Curisinchi, interview in the district of Acolla, September 10, 1996.

12. Rubén Valenzuela, personal communication, Lima, August 10, 1996.

13. Compare this concept to Aymara's musical ideal of "playing as one," which Thomas Turino interprets as an indication of the desire for a "dense sound quality." "Playing like one instrument" implies that the performer should not "escape from the dense, integrated fabric of the ensemble performance" (Turino 1993:55). In spite of the affinity of musical metaphors used in both cases, there is a substantial difference. Both ensembles use different techniques and instrumental configurations. Panpipe groups play single instruments in pairs, and the main challenge is to achieve fluidity while rendering a melodic line between two interdependent performers. Conversely, the orquesta típica combines different types of instruments and their members execute the same tune independently of one another, sometimes in a highly heterophonic texture.

14. A more elaborate analysis of sound and aesthetics of the saxophone in the Mantaro Valley is available in Romero 1999a.

15. Juan Santos, from Orcotuna, interview in Lima, August 1996.

16. The reader may listen to excerpts of the tunantada and the chonguinada accompanied by an orquesta típica on the record *Traditional Music of Peru 2: The Mantaro Valley* (Smithsonian Folkways, CD SF 40467).

17. This perception is so widely accepted that the radio stations in Lima that present Andean folklore widely use the term *tunantero*, taken from the *tunantada*, in referring to any melancholy song in a slow tempo.

18. Not to be confused with the name of the musical genre. The musical genre of the huayno is generally comprised of three sections as well (A + B + *fuga*). In this case, the local custom prescribes that each of these musical sections should be called a huaynos.

19. The importance of music as a professional alternative in the Mantaro Valley and its significance as a source of supplementary salary have even been highlighted in the following: Mallon 1983 (145), Hutchinson 1973 (157–173), and Sánchez 1987 (90).

20. Similar patterns of social behavior have been reported for the case of

Aymara panpipe ensembles. In Conima, where the composition of new tunes also takes place during rehearsals, "implicit consensus" is achieved through the subtle and passive rejection of the ideas that are not considered adequate (see Turino 1993:77). In Conima, however, the group of musicians themselves decides on acceptance or dismissal of the proposed new tunes, while in the Mantaro Valley there is a coordination between musicians and the hiring committee.

21. Rubén Valenzuela, interview in Lima, August 10, 1996.

22. Mencio Sovero, interview in Lima, June 12, 1995.

23. Anonymous, interview in Lima, July 1996.

24. Interview in Huancayo, September 12, 1996.

25. Interview in Huancayo, September 2, 1996.

26. Zenobio Dagha, interview in Chupuro, September 10, 1996.

27. Along the same lines, the town of Acolla in the valley is known as *pueblo de músicos* (town of musicians), coastal Trujillo as *la capital de la marinera* (the capital of La Marinera), and Puno as *la capital folklórica del Perú* (the Peruvian capital of folklore).

28. The notion of lo antiguo also concerns the choreography of the dance. In Huaripampa it is considered "authentic" to dance with the head up, with arrogance, and holding the cane upward.

29. Máximo Salazar, interview in Huaripampa, September 13, 1996.

30. The absence of women from the tunantada in the town of Huaripampa does not reflect a general trend. Women do perform with men in many other dance-dramas, as in the widely popular chonguinada.

31. Máximo Salazar, interview in Huaripampa, September 13, 1996.

32. The consequences of the railroad for the regional economy of the Cuzco region in southern Peru have also been addressed by José Luis Rénique in *Los Sueños de la Sierra: Cuzco en el Siglo XX* (1991: 43).

## Chapter 4

1. This chronology coincides with Teófilo Altamirano's assertion that until the 1940s migration from the Mantaro Valley to Lima was limited to elite groups. From that date onward, it became a generalized practice (1984b).

2. The celebrated popular Festival of the Pampa de Amancaes, coincidental with the Festival of Saint John (June 24), in Rimac, an area of downtown Lima, was the first significant occasion for Andean music in Lima. In 1927 migrant Andean musicians participated for the first time in the festival. By 1928 Amancaes had become a national musical contest of "Inca style, Andean, and criollo" music (Vivanco 1973:34). The festival became an almost official event with the presence of President Leguía, who witnessed the final phase of the contest with almost 50,000 people gathered around the event (Vivanco 1973:36). From 1935 to 1945 the fiesta of Amancaes became larger and larger, but its importance began to decrease when alternative forums emerged, like *coliseos* and radio programs. However, Amancaes was still active, with numerous awards being offered each year. In 1963 Amancaes ceased to exist due to

the withdrawal of state sponsorship (Vivanco 1973:39; see also Nuñez and Lloréns 1981:56 and Turino 1988:132).

3. Nuñez and Lloréns (1981), Lloréns (1983), and Turino (1988) have included in this initial phase of Andean music as "Incaic" the work of Peruvian academic composers of the nationalist period (1900–1940) who used Andean musical materials for their art music compositions. I contend, however, that though Peruvian academic music is a related phenomenon, it is misleading to blend the works and performances of these composers, who primarily came from provincial intellectual elites, and molded their art mainly around avantgarde musical currents of the era (post-Romanticism, French impressionism, and polytonality), with those of Andean Indian and mestizo performers of regional musical traditions. For more on nationalism and art music academic composers in Peru and Latin America see Béhague (1979).

4. The word *serrucho* (literally handsaw) in the quoted passage was a derogatory term used frequently by Limeños to insult persons of Andean origins.

5. The singer is Agripina Castro de Aguilar (1921–1996), who later became a successful soloist at coliseos and participated in the first recordings of Andean music, collaborating in this endeavor with José María Arguedas. Agripina Castro de Aguilar was born in the area of Huancayo, and after she became a well-known singer in Lima she became a renowned collector of Andean quotidian and ritual dresses, which she rented to dancers for a living. I am grateful to Lucy Nuñez for letting me use portions of this as yet unpublished interview she had with the singer in March 1989. The interview was conducted as part of a project of the Center for Andean Ethnomusicology of the Catholic University of Peru.

6. Turino, for example, when considering the effects of theater-stage presentations of "folklore" in Lima, asserts that "Andean arts are highly influenced by urban-Western aesthetics and criollo stereotypes regarding Andeans. Legitimacy indeed enhanced but on criollo terms and within their control" (1991:272). Nuñez and Lloréns suggest as well a similar viewpoint in defining the coliseo as "an imposition of the urban model upon the migrant" (1981:72).

7. Richard P. Schaedel speaks of a "new ideology to replace the shattered criollo image" (1979:410), Matos Mar of the "consolidation and development of the new pan-Peruvian culture" (1984:86), and Turino of the "construction of a new identity" (1993:178).

8. A taxi driver in the valley who turned to Wanka folklore after playing tropical music in his teens, the youngsters in distant rural districts who attend chicha dances the morning after they participate in the traditional festival, the Picaflor de los Andes singing Mexican *rancheras* in his youth, the violinist of an orquesta típica growing up watching Gary Cooper films: all are examples of the continuous exposure of Andean peoples to "different" musics and cultures, which does not necessarily turn into processes of "assimilation" or "homogenization," just as globalization processes have not precipitated these processes in other parts of the world, either (Appadurai 1990). In this sense, perceiving Andean peoples as "others" and exaggerating their differences from

Westerners, while hiding their "sameness" (Agawu 1995:393), have prompted fears of or desires for a surge of a "new" identity for all Andean migrants in the midst of the "cultural mosaic" of Lima.

9. The Folklore and Popular Arts Section was founded by a state resolution (Number 3479, October 30, 1945) with the following aims: (1) to conduct and coordinate research on folklore and popular arts in the country; (2) to collect material through the cooperation of competent representatives, especially teachers and students, in all the Republic; (3) to establish the corresponding archive, including photographic sections and documentary film; (4) to promote the creation of the Folklore Museum in the National Museum of History and of the Folk Music Archive in the National School of Music; (5) to elaborate educational materials; (6) to contribute to the development of popular arts; (7) to organize a library of folklore; (8) to encourage the publication of a journal of Peruvian folklore and others journals related to folklore; and (9) to sponsor events, representations, auditions, conferences, expositions, and other mediums to intensify and disseminate folklore and popular arts. This list of objectives has been reproduced in Quijada Jara 1961 (75).

10. Arguedas's individual efforts from a state-sponsored organization should not be likened, therefore, to other state-supported ventures that used folklore to foster specific political programs, however short-lived and unsuccessful, such as the Festival of Amancaes during the Leguía regime (1919–1930) and the Inkarri festivals during Velasco's revolutionary government (1969–1978).

11. Arguedas did, however, disseminate his ideas in several newspaper articles written since the 1940s. In the 1960s, however, he published more intensively and explicitly on the problem of "authenticity" and "deformation" of Andean folklore (see Arguedas 1976 and 1977).

12. This set of rules and regulations, referred to as Rules for Music and Dance Performers of National Folklore, was made official on February 27, 1964, by a *resolución suprema* (legal decree) of the Ministry of Education.

13. Interview with Lucy Nuñez in Lima, March 3, 1989.

14. Turino, for example, concludes that "Arguedas and those that followed him were still involved with the romantic 'folklorization' of Andean arts initiated within the indigenismo movement" and, furthermore, that in promoting theater-staged presentations Arguedas was "bowing to the greater prestige of urban-Western values and institutions by suggesting that such contexts are the final proving ground for performers and art forms" (Turino 1991: 272).

15. Interview with Agripina Castro de Aguilar in Lima, March 3, 1989 (courtesy Lucy Nuñez).

16. Recent studies on migration have attempted to overcome these shortcomings by emphasizing case studies rather than general theories and representing local and regional diversity rather than universal trends. It has been understood that different Andean regions relate in diverse ways to the nation's capital and, consequently, its migrants maintain different types of relationships with their original towns and regional associations, with distinct objectives

and activities and separate reciprocity networks (see Altamirano 1984). Jorge P. Osterling's study on Huayopampino migrants in Lima was an early forerunner in this new trend (1980), as were Altamirano's studies on Quechua-speaking groups from Ayacucho and the Mantaro Valley and on Aymara-speaking migrants from Puno (1984b, 1988). Carlos Degregori, Cecilia Blondet, and Nicolás Lynch have documented numerous migrant experiences in one squatter settlement in Lima (1986), and Golte and Adams have analyzed and presented group and individual cases from four different Andean regions in comparison (1987). Specific cultural practices of Andean migrants in Lima have been addressed by Nuñez in her book on scissor dancers from Ayacucho (1990), by Michelle Bigenho in her article about the Negrito and scissors dances also from Ayacucho (1993), and by Turino in his chapter on an Aymara regional association and its festive activities around panpipe music (1993).

17. Rural–urban migration has been not only one of the most studied topics in Peruvian social studies but also one in which generalizations have been applied to the entire Andean area, concealing many complexities and nuances that, for example, the Mantaro Valley seems to inculcate. In a recent bibliographical survey Héctor Martínez counted 678 publications that dealt with the matter (1980:17). Most of these studies have been published since the 1960s, as by that time migration as a social process had already altered in significant ways the previous rural–urban relationships in the nation. Before the 1960s, migration had also been seriously considered as a subordinate topic within statistical and geographical studies. In examining the literature Martínez has noted that it is impossible to distinguish a dominant trend, since a variety of theoretical frameworks have been used to study migration, from Robert Redfield's folk–urban continuum to the "theory of marginality" and from Oscar Lewis's "poverty of culture" concept to Ralph Linton's theories on social stress (Martínez 1980:24). Carlos E. Aramburú, in another evaluation of the literature of rural–urban migration in Peru, has categorized most of the theoretical studies as "dualist" perspectives that stressed "integration" or "adaptation" through migration between a group considered "traditional" (Indian) and another considered modern, representing the "national culture" (1981:4). For Aramburú, the difference between "dualist" migration studies and others that emphasize historical-structural perspectives (Marxist) is that the former consider migration without a critical evaluation of the social and economic systems to which subordinate migrant groups are supposed to adapt. Nevertheless, the studies that fall into this trend have been the most influential in Andean migration studies around the world, especially the widely cited works of Paul L. Doughty (1970, 1972) and William Mangin (1959, 1970, 1973).

18. Doughty's insistence on the determining role of voluntary associations as mechanisms of integration and adaptation has been criticized over time. In addition to Aramburu, whose criticism of the "neutrality" of Doughty's approach has already been mentioned, authors like Fred Jongkind (1974) have openly disagreed. In his research, Jongkind found that regional associations were elitist, driven more by prestige than by solidarity, that few of them maintained rural customs, but most followed a "Western" pattern, and that

the associations were so horizontally and vertically divided that they contributed little to the "integration" of Peruvian society (1974:481). Jongkind's conclusions, however, seem extreme, and his research suffers from an empiricist
approach. But other authors have also seen important limitations to Doughty's
view. Golte and Adams have called attention to other forms of association for
migrants outside the regional organization, such as festivals, kinship ties,
neighborhood leagues, and labor guilds (1987:67). Schaedel, while not directly
referring to Doughty's views, in calling attention to "disengagement spheres"
like the *barriadas* (shantytowns) as substitutes for previous urban contexts
that migrants were supposed to adapt to has suggested that "national society"
should not be taken for granted as Doughty does (Schaedel 1979:405). In fact,
in the barriada other mechanisms beyond the strict borders of the formal regional clubs were at play, especially those mechanisms enclosed in what Larissa
Adler Lomnitz has called the "network of reciprocal exchange" (Lomnitz 1977:
3). Studies on barriadas and *tugurios* (run-down urban homes) in Lima have
further documented how these networks perform for the Andean migrant (see
the forerunner studies of Matos Mar 1961 and 1977 and the more recent ones
in Lobo 1982; Millones 1978; Golte and Adams 1987; and Degregori, Blondet,
and Lynch 1986).

19. See, for example, Luis E. Valcárcel's classic portrait of the Andean
mestizo as a tragic and lonely individual, which dominated much of the social
thought in Peru before the 1960s (1925). However, this vision has its contem-
poraneous counterpart in more recent anthropological literature from the 1970s
onward, which continues to define ethnic groups in Peru as separate entities
in which mestizo, Indian, and white ethnic groups appear segregated in history, with no interconnections among them. For an explanation of the distinctive qualities of the Wanka mestizo see Arguedas 1953:121–123.

20. Altamirano, a Peruvian anthropologist, affirms that "Mantaro Valley
people in Lima are proud of the 'progressive' reputation of their region and
see themselves as a cut above other highlands migrants" (1984b:212).

21. Edwin Montoya, recording artist of Andean music, interview in Lima,
June 19, 1996.

22. There were nearly 100 regional associations of the Mantaro Valley in
Lima in the mid-1980s at the level of the department, the province, and the
district. The organization of these associations is highly complex, since there
may be several organizations of one district that claim local representation.
There are also higher level federations in Lima that embrace many of these
associations as affiliates, such as the Federación Departamental de Junín, the
Asociación Inter-distrital de la Provincia de Huancayo, and the Central de
Entidades Regionales del Departamento de Junín. The existence of these federations at the regional level of the Mantaro Valley determines a high degree
of interaction among members of lower level associations (see Altamirano
1984b:201).

23. There are other locales around the city as well, since any entrepreneur
is entitled to organize a public event and imagine new spaces for Wanka folk-

lore. Folklore *salones* (saloons) are also used for these types of "urban festivals," usually located in downtown Lima (as of 1996) and in industrial zones.

24. The ticket cost the equivalent of U.S. $2.00 when I attended the Hatunhuasi in June 1996.

25. Anonymous informant from the Mantaro Valley, interview in Lima, June 12, 1996.

26. This is later than in other parts of the Third World, where the record industry developed a market for traditional local musics as early as the first decade of the twentieth century. See Pekka Gronow's report on the development of the record industry in the "Orient" (1981) and Ali Jihad Racy's on Egypt (1976). For a broader picture of the development of recording technologies see Shelemay (1991).

27. From an interview with Lucy Nuñez held in Lima on March 3, 1989. Years later, while residing in Santiago de Chile, Arguedas recalled details of this affair in a letter from December 1, 1968, that he wrote to Agripina Castro de Aguilar, in which he said to her: "I enjoy myself greatly when I remember that I was, perhaps, the first person to appreciate your talent and understand that you would do a lot for the folkloric music and dances. Do you remember how much we fought from the Section of Folklore when it was in Puno Street? Then we convinced Mr. Vich to press the first Wanka record" (unpublished letter, courtesy of Lucy Nuñez).

28. This according to an interview that Lucy Nuñez had on January 17, 1989, with Juan de la Cruz Fierro, a musician elder from the valley who witnessed many of these events.

29. The 78 RPM format continued to dominate the market for most of the decade of the 1950s until the advent of the 33 RPM LP format, which in the early 1960s became the standard form. The 45 RPM format was also very popular, especially among the less affluent people, because it was much cheaper than the LP and also because it featured only the most popular tunes.

30. There are no official figures on the sales of record companies in Peru. These estimates have been obtained through informal conversations with Ezequiel Soto, an executive in charge of sales at IEMPSA, in Lima, on multiple occasions during 1986.

31. On the phenomenon of Andean recording stars and migrant music in Lima see the several short newspaper articles by Arguedas published from the 1940s through the 1960s, which contain not only descriptions but musical criticism as well (reprinted in Arguedas 1976, 1977, and 1985). For a raw display of data, detailed listing, and directory of musicians and locales, radio stations, and record production, see the bachelor's thesis of Alejandro Vivanco, a folklore musician in his own right who graduated from San Marcos University relatively late in his life (1973). A general survey of migrant music in Lima has been provided by Nuñez and Lloréns (1981) and Turino (1988).

32. See recordings of the huaconada on a Victor record, 30099-B (Camden, New Jersey), the huaylijia on a Smith record, 7634-A (Peru), the pachahuara on an Odeon record, 1723 (Peru), the toril on Odeon P-1021-A (Peru), and the

chonguinada on Odeon P-1016-A (Peru). I was able to locate these examples in the 78 RPM record collection of Hugo Orellana from Ataura, Jauja.

33. Arguedas left aside the LP recordings from his inventory because to him "the LP is the aristocratic disc of folklore music. It is directed to the affluent serrano, to the instructed and sensitive follower and the tourist. The laborer serrano, factory worker or domestic servant, does not buy them. A 45 rpm disc costs $25 soles, an LP $150" (1969:21).

34. Actually, the perception of nonstandard Spanish emerges from the noncorrespondence between the syllabic sung accent and the musical and rhythmic accent of the piece. As a result, Spanish words appear accented in the "wrong" places, which is an effect perceived by most non-Andean Limeños as a sign of "bad" Spanish, of definite rural origins.

35. These observations reflect only general impressions and general trends, since there are no strict rules for the correspondence between lyrics and the character of musical genres. For an extensive collection and analysis of lyrics of Andean song genres see Rodrigo Montoya's *La Sangre de los Cerros* (1987b).

## Chapter 5

1. In his declaration from August 27, 1821, San Martín asserted: "From now on the natives will not be denominated *Indians* or *natives*: they are sons and citizens of Peru, and by the name of Peruvians they shall be called" (Bustamante Cisneros 1918:39).

2. From Bolívar's decree of April 8, 1824. Bolívar's decrees of April 8, 1824, and July 4, 1825, as well as other related official documents, are reproduced in Bustamante 1918. They have also been reproduced in Philip A. Means 1920.

3. Indigenous communities in Peru are associations of peasants who reside in a rural hamlet or village and retain legal or moral rights to their land and a certain degree of political autonomy in their local affairs.

4. The literature on Peruvian indigenismo is extensive. An overview can be found in Davies (1974), Alfageme et al. (1978), Tord (1978), Tamayo (1980), and Krystal (1987).

5. For an analysis of Leguía's government see Cotler 1978, chapters 3–5.

6. For a more detailed commentary on the Indian legislation in the 1933 constitutional chart see Dobyns 1969.

7. Today there are 4,842 indigenous communities officially registered, of which the government has officially recognized 4,140 as such. Most of these comunidades are in the Andes, nearly 97.32 percent. See *Atlas del Peru* (Lima: Instituto Geográfico Militar, 1989), p. 210.

8. See Tudela y Varela's book *Socialismo Peruano* (cited in Bustamante Cisneros 1918:85).

9. Cited in Bustamante Cisneros 1918:86.

10. See Villarán's *Condición Legal de las Comunidades Indígenas*, published in 1907 (cited in Bustamante Cisneros 1918:86).

11. This survey included previously written works as well as interviews specifically done for Bustamante Cisneros's Bachelor thesis (see Bustamante Cisneros's chapter "Disolución o Conservación de las Comunidades").

12. In Mariátegui's own words: "I consider that our agrarian problem has a special character due to an indisputable and concrete factor: the survival of the Indian 'community' and of elements of practical socialism in indigenous agriculture and life" (1971:33).

13. In postrevolutionary Mexico, according to Alan Knight, "the new regime, raising the standard of the 1917 constitution and consolidating itself through the 1920's, incorporated indigenismo into its official ideology. It claimed, in other words, to seek the emancipation and integration of Mexico's exploited Indian groups: emancipation from the old oppression of landlord, cacique, and cura (priest)" (1990:80).

14. Despite the efforts of the Leguía regime to establish a "space" for the Indian within the modern nation-state of Peru (such as the founding of the Indian Affairs Section, the patronage of the Indian race, and the establishment of the Day of the Indian; see Cotler 1978:185–226), his national project of Patria Nueva (New Nation) succumbed after a few years and never achieved its initial objectives.

15. However, I differ from the notion that the 1968 military revolution attempted to construct a mestizo hegemony, as Mallon affirms (1992:47). With the sole exception of the agrarian reform, which was more of an economic measure than one predestined to revive Indian identities, the uses of Indian symbols were inconsistent; nor was there an organic project to build a nation based on Indian/Andean values. The symbols that Mallon mentions (for example, making Quechua official and the Inkarri folklore festivals) were barely significant in the complex scenery of the military revolution. They never received consistent support and failed to fulfill their original promises. I would clarify, however, that when I say "frustrated attempt" I am thinking mostly in terms of the development of national and regional Andean cultural identities. Turino, nevertheless, affirms that for certain migrant communities, as in the case of Conima, which he studies, the Velasco government and its "nationalist" policies inspired them to assume openly their local and musical identities in the nation's capital (see Turino 1993:140–144).

16. Basadre 1968:123, vol. II. Creole society and creole culture arise as an obscure notion based on colonial history but constructed in contemporary times to allude broadly to a social sector that is perceived as dominant and as claiming an alliance to a Hispanic origin but is far from homogenous and solid, as has been assumed in the literature. Ozzie G. Simmons has accurately highlighted its ambiguous quality, stating that by definition "criollismo is capable of appropriating any element of foreign origin and 'reworking' it in a criollo mold, just as any foreigner who acculturates enough to display evident orientations to criollo symbols and to participate meaningfully in criollo patterns is hailed as becoming 'creolized' " (1955:109). The concept of lo criollo is, then, highly dynamic and much more complex than is suggested by the simple definition of criollo: "an urban type of behavior that is expressed through fast

talking, alertness, and 'cute' or deceitful acts through which one escapes obligations" (Doughty 1972:39). If, in fact, this definition corresponds to one of the principal meanings of the criollo concept in Peru, its portrayal as a univocal and universal notion within Peruvian society is deceitful in itself. Simmons has adequately recalled that criollismo takes on different meanings according to which social class claims its parentage. According to Simmons, Peruvian higher classes do not necessarily identify themselves with the criollismo of the lower and emergent classes and only occasionally claim some aspects of it in relation to their own interests in time and place (1955:113–114). The assimilation to or the dominance of a criollo culture is, then, more of an imagined process than an actual mechanism and definitely a limitation in studies of migration as "assimilation" and "integration." (See also Tschopik 1948.)

17. Various dances that are very popular in the valley celebrate aspects of the national wars. For example, the dance of the avelinos connects to the war between Peru and Chile, but it actually represents the local peasants who fought guerrilla-style combat at the regional level (see Mendoza-Walker 1989).

18. Similar processes have been observed elsewhere. For example, Michel De Certeau, as cited by García Canclini, had observed while living in California that among emigrants from other countries "roles are taken and changed with the same versatility as cars and houses" and that life "consists in constantly crossing borders" (1996:232). García Canclini cited De Certau in the context of his own argument on "deterritorializing," in which there is a "loss of the 'natural' relation of culture to geographical and social territories" (García Canclini 1995:229).

19. In this case I use a pseudonym.

20. For a critical review of the development of mass media in Latin America see Rowe and Schelling 1991.

21. Due to the controversial attributes of their testimonies, I prefer to maintain the anonymity of my informants and the district where they reside, since it would easy to guess their identity if I named the district. Their testimonies were obtained during interviews given in the Mantaro Valley and in Lima during the years 1995 and 1996.

22. My observations in Paccha were obtained during 1985, jointly with the late Peruvian anthropologist Mary Fukomoto. Today chicha music is still very popular in Paccha and it is frequently performed during patronal festivals at private venues where only young single men and women assist. For more material on this topic see Romero 1989.

23. I have elaborated elsewhere on the role of the mass media and its impact on traditional culture and music (see Romero 1992).

# Glossary

*Asociación*  An association or committee that is in charge of organizing a public festival.

*Barriada*  squatter settlement located on the borders of the city of Lima.

*Cabildos*  Colonial term for local governments or municipalities.

*Cacho*  Spanish name of the musical instrument *wakrapuku*, a spiral-shaped cattle horn trumpet.

*Cacique*  An Indian or mestizo who was a local authority that represented the colonial administration.

*Cargo*  A Spanish word adopted in the Andes to designate community or ritual offices and responsibilities. In the festival system the holder of a cargo assumes the obligation to sponsor all or part of the festival events. A cargo may be designated by diverse names such as mayordomo, prioste, and alférez.

*Chicha*  A novel urban musical style that is a blend between the Colombian cumbia and the Andean huayno.

*Cholo*  An ethnic term applied to the rural Indian peasant who moves into the cities and adopts urban habits and values.

*Chonguinada*  One of the most popular dances in the Mantaro Valley.

*Chuto*  A pejorative name for the rural Indian. Also used in dance-dramas in reference to an Indian character.

*Cofradía*  A religious brotherhood introduced during the colonial period. The cofradía was responsible for the organization of festivals until its disappearance.

*Coliseo*  An open theater where Andean musical ensembles and vocalists performed on Sundays and holidays in Lima. Coliseos were very popular from 1940 to 1970.

*Compañías folklóricas*  Folk companies that performed in movie theaters around Lima and, since the 1940s, in coliseos.

*Comunidad indígena*  An Indian community. It had legal status and the right to own land. Liberal politicians periodically have attempted to dismantle the lands of the Indian community in the name of progress and private property.

*Concurso*   A contest of traditional music or dance. Concursos are widely popular throughout urban and rural Peru and are formal competitions with
strict rules and an uncompromising jury.

*Conjunto*   The name by which large ensembles that consisted of harp, violins,
quenas, guitars, and *mandolinas* were called in the Mantaro Valley around
the beginnings of the century (English: *group*).

*Criollo*   During the colonial period the European born in the New World.
During the Republic and at the beginning of the twentieth century the
term was applied to the Hispanic-derived cultural manifestations. By ex-
tension, it was also applied to the "white" national elites.

*Encomienda*   A colonial system by which land was allotted to Spanish administrators for their personal use.

*Faena*   In the Andes, communal work. All the members of an Indian community participate in such events.

*Gamonal*   The name given to an abusive landlord in the Andes. They were
accused of exploiting the Indian labor force and manipulating the law for
their benefit.

*Haciendas*   Large landholdings that were the base for the power of Peruvian
ruling classes until the agrarian reform of 1968.

*Harawi*   An Indian monophonic genre of pre-Hispanic origins.

*Huaylas*   Musically derived from the huayno, one of the most popular dances
in the Mantaro Valley. It is a Spanish derivation of the Quechua *waylarsh*,
which is used here in reference to a private ritual.

*Huayno*   The most popular song genre in the Andes.

*Indigenismo*   A pro-Indian political, intellectual, and artistic movement whose
focal point occurred during the 1920s in Peru.

*Jija, La*   A dance in the Mantaro Valley that depicts agricultural work.

*Latifundismo*   The system by which private property in the Andes gave rise
to the large haciendas.

*Limeño*   Resident of Lima, the nation's capital.

*Mayordomo*   A cargo holder.

*Mestizo*   A racial term in colonial times, designating a half-breed of Spanish
and Indian heritage. In the twentieth century, the term *mestizo* (in the
case of an individual) or *mestizaje* (in the case of a cultural process) designates a cultural trend that blends rural Indian practices with modern
urban conventions.

*Misti*   Quechua name given to mestizos in certain areas of southern Peru.

*Muliza*   A slow, lyrical musical song genre popular in the central Peruvian
Andes.

*Octava*   A celebration that takes place one week after the central day of a
festival. It generally marks the conclusion of the festival.

*Orquesta típica*   A musical ensemble of saxophones, clarinets, a harp, and a
violin that the inhabitants of the Mantaro Valley claim to be the most
representative and traditional ensemble of the region.

*Pago*   An offering made to Andean deities.

*Pasacalle* A generic name given in the Andes to designate parts of the music or of the dance that take place while the performing group strolls through the streets of a town. It bears no relation to the pasacaglia.

*Peñas* Austere and popular restaurant-bars in the cities of Peru, generally attended by an urban audience and tourists. While the peñas became popular featuring Andean music reelaborated by urban middle-class ensembles, today the peñas are open to a variety of musical styles.

*Pincullo* An Andean vertical flute of different sizes.

*Prioste* A cargo holder.

*Quechua* The most widely spoken indigenous language in the Andean countries in South America.

*Quena* An end-notched flute of pre-Hispanic origins.

*Reducciones* Spanish word that designates the compulsory congregation of Indian populations into communities.

*Santiago* The name of a saint but also of a musical genre in the Mantaro Valley. *Santiago* is often used as a synonym for *herranza* but also as the designation of a song that has been de-contextualized from the santiago or herranza ritual.

*Serrano* A resident of the mountains of Peru. In urban contexts it was used as a pejorative term.

*Tinya* A small Andean drum of different sizes.

*Tonadas* Herranza musicians' term to refer to song or melodies of the ritual.

*Tunantada* One of the most popular dances in the Mantaro Valley.

*Wakrapuku* A spiral-shaped cattle horn trumpet used in the central Andes of Peru.

*Wamani* An Andean deity who is thought to inhabit the mountains.

*Wanka* The pre-Hispanic ethnic group that inhabited the Mantaro Valley. The contemporary residents of the valley have adopted this name to identify their regional culture.

*Waylarsh* A ritual in which young and unmarried men and women danced on a mound of grains. Some people in the Mantaro Valley continue to use this Quechua name for the festival dance huaylas.

*Zapateo* Shoe tapping. It is used to designate sections of a dance that use this feature.

# Bibliography

Abu-Lughod, Lila. 1986. *Veiled Sentiments: Honor and Poetry in a Bedouin Society*. Berkeley: University of California Press.

——. 1990. "The Romance of Resistance: Tracing Transformations of Power through Bedouin Women." *American Ethnologist* 17(1): 41–55.

——. 1991. "Writing against Culture." In *Recapturing Anthropology: Working in the Present*. Richard G. Fox, ed. Santa Fe: School of American Research Press.

Adams, Richard. 1959. *A Community in the Andes: Problems and Progress in Muquiyauyo*. Seattle: University of Washington Press.

Agawu, Kofi. 1995. "The Invention of African Rhythm." *Journal of American Musicological Society* 48(3): 380–395.

Alberti, Giorgio, and Rodrigo Sanchez. 1974. *Poder y Conflicto Social en el Valle del Mantaro*. Lima: Instituto de Estudios Peruanos.

Albó, Xavier. 1974. "Santa Vera Cruz Taitita." *Allpanchis* 7:163–215.

Augusta Alfageme, Carlos Iván Degregori, Marfil Francke, and Mariano Valderrama. 1978. *Indigenismo, Clases Sociales y Problema Nacional*. Lima: CELATS.

Alonso, Ana María. 1994. "The Politics of Space, Time, and Substance: State Formation, Nationalism, and Ethnicity." *Annual Review of Anthropology* 23:379–405.

Altamirano, Teófilo. 1984a. *Presencia Andina en Lima Metropolitana*. Lima: Pontificia Universidad Católica del Perú.

——. 1984b. "Regional Commitment among Central Highland Migrants in Lima." In *Miners, Peasants and Entrepreneurs: Regional Development in the Central Highland of Perú*. Norman Long and Brian Roberts, eds. Cambridge: Cambridge University Press.

——. 1988. *Cultura Andina y Pobreza Urbana: Aymaras en Lima Metropolitana*. Lima: Pontificia Universidad Católica del Perú.

Anderson, Benedict. 1991. *Imagined Communities: Reflections on the Origin and Spread of Nationalism*. London: Verso.

Appadurai, Arjun. 1981. "The Past as a Scarce Resource." *Man* 16(2): 201–219.

——. 1990. "Disjuncture and Difference in the Global Cultural Economy." *Public Culture* 2(2): 1–23.

————. 1996a. "Here and Now." In *Modernity at Large: Cultural Dimensions of Globalization.* Minneapolis: University of Minnesota Press.

————. 1996b. "Life after Primordialism." In *Modernity at Large: Cultural Dimensions of Globalization.* Minneapolis: University of Minnesota Press.

Aramburú, Carlos E. 1981. *Migraciones Internas; Perspectivas Teóricas y Metodológicas.* Lima: Instituto Andino de Estudios en Población y Desarollo.

Arguedas, José María. 1953. "Folklore del Valle del Mantaro." *Folklore Americano* I(I): 101–293.

————. 1957a. *Estudio Etnográfico de la Feria de Huancayo.* Lima: Oficina Nacional de Planeamiento y Urbanismo. Ms.

————. 1957b. "Evolución de la Comunidades Indígenas. El valle del Mantaro y la Ciudad de Huancayo." *Revista del Museo Nacional* 26:105–196.

————. 1969. "La Difusión de la Musica Folklórica Andina." *Ciencias Antropológicas* I (Seminario de Antropología, Instituto Riva-Aguero, Pontificia Universidad Católica del Perú): 17–33.

————. 1975. *Formación de una Cultura Nacional Indoamericana.* Mexicó City: Siglo XXI.

————. 1976. *Señores e Indios: Acerca de la Cultura Quechua.* Montevideo: Calicanto.

————. 1977. *Nuestra Música Popular y sus Intérpretes.* Lima: Mosca Azul y Horionte Editores.

————. 1985. *Indios, Mestizos y Señores.* Lima: Horizonte.

————. 1989. *Canto Kechua.* Lima: Horizonte [first edition in 1938].

Arriaga, Pablo Joseph de. 1920 [1621]. *La Extirpación de la Idolatría en el Perú.* Lima: Horacio Urtega Editores.

Asad, Talal, ed. 1973. *Anthropology and the Colonial Encounter.* London: Ithaca.

Averill, Gage. 1997. *A Day for the Hunter, a Day for the Prey: Popular Music and Power in Haiti.* Chicago: University of Chicago Press.

Barth, Fredrik. 1969. "Introduction." In *Ethnic Groups and Boundaries: The Social Organization of Cultural Difference.* Boston: Little, Brown.

Basadre, Jorge. 1968. *Historia de la República del Perú.* Lima: Editorial Universitaria.

Béhague, Gerard. 1979. *Music in Latin America: An Introduction.* Englewood Cliffs, NJ: Prentice-Hall.

Bennoune, Mafhoud. 1985. "What Does It Mean to Be a Third World Anthropologist?" *Dialectical Anthropologist* 9(1–4): 357–364.

Bigenho, Michelle. 1993. "El Baile de los Negitos y la Danza de las Tijeras: Un Manejo de Contradicciones." In *Música, Danzas y Máscaras en los Andes.* Rául R. Romero, ed. Lima: Pontificia Universidad Católica del Perú.

Blacking, John. 1977. "Some Problems of Theory and Method in the Study of Musical Change." *Yearbook of Traditional Music* 9:1–26.

Bonilla, Heraclio. 1974. *El Minero de los Andes.* Lima: Instituto de Estudios Peruanos.

————. 1978. "The War of the Pacific and the National and Colonial Problem in Perú." *Past and Present* 81:92–118.

————. 1987. "The Indian Peasantry and 'Perú' during the War with Chile." In *Resistance, Rebellion and Consciousness in the Andean Peasant World, 18th and 20th Centuries*. Steve J. Stern, ed. Madison: University of Wisconsin Press.

Bourricaud, François. 1971. "La Clase Dirigente Peruana: Oligarcas e Industriales." In *La Oligarquía en el Perú (Serie Perú Problema no. 2)*. Lima: Instituto de Estudios Peruanos.

————. 1975. "Indian, Mestizo and Cholo as Symbols in the Peruvian System of Stratification." In *Ethnicity: Theory and Experience*. Nathan Glazer and Daniel P. Moynihan, eds. Cambridge, MA: Harvard University Press.

Brown, Michael F. 1976. "Notas Sobre la Chonguinada de Junin." *América Indígena* 36(2):375–384.

Burga, Manuel. 1988. *Nacimiento de una Utopía: Muerte y Resurrección de los Incas*. Lima: Instituto de Apoyo Agrario.

Burga, Manuel, and Flores Galindo, Alberto. 1979. *Apogeo y Crisis de la República Aristocrática*. Lima: Ediciones Rikchay Peru.

Bustamante Cisneros, Ricardo. 1918. *Condición Jurídica de las Comunidades de Indígenas en el Perú*. Bachelor's thesis (San Marcos University, Faculty of Justice).

Cancian, Frank. 1965. *Economics and Prestige in a Maya Community: The Religious Cargo System of Zinacantán*. Stanford: Stanford University Press.

Cánepa-Koch, Gisela. 1992. "Una Propuesta Teórica para el Estudio de la Máscara Andina." *Anthropologica* 10:139–170.

————. 1993. "Máscara y Transformación: La construcción de la Identidad en la Fiesta de la Virgen del Carmen en Paucartambo." In *Música, Danzas y Máscaras en los Andes*. Raúl R. Romero, ed. Lima: Pontificia Universidad Católica del Perú.

————. 1998. *Máscara, Identidad y Transformación en los Andes*. Lima: Pontificia Universidad Católica del Perú.

Cavero, Jesús A. 1985. "El Qarawi y su Función Social." *Allpanchis* 25:233–270.

Celestino, Olinda, and Alfred Meyers. 1981. *Las Cofradías en el Perú: Región Central*. Frankfurt: Verlag Klaus Dieter Vervuert.

Chaterjee, Partha 1993. *The Nation and Its Fragments: Colonial and Post-Colonial Histories*. Princeton, NJ: Princeton University Press.

Chavez Molina, Juan. 1954. "La Comunidad Indígena, Estudio Económico, Social y Jurídico." *Perú Indígena* 5(13):33–46.

Clifford, James. 1986. "Introduction: Partial Thruths." In *Writing Culture: The Poetics and Politics of Ethnography*. Berkeley: University of California Press.

————. 1988. *The Predicament of Culture: Twentieth Century Ethnography, Literature and Art*. Cambridge, MA.: Harvard University Press.

Comaroff, Jean. 1985. *Body of Power, Spirit of Resistance: The Culture and History of a South African People*. Chicago: University of Chicago Press.

Comaroff, Jean, and John Comaroff. 1992. "Of Totemism and Ethnicity." In *Ethnography and the Historical Imagination*. Boulder: Westview.

————. 1993. "Introduction." In *Modernity and Its Malcontents: Ritual and Power in Post-Colonial Africa*. Chicago: University of Chicago Press.

Cotler, Julio. 1968. "La Mecánica de la Dominación Interna y del Cambio Social en el Perú." In *Perú Problema*. Lima: Moncloa Editores e Instituto de Estudios Peruanos. (Translated as "The Mechanics of Internal Domination and Social Change in Perú." *Studies in Comparative International Development* 3(12): 229–246, 1968.)

————. 1978. *Clases, Estado y Nación en el Perú*. Lima: Instituto de Estudios Peruanos.

DaMatta, Roberto, and David Hess. 1995. *The Brazilian Puzzle: Culture on the Borderlands of the Western World*. New York: Columbia University Press.

Davies, Thomas. 1974. *Indian Integration in Perú: A Half Century of Experience 1900–1984*. Lincoln: University of Nebraska Press.

Degregori, Carlos, Cecilia Blondet, and Nicolas Lynch. 1986. *Conquistadores de un Nuevo Mundo: De Invasores a Ciudadanos en San Martín de Porres*. Lima: Instituto de Estudios Peruanos.

————. 1995. "El Estudio del Otro: Cambios en los Análisis sobre Etnicidad en el Perú." In *Perú 1964–1994: Economía, Sociedad y Política*. Julio Cotler, ed. Lima: Instituto de Estudios Peruanos.

de la Cadena, Marisol. 1990. "De Utopías y Contrahegemonías: El Proceso de la Cultura Popular." *Revista Andina* 8 (1):65–75.

————. 1995. "Women Are More Indian: Ethnicity and Gender in a Community near Cuzco." In *Ethnicity, Markets and Migration in the Andes: At the Crossroads of History and Anthropology*. Brooke Larson and Olivia Harris, eds. Durham: Duke University Press.

————. 1996. "The Political Tensions of Representations and Misrepresentations: Intellectuals and Mestizas in Cuzco (1919–1990)." *Journal of Latin American Anthropology* 2(1):112–147.

Deustua, José and José Luis Rénique. 1984. *Intelectuales, Indigenismo y Descentralismo en el Perú, 1897–1931*. Cusco: Centro de Estudios Rurales Andinos Bartolome de las Casas.

Dobyns, Henry. 1969. *The Social Matrix of Peruvian Indigenous Communities*. Ithaca: Cornell-Perú Project Monograph, Department of Anthropology.

Dobyns, Henry E., and Paul L. Doughty. 1976. *Perú: A Cultural History*. New York: Oxford University Press.

Doughty, Paul L. 1970. "Behind the Back of the City: Provincial Life in Lima, Perú." In *Peasants in Cities*. William Mangin, ed. Boston: Houghton Mifflin.

————. 1972. "Peruvian Migrant Identity in the Urban Milieu." In *The Anthropology of Urban Environments*. Thomas Weaver and Douglas White, eds. Washington, DC: Society for Applied Anthropology (Monograph Series no. 11).

Eickelman, Dale. 1989. *The Middle East: An Anthropological Approach*. Englewood Cliffs, NJ: Prentice-Hall.

Erasmus, Charles J. 1978. "Culture Change in Northwest Mexico." In *Contem-*

*porary Change in Traditional Communities of México and Perú*. Charles Erasmus, Solomon Miller, and Louis Faron, eds. Urbana: University of Illinois Press.

Erlmann, Veit. 1991. *African Stars: Studies in Black African Performance*. Chicago: University of Chicago Press.

Escobar, Gabriel. 1974. *Sicaya: Cambios Culturales en una Comunidad Mestiza Andina*. Lima: Instituto de Estudios Perúanos.

Espinoza Soriano, Waldemar. 1973. *Historia del Departamento de Junín*. Huancayo: Editor Enrique Chipoco Tovar.

Fahim, Hussein, ed. 1982. *Indigenous Anthropology in Non-Western Countries*. Durham: Carolina Academic Press.

Feld, Steven. 1982. *Sound and Sentiment: Birds, Weeping, Poetics and Song in Kaluli Expression*. Philadelphia: University of Pennsylvania Press.

Flores Galindo, Alberto. 1974. *Los Mineros de la Cerro de Pasco*. Lima: Pontificia Universidad Católica del Perú.

———. 1986. *Buscando un Inca: Identidad y Utopía en los Andes*. La Habana: Casa de las Américas.

———. 1992. *Dos Ensayos sobre José María Arguedas*. Lima: Sur-Casa de Estudios del Socialismo.

Flores Ochoa, Jorge. 1974. " 'Mistis and Indians: Their Relations in a Micro-Economic Region of Cusco." In *Class and Ethnicity in Perú*. Pierre van den Bergue, ed. Leiden: E. J. Brill.

Foster, George M., Thayer Scudder, Elizabeth Colson, and Robert V. Kemper, eds. 1979. *Long-Term Field Research in Social Anthropology*. New York: Academic Press.

Foucault, Michel. 1978. *The History of Sexuality: An Introduction* (Vol. I). New York: Vintage.

———. 1970. "Poder, Raza y Etnia en el Perú Contemporáneo." In Fernando Fuenzalida, Enrique Mayer, Gabriel Escobar, Francois Bourricaud, and José Matos Mar, *El Indio y el Poder en el Perú Rural*. Lima: Instituto de Estudios Peruanos.

———. 1980. "Santiago y el Wamani: Aspectos de un Culto Pagano en Moya." *Debates en Antropología* 5:155–187.

García Canclini, Néstor. 1993. *Transforming Modernity: Popular Culture in Mexico*. Austin: University of Texas Press.

———. 1995. *Hybrid Cultures: Strategies for Entering and Leaving Modernity*. Minneapolis: University of Minnesota Press.

Geertz, Clifford. 1973. "Person, Time and Conduct in Bali." In *The Interpretation of Cultures*. New York: Basic Books.

Gellner, Ernest. 1983. *Nations and Nationalism*. Ithaca: Cornell University Press.

Golte, Jurgen, and Norma Adams. 1987. *Los Caballos de Troya de los Conquistadores: Estrategias Campesinas en la Conquista de la Gran Lima*. Lima: Instituto de Estudios Perúanos.

Gronow, Pekka. 1981. "The Record Industry Comes to the Orient." *Ethnomusicology* 25(2):251–284.

Guilbault, Jocelyne. 1993. *Zouk: World Music in the West Indies*. Chicago: University of Chicago Press.

Gupta, Akhil, and James Ferguson. 1992. "Beyond 'Culture': Space, Identity, and the Politics of Difference." *Cultural Anthropology* 7(1):6–23.

———. 1997. "Discipline and Practice: 'The Field' as Site, Method, and Location in Anthropology." In *Anthropological Locations: Boundaries and Grounds of a Field Science*. Berkeley: University of California Press.

Hannerz, Ulf. 1996. *Transnational Connections: Culture, People, Places*. London: Routledge.

Herzfeld, Michael. 1985. *The Poetics of Manhood: Contest and Identity in a Cretan Mountain Village*. Princeton, NJ: Princeton University Press.

———. 1991. *A Place in History: Social and Monumental Time in a Cretan Town*. Princeton, NJ: Princeton University Press.

———. 1996. "National Spirit or the Breath of Nature? The Expropriation of Folk Positivism in the Discourse of Greek Nationalism." In *Natural Histories of Discourse*. Michael Silverstein and Greg Urban, eds. Chicago: University of Chicago Press.

Hobsbawm, Eric J. 1983. "Introduction: Inventing Traditions" In *The Invention of Tradition*. Eric J. Hobsbawm, and Terence O. Ranger, eds. Cambridge: Cambridge University Press.

———. 1990. *Nations and Nationalism since 1780: Programme, Myth, Reality*. Cambridge: Cambridge University Press.

Hutchinson, William B. 1973. *Socio-Cultural Change in the Mantaro Valley of Perú: Acolla, a Case Study*. Ph.D. thesis (University of Indiana, Bloomington).

Hurtado Suárez, Wilfredo. 1995. *Chicha Peruana: Música de los Nuevos Migrantes*. Lima: Eco-Grupo de Investigaciones Económicas.

Instituto Nacional de Cultura. 1978. *Mapa de los Instrumentos de Uso Popular en el Perú*. Lima: Instituto Nacional de Cultura, Oficina de Música y Danza.

Isbell, Billie Jean. 1978. *To Defend Ourselves: Ecology and Ritual in an Andean Village*. Austin: University of Texas Press.

Ivy, Marilyn. 1995. *Discourses of the Vanishing: Modernity, Phantasm, Japan*. Chicago: University of Chicago Press.

Jameson, Fredric, and Masao Miyoshi, eds. 1998. *The Cultures of Globalization*. Durham, NC: Duke University Press.

Jones, Delmos J. 1970. "Towards a Native Anthropology." *Human Organization* 29(4):251–259.

Jongkind, Fred. 1974. "A Reappraisal of the Role of the Regional Associations in Lima, Perú." *Comparative Studies in Society and History* 16(4):471–482.

Kay Trask, Haunani. 1991. "Natives and Anthropologists: The Colonial Struggle." *Contemporary Pacific* 3:159–167.

Karrer, Wolfgang. 1994. "Nostalgia, Amnesia, and Grandmothers: The Uses of Memory in Albert Murray, Sabine Ulbarri, Paula Gunn Allen, and Alice Walker." In *Memory, Narrative, and Identity*. Amritjit Singh, Joseph T.

Skerret, Jr., and Robert E. Hogan, eds. Boston: Northeastern University Press.

Kelly, John D., and Martha Kaplan. 1990. "History, Structure, and Ritual." *Annual Review of Anthropology* 19:119–150.

Knight, Alan. 1990. "Racism, Revolution and Indigenismo: México 1910–1940." In *The Idea of Race in Latin America*, Richard Graham, ed. Austin: University of Texas Press.

Krystal, Efraín. 1987. *The Andes Viewed from the City: Literary and Political Discourse on the Indian in Perú 1848–1930.* New York: Peter Lang.

Kubler, George. 1963. "The Quechua in the Colonial World." In *Handbook of South American Indians.* Julian Steward, ed. New York: Cooper Square.

Laite, Julian, and Norman Long. 1987. "Fiestas and Uneven Capitalist Development in Central Perú." *Bulletin of Latin American Research* 6(1): 27–53.

Lan, David. 1985. *Guns and Rain: Guerrillas and Spirit Mediums in Zimbabwe.* Berkeley: University of California Press.

Lloréns, José Antonio. 1983. *Música Popular en Lima: Criollos y Andinos.* Lima: Instituto de Estudios Peruanos.

———. 1991. "Andean Voices on Lima Airwaves: Highland Migrants and Radio Broadcasting in Perú." *Studies in Latin American Popular Culture* 10: 177–189.

Lobo, Susan. 1982. *A House of My Own: Social Organization in the Squatter Settlements of Lima, Perú.* Tucson: University of Arizona Press.

Lomnitz, Larissa Adler. 1977. *Networks and Marginality: Life in a Mexican Shantytown.* New York: Academic Press.

Lomnitz-Adler, Claudio. 1992. *Exits from the Labyrinth: Culture and Ideology in the Mexican National Space.* Berkeley: University of California Press.

Long, Norman and Brian Roberts, eds. 1978. *Peasant Cooperation and Capitalist Expansion in Central Perú.* Austin: University of Texas Press.

———. 1984. *Miners, Peasants and Entrepreneurs: Regional Development in the Central Highland of Perú.* Cambridge: Cambridge University Press.

Mallon, Florencia E. 1983. *The Defense of Community in Perú's Central Highlands.* Princeton, NJ: Princeton University Press.

———. 1992. "Indian Communities, Political Cultures, and the State in Latin America." *Journal of Latin American Studies* 24:35–53.

———. 1995. *Peasant and Nation: The Making of Postcolonial Mexico and Perú.* Berkeley: University of California Press.

———. 1996. "Constructing 'Mestizaje' in Latin America: Authenticity, Marginality, and Gender in the Claiming of Ethnic Identities." *Journal of Latin American Anthropology* 2(1):170–181.

Mangin, William. 1959. "The Role of Regional Associations in the Adaptation of Rural Populations in Perú." *Sociologus* 9:21–36.

———. 1970. "Tales from the Barriadas." In *Peasants in Cities.* Boston: Houghton Mifflin.

———. 1973. "Sociological, Cultural and Political Characteristics of Some Urban Migrants in Perú." In *Urban Anthropology: Cross-Cultural Studies in Urbanization.* London: Oxford University Press.

Manrique, Nelson. 1981. *Campesinado y Nación: Las Guerrillas Indígenas en la Guerra con Chile*. Lima: Centro de Investigación y Capacitacion/Editora Ital Perú.

———. 1987. *Mercado Interno y Región: La Sierra Central 1820–1930*. Lima: DESCO.

———. 1998. "The War for the Central Sierra." In *Shining and Other Paths: War and Society in Perú, 1980–1995*. Steve Stern, ed. Durham: Duke University Press.

Mariátegui, Jose Carlos. 1971. *Seven Interpretive Essays on Peruvian Reality*. Austin: University of Texas Press.

Martínez, Héctor. 1959. "Vicos: Las Fiestas en su Integración y Desintegración Cultural." *Revista del Museo Nacional* 28: 189–247.

———. 1980. *Migraciones Internas en el Perú: Aproximación Crítica y Bibliografía*. Lima: Instituto de Estudios Peruanos.

Matos Mar, Jose. 1961. "Migration and Urbanization: The Barriadas of Lima." In *Urbanization in Latin America*. Philip Hauser, ed. Liège, Belgium: UNESCO.

———. 1977. *Estudio de las Barriadas Limeñas, 1955*. Lima: Instituto de Estudios Peruanos.

———. 1984. *Desborde Popular y Crisis del Estado*. Lima: Instituto de Estudios Perúanos.

Maybury-Lewis, David. 1984. "Living in Leviathan: Ethnic Groups and the State." In *The Prospects for Plural Societies*. Washington, DC: American Ethnological Society.

Mayer, Enrique. 1970. "Mestizo e Indio: El Contexto Social de las Relaciones Interétnicas." In Fernando Fuenzalida, et al., *El Indio y el Poder en el Perú Rural*. Lima: Instituto de Estudios Peruanos.

Mayer, Enrique. 1981. *Uso de la Tierra en los Andes: Ecología y Agricultura en el Valle del Mantaro del Perú con Referencia Especial a la Papa*. Lima: Centro Internacional de la Papa.

Means, Philip Ainsworth. 1920. "Indian Legislation in Perú." *Hispanic Historical Review* 3(4): 509–534.

Mendoza-Walker, Zoila. 1989. "La Danza de los Avelinos." *Revista Andina* 1(14): 501–521.

Merino de Zela, Mildred. 1977. "Folklore Coreográfico e Historia." *Folklore Americano* 24:67–94.

Millones, Luis. 1978. *Tugurios: La Cultura de los Marginados*. Lima: Instituto Nacional de Cultura.

Mishkin, Bernard. 1963. "The Contemporary Quechua." In *Handbook of South American Indians*. Julian Steward, ed. New York: Cooper Square.

Montoya, Rodrigo. 1987a. *La Cultura Quechua Hoy*. Lima: Mosca Azul.

———. 1987b (with Luis and Edwin Montoya). *La Sangre de los Cerros*. Lima: CEPES/Mosca Azul/Universidad Nacional Mayor de San Marcos.

Murra, John. 1984. "The Cultural Future of the Andean Majority." In *The Prospect for Plural Societies*. David Maybury-Lewis, ed. Washington, DC: American Ethnological Society.

Narayan, Kirin. 1993. "How Native Is a 'Native' Anthropologist?" *American Anthropologist* 95(3): 671–686.

Nettl, Bruno. 1983. *The Study of Ethnomusicology: Twenty-nine Issues and Concepts.* Urbana: University of Illinois Press.

———. 1985. *The Western Impact on World Music: Change Adaptation and Survival.* New York: Schirmer.

Nuñez, Lucy. 1990. *Los Dansaq.* Lima: Museo Nacional de la Cultura Peruana.

Nuñez Rebaza, Lucy and Jose A. Llorens. 1981. "La Música Tradicional Andina en Lima Metropolitana." *America Indígena* 41(1): 53–74.

Olsen, Dale A. 1986–1987. "The Peruvian Folk Harp Tradition: Determinants of Style." *Folk Harp Journal* 53:48–54, 54:41–48, 55:55–59, 56:57–60.

Orellana, Simeon. 1972a. "La Huaconada de Mito." In *Anales Científicos de la Universidad Nacional del Centro-Perú,* vol. 1. Huancayo: Universidad Nacional del Centro.

———. 1972b. "Las Huatrilas de Jauja." *Folklore Americano* 17:230–237.

———. 1976. "La Pachahuara de Acolla: Una Danza de los Esclavos Negros en el Valle de Yanamarca." *Boletín del Instituto Francés de Estudios Andinos* 5(1–2):149–165.

Ortner, Sherry B. 1991. "Reading America: Preliminary Notes on Class and Culture." In *Recapturing Anthropology: Working in the Present.* Richard G. Fox, ed. Santa Fe: School of American Research.

Ossio, Juan M. 1978. "Relaciones Interétnicas y Verticalidad en los Andes." *Debates en Antropología* 2:1–23.

———. 1995. "Etnicidad, Cultura y Grupos Sociales." En *El Perú Frente al Siglo XXI.* Gonzalo Portocarrero and Marcel Valcarcel, eds. Lima: Pontificia Universidad Católica del Perú.

Osterling, Jorge P. 1980. *De Campesinos a Profesionales: Migrantes de Huayopampa en Lima.* Lima: Pontificia Universidad Católica del Perú.

Peñaloza Jarrín, José Benigno. 1995. *Huancayo: Historia, Familia y Región.* Lima: Pontificia Universidad Católica del Perú, Instituto Riva-Agüero.

Poole, Deborah A. 1990. "Accommodation and Resistance in Andean Ritual Dance." *Drama Review* 34(2):98–126.

———. 1994. "Performance, Domination, and Identity in the 'Tierras Bravas' of Chumbivilcas (Cusco)." In *Unruly Order: Violence, Power, and Cultural Identity in the High Provinces of Southern Perú.* Boulder: Westview.

Quijada Jara, Sergio. 1957. *Canciones del Ganado y Pastores.* Huancayo: Talleres Gráficos Villanueva.

———. 1961. "Estado Actual de los Estudios Folklóricos en el Perú." *Perú Indígena* 9(20–21):73–81.

Quispe, Ulpiano. 1969. *La Herranza en Choque Huarcaya y Huancasancos, Ayacucho.* Lima: Instituto Indigenista Peruano.

Racy, Ali Jihad. 1976. "Record Industry and Egyptian Traditional Music." *Ethnomusicology* 21(1):23–48.

Ráez, Nemesio. 1899. *Monografía de la Provincia de Huancayo.* Huancayo: Imprenta del Colegio de Santa Isabel. Reprinted in *Monografía de Huancayo y Otros Estudios.* Huancayo: Centro Cultural José María Arguedas, 1995.

Rappaport, Joanne. 1998. *The Politics of Memory: Native Historical Interpretation in the Colombian Andes*. Durham, NC: Duke University Press.

Rénique, José Luis. 1991. *Los Sueños de la Sierra: Cuzco en el Siglo XX*. Lima: Centro Peruano de Estudios Sociales.

Reyes-Schramm, Adelaida. 1979. "Ethnic Music, the Urban Area, and Ethnomusicology." *Sociologus* 29:1–21.

Rice, Timothy. 1994. *May It Fill Your Soul*. Chicago: University of Chicago Press.

Roel, Josafat. 1959. "El Wayno del Cuzco." *Folklore Americano* 6–7: 129–245.

Romero, Emilio. 1949. *Historia Económica del Perú*. Buenos Aires: Editorial Sudamericana.

———. 1969. "En Torno al Regionalismo y Centralismo." In *Regionalismo y Centralismo*. Emilio Romero and César Lévano, eds. Lima: Biblioteca Amauta.

Romero, Raúl R. 1988. "Development and Balance of Peruvian Ethnomusicology." *Yearbook of Traditional Music* 20:146–157.

———. 1989. "Música Urbana en un Contexto Rural: Tradición y Modernidad en Paccha (Junín)." *Anthropologica* 7:119–133.

———. 1990. "Musical Change and Cultural Resistance in the Central Andes of Perú." *Latin American Music Review* 11(1):1–35.

———. 1992. "Preservation, the Mass Media and Dissemination of Traditional Music: The Case of the Peruvian Andes." In *World Music, Musics of the World: Aspects of Documentation, Mass Media and Acculturation*. Max Peter Baumann, ed. Wilhelmshaven: Florian Noetzel.

———. (Ed.) 1993. *Música, Danzas y Máscaras en los Andes*. Lima: Pontificia Universidad Católica del Perú.

———. 1998. "Perú." In *Garland Encyclopedia of World Music: South America, Mexico, Central America and the Caribbean*. New York: Garland.

———. 1999a. "Aesthetics of Sound and Listening in the Andes: The Mantaro Valley in Central Perú." *World of Music* 41(1):53–58.

———. 1999b. "Andean Perú." In *Music in Latin American Culture: Regional Traditions*. John Schechter, ed. New York: Schirmer.

Rowe, William. 1996. *Ensayos Arguedianos*. Lima: Universidad Nacional Mayor de San Marcos and SUR-Casa de Estudios del Socialismo.

Rowe, William, and Vivian Schelling. 1991. *Memory and Modernity: Popular Culture in Latin America*. London: Verso.

Sahlins, Marshall. 1976. *Culture and Practical Reason*. Chicago: University of Chicago Press.

Said, Edward. 1990. "Third World Intellectuals and Metropolitan Culture." *Raritan* 9(3): 27–50.

Sánchez, Rodrigo. 1987. *Organización Andina, Drama y Posibilidad*. Huancayo: Instituto Regional de Economía Andina.

Schaedel, Richard P. 1979. "From Homogenization to Heterogenization in Lima, Perú." *Urban Anthropology* 8(3/4): 399–420.

Schechter, John. 1982. *Music in a Northern Ecuadorian Highland Locus: Diatonic*

*Harp, Genres, Harpists, and Their Ritual Junction in the Quechua Child's Wake*. Ph.D. dissertation (University of Texas at Austin).

————. 1992. *The Indispensable Harp: Historical Development, Modern Roles, Configurations and Performance Practices in Ecuador and Latin America*. Kent, Ohio: Kent State University Press.

Scott, James. 1990. *Domination and the Arts of Resistance: Hidden Transcripts*. New Haven: Yale University Press.

Seeger, Anthony. 1987. *Why Suyá Sing: A Musical Anthropology of an Amazonian People*. Cambridge: Cambridge University Press.

Shelemay, Kay. 1991. "Recording Technology, the Record Industry and Ethnomusicology Scholarship." In *Comparative Musicology and Anthropology of Music*. Bruno Nettl and Philip V. Bohlman, eds. Chicago: University of Chicago Press.

Silverblatt, Irene. 1988. "Political Memories and Colonizing Symbols: Santiago and the Mountain Gods of Colonial Perú." In *Rethinking History and Myth: Indigenous South American Perspectives on the Past*. Jonathan D. Hill, ed. Urbana: University of Illinois Press.

Simmons, Ozzie G. 1955. "The Criollo Outlook in the Mestizo Culture of Coastal Perú." *American Anthropologist* 57(1): 107–117.

Smith, Gavin. 1989. *Livelihood and Resistance: Peasants and the Politics of Land in Perú*. Berkeley: University of California Press.

Smith, Waldemar R. 1977. *The Fiesta System and Economic Change*. New York: Columbia University Press.

Stern, Steve J. 1982. *Perú's Indian Peoples and the Challenges of Spanish Conquest*. Madison: University of Wisconsin Press.

————. 1987. *Resistance, Rebellion and Consciousness in the Andean Peasant World, 18th and 20th Centuries*. Madison: University of Wisconsin Press.

Stevenson, Robert. 1960. *The Music of Perú*. Washington, DC: Organization of American States.

————. 1968. *Music in Aztec and Inca Territories*. Berkeley: University of California Press.

Stokes, Martin. 1994. "Introduction: Ethnicity, Identity and Music." In *Ethnicity, Identity and Music: The Musical Construction of Place*. Oxford: Berg.

Sutton, David E. 1991. "Is Anybody Out There? Anthropology and the Question of Audience." *Critique of Anthropology* 11(1): 91–104.

Tamayo Herrera, José. 1980. *Historia del Indigenismo Cuzqueño, Siglos XVI–XX*. Lima: Instituto Nacional de Cultura.

————. 1981. *Historia Social del Cuzco Republicano*. Lima: Editorial Universitaria.

Tambiah, Stanley. 1979. "A Performative Approach to Ritual." *Proceedings of the British Academy* 40:113–169.

Tord, Luis Enrique. 1978. *El Indio en los Ensayistas Peruanos 1848–1948*. Lima: Unidos.

Tschopik, Harry. 1947. *Highland Communities in Central Perú*. Washington, DC: Smithsonian Institution.

————. 1948. "On the Concept of Creole Culture in Perú." *Transactions of the New York Academy of Sciences* 10:252–261.

Turino, Thomas. 1988. "The Music of Andean Migrants in Lima, Perú: Demographics, Social Power and Style." *Latin American Music Review* 9(2): 127–150.

————. 1990. "Somos el Perú: Cumbia Andina and the Children of Andean Migrants in Lima, Perú." *Studies in Latin American Popular Culture* 9:15–37.

————. 1991. "The State and Andean Musical Production in Perú." In *Nation-States and Indians in Latin America*. Greg Urban and Joel Sherzer, eds. Austin: University of Texas Press.

————. 1993. *Moving Away from Silence: Music of the Perúvian Altiplano and the Experience of Urban Migration*. Chicago: University of Chicago Press.

————. 1998. "Quechua and Aymara." In *Garland Encyclopedia of World Music: South America, Mexico, Central America and the Caribbean*. New York: Garland.

Turner, Victor. 1967. *The Forest of Symbols: Aspects of Ndembu Ritual*. Ithaca: Cornell University Press.

————. 1969 *The Ritual Process: Structure and Anti-Structure*. Chicago: Aldine.

Valcárcel, Luis E. 1927. *Tempestad en los Andes*. Lima: Minerva (Biblioteca Amauta).

————. 1951. "Introducción." In *Fiestas y Danzas en el Cuzco y en los Andes*. Pierre Verger, ed. Buenos Aires: Editorial Sudamericana.

Valenzuela, Rubén. 1984. *La Orquesta Típica del Centro del Perú*. Thesis (National Conservatory of Music, Lima).

van den Bergue, Pierre, ed. 1974. *Class and Ethnicity in Perú*. Leiden: E. J. Brill.

Varallanos, Jose. 1989. *El Harahui y el Yaraví: Dos Canciones Populares Peruanas*. Lima: Consejo Nacional de Ciencia y Tecnología.

Vilcapoma, Jose Carlos. 1995. *Waylarsh: Amor y Violencia de Carnaval*. Lima: Pakarina.

Vivanco, Alejandro. 1973. "El Migrante de Provincias como Intérprete del Folklore Andino en Lima." Bachelor's thesis (San Marcos University, Lima).

Wagley, Charles. 1965. "On the Concept of Social Race in the Americas." In D. Heath and R. Adams, eds. *Contemporary Cultures and Societies in Latin America* New York: Random House.

Waterman, Christopher. 1990. *Juju: A Social History and Ethnography of an African Popular Music*. Chicago: University of Chicago Press.

Williams, Raymond. 1977. *Marxism and Literature*. Oxford: Oxford University Press.

Wolf, Eric. 1955. "Types of Latin American Peasantry." *American Anthropologist* 57(3): 452–471.

————. 1966. *Peasants*. Englewood-Cliffs, NJ: Prentice-Hall.

# Index